FINE
Embellishment
TECHNIQUES

FINE
Embellishment
TECHNIQUES

Classic Details
for Today's Clothing

JANE CONLON

The Taunton Press

Cover photo: Jack Deutsch

Publisher: Jim Childs
Acquisitions editor: Jolynn Gower
Publishing coordinator: Sarah Coe
Editor: Thomas McKenna
Indexer: Lynda Stannard
Cover Designer: Ann Marie Manca
Designer: Mary Terrizzi
Layout artist: Lynne Phillips
Photographer: Jack Deutsch, except where noted
Illustrator: Christine Erickson
Typeface: Weiss
Paper: 70-lb. Patina
Printer: R. R. Donnelley, Willard, Ohio

The Taunton Press
Inspiration for hands-on living™

Text © 2001 by Jane Conlon
Photographs © 2001 by The Taunton Press, Inc.
Illustrations © 2001 by The Taunton Press, Inc.

Printed in the United States of America
10 9 8 7 6 5 4 3 2 1

Fine Embellishment Techniques was originally published in hardcover in 1999
by The Taunton Press, Inc.

The Taunton Press, Inc., 63 South Main Street, PO Box 5506, Newtown, CT 06470-5506
e-mail: tp@taunton.com

Distributed by Publishers Group West

Library of Congress Cataloging-in-Publication Data
 Conlon, Jane.
   Fine embellishment techniques : classic details for today's clothing /
Jane Conlon.
     p.   cm.
   Includes index.
   ISBN 1-56158-496-7 paperback
   ISBN 1-56158-231-X hardcover
   1. Fancy work. 2. Clothing and dress. I. Title.
 TT750.C63   1999
 646.4—dc21   98-34694 CIP

For Kaliisa and Wren, with love

ACKNOWLEDGMENTS

I would like to thank the tremendous team at The Taunton Press for their efforts on behalf of this book. In particular, I am indebted to Jolynn Gower for inspiring confidence, for cultivating interest and enthusiasm, and for imparting her calm energy and clear insight throughout the duration of the project; to Sarah Coe for pulling so many important details together so effectively; to Tom McKenna for his positive demeanor and discerning eye; and to Mary Terrizzi for the efficient layout and beautiful design.

Thanks also to photographer Jack Deutsch for his consummate artistry; to illustrator Christine Erickson for the lovely drawings; and to Karen Morris for initial encouragement.

Maggie Backman of Things Japanese, Kaethe Kliot of Lacis, and Irene Jones of Exim Marketing indulged my questions regarding materials and techniques, each offering generous contributions of time and expertise that benefited the manuscript and for which I am grateful.

Likewise, I am indebted to the profoundly talented and eclectic circle of sewing friends that make 27th Street Fabrics, in Eugene, Oregon, such a unique and wonderful place: Mary Enos for her wisdom, perspective, and generosity; and Mary Goodson, Terri Mitchell, Sylvia Mitchell, Celeste Percy, and Millie Schwandt for sharing their creative insights, as well as valuable knowledge, opinions, and ideas. I have learned, grown, and benefited immensely from this exchange and am beholden to you all.

Finally, in the realm of friends and family, no one is more blessed than me. I would especially like to thank my mother, Judith Stensland, and acknowledge the memory of my father, Donald Stensland, for providing love, latitude, and boundaries as well as guidance and encouragement. In a similar vein, my soul sisters Kathleen Gent, Maia Penfold, Lisa Price, Karen Powers, and Jamileh Stroman have always been—and continue to be— a wellspring of unconditional love, support, and persistent enthusiasm for the dreams I hold dear. I am utterly grateful for friends so divine.

I would also like to thank Harmony Eberhardt for contributing time, skill, and effort when it mattered most; it made such a difference!

At the center of my life, my daughters, Kaliisa Conlon and Peregrine Facaros, and my lifelong partner, Nickolas Facaros, fill my days with purpose, inspiration, and wonder. I am especially thankful for the web of support they created during the acute phases of this project. Kaliisa's generous contributions of time, skill, energy, and creative input; Wren's big heart and youthful spirit, and Nick's enduring love, support, and acceptance were abundant and sustaining.

CONTENTS

 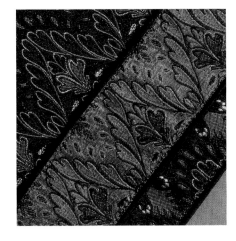

INTRODUCTION

Fine Embellishment Techniques will teach you classic techniques for beautifully embellished garments. Whether you are a beginning, intermediate, or advanced sewer, this book is designed to provide you with a wealth of embellishment inspirations as well as step-by-step instructions so you can achieve outstanding results on projects large and small.

My main inspiration for the techniques featured in this book is the tradition of embellishment used to adorn clothing from the '20s, '30s, and '40s. Worked in high-quality, natural fiber fabrics, with consummate attention to craftsmanship and detail, garments of this vintage feature rich embellishments that enhance both the garment *and* its wearer. Many of the techniques favored in this bygone era are delightfully easy to master. What's more, up-to-date interpretations translate well to today's fashions and can be used to introduce signature elements into everyday wear or worked for dramatic effect on garments for special occasions. Using the embellishment techniques to best advantage, however, demands fine-tuning your sewing skills, utilizing the best products and notions available, exploiting the full capacity of your sewing machine, and settling for nothing less than quality as the foundation for superior workmanship.

If this sounds intimidating, cast your doubts aside. This book will help you master the techniques of embellishment with predictable, professional results. It will also encourage the artful use of these techniques and promote a better understanding of how to select and effectively use the tools and materials worthy of your best endeavors. Included, of course, is source information and a list of suppliers to indicate where you can find unique notions and tools.

The book is organized by topic in a manner designed to be as instructive, inspirational, and user-friendly as possible. You'll find step-by-step instructions for individual techniques, along with specific references to tools and materials that will make the most of your sewing time and produce the best results possible. Ideas for ways to use the techniques presented in this book are plentiful, featuring numerous sample garments, close-up photographs of embellishment details, and text and illustrations designed to inspire a wealth of ideas for simple to elaborate applications.

As you explore the methods and ideas presented in *Fine Embellishment Techniques*, I hope you will discover ways to make your sewing more creative, fun, and, ultimately, more rewarding. Over the years I have pursued and perfected numerous ways to embellish garments that meet my creative expectations and suit my personal style. Perhaps you will find, as I have, that embellishments are not only the key to creating exquisite garments but also to developing a style uniquely your own.

Beading

Bead-embellished garments can be irresistibly gorgeous, but as anyone who's made or worn one knows, the visual allure of the beaded garment is only half the picture. With their perfect weight, drape, and dazzle, beaded garments feel beautiful. They hang right. They're substantial. They catch the light. And if you've made them, they reveal something radiant in your personality.

Fortunately for embellishment enthusiasts, beading presents yet another set of enticements. Not only is it downright addictive, but it's also exponentially satisfying, since even a sprinkling of beadwork can infuse a garment with elegance and charm. It's also versatile. Beading marries equally well with leather, velvet, and silk chiffon and is compatible with every fiber, weight, and texture in between. Likewise, many blouse, dress, jacket, and vest patterns lend themselves to the distinctive touch of beading.

Beading bestows timeless beauty to garments. Its effect can be ethereal, whimsical, or weighty. As an accessory to other embellishments or as the embellishment focus, beading enriches the overall design. Best of all, beading techniques are easy to master and, depending upon the scope of the project, require very little investment in tools and materials.

MATERIALS AND EQUIPMENT

A beaded-garment project requires, first and foremost, selecting fabrics, beads, and garment styles that are compatible in terms of practicality and overall design. Familiarity with beading terminology and with materials and equipment will help you make appropriate and price-wise decisions for your projects.

In this chapter I will discuss the many types of beads you can use for your beading projects and the beading supplies you need to complete those projects. (For information on where to buy beads and beading supplies, see the sidebar on the facing page and the source list on p. 168.)

I will also guide you through five different beading methods, including bead embroidery, tambour beading, beaded edges and fringe, beaded buttons, and beadweaving. Rather than include specific projects, I have provided step-by-step instructions for each of these beading techniques that can be adapted to your own projects.

Beads

Beads come in an infinite array of colors, shapes, and sizes. Wood, bone, shell, metal, gemstones, seeds—even rose petals—are some of the natural materials used in bead production. Their man-made counterparts include glass, crystal, paper, and plastic, with glass heading the list of beads produced for commercial consumption. Glass rocaille beads are the most pertinent bead category in relation to the bead-embellished garment, with crystals, pearls, spangles, and paillettes (also known as sequins) in tow. While selective use of other bead categories will, at times, be appropriate for various garment applications, techniques featured in this chapter center around creative use of the following types of beads.

Buying Beads

Beads can be purchased from specialty bead stores and mail-order suppliers, as well as from some sewing and craft stores. A well-stocked local bead store is a real treat because it offers the advantage of direct selection and the luxury of firsthand experimentation with possible bead combinations.

Mail-order suppliers generally offer better prices and a larger number of products to choose from. Most suppliers have color catalogs, and some offer color cards that feature actual beads (suppliers often charge extra for the color cards). Many offer quantity price breaks on rocailles as well as spe-

cialty beads, which are especially welcome if you know what you want and need large quantities. (Some mail-order suppliers have minimum-order requirements, but I've never had a problem coaxing a friend or two to go in on an order of beads!) Mail-order suppliers are also a good backup source to consult if you run out of beads midway through a project and can no longer purchase them locally.

Regardless of where you shop for beads, be sure you buy the right amount for the project at hand. Predict bead quantities in advance and buy more than you think you need. Nothing's worse than coming

up short on supplies midway through a project. Likewise, if your garment ever needs repair, you'll want to have extra beads on hand. If you're lucky, you may find the same bead twice, but keep in mind that bead production is not consistent from year to year, and even among colors that are readily available, dye lots can vary. To avoid this risk, purchase too many beads rather than too few. Some suppliers will allow you to return unbroken bead hanks or packages for exchange or credit. Ask in advance if this is an option.

ROCAILLES

Rocailles are the foundation of the bead embroiderer's palette. Made to uniform standards and classified according to size (the larger the number, the smaller the bead), shape, color (see the sidebar on p. 8), and sheen, they provide the consistency required for beaded garments.

Various types of rocailles work well for embroidery, fringe, beadweaving, button making, and tambour applications. Seed beads are round rocailles with round holes. Charlottes are faceted seed beads with lovely, light-reflective properties (see the left photo at right). Charlottes that I have purchased have been size 13 beads with two cuts, but the term charlotte may be extended to tricut beads as well. (Unlike two-cut beads, which are faceted only on the side, tricuts are faceted on the ends as well, which increases their light-reflective capacity.)

Rocailles are also classified according to their shape. Common classifications include hex beads, square rocailles, and delica seed

Charlottes are faceted seed beads that reflect light.

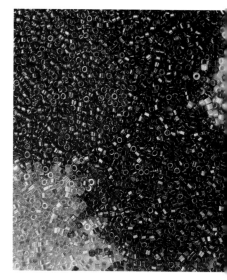

Delica beads are the most uniform of all seed beads.

beads (from Japan). It is worth noting that delicas (see the right photo above) are the most uniform of the seed beads. They are square and have larger holes than round rocailles of comparable size, making them ideal for bead-weaving applications. Rocailles are sold by the strand, hank, or weight.

Bead Colors

Color is imparted to beads by way of colored glass, linings, and surface coatings. Colors may be transparent or opaque, and the degree of luster is dictated by various treatments used to produce matte, satin, pearl, or reflective surfaces. Surface coatings are applied to glass beads to affect the color, complexity, degree of sheen, and transparency. Metallic, luster, and rainbow (referred to as iris or aurora borealis) coatings are used on the outside of beads for effect. Linings, metallic or otherwise, coat the interior hole of a transparent bead, affecting bead color from the inside out.

Before purchasing beads, it is important to know how the surface coating (if any) was applied. Generally, surface coatings are fired, electroplated, dipped, or dyed. Fired coatings are similar to glazes used in pottery and are more or less permanent. Electroplated coatings are not necessarily permanent over time but wear longer than dipped or dyed coatings, which can rub off. Beads that have been dipped or dyed tend to look shoddy over time and are not recommended for garments. Obviously, before putting a lot of energy toward a project, you want to be sure that the beads you select will retain their color and luster over time and won't stain or discolor fabric.

Bugles are made of glass or metal with smooth or ridged surfaces.

BUGLES

Bugles are tube-shaped beads made of glass or metal with smooth or ridged surfaces (see the photo above). They can be used alone or combined with rocailles and are well suited to embroidery, fringe, and tambour applications. Bugles vary in width (degree of thickness) and are available in plain, faceted, or twisted lengths, ranging from 2mm to 35mm. Beware when purchasing bugles from catalogs: Size designations do not always correspond to the length of the bugle. Color and surface treatments for bugles are the same as for rocailles. In fact, it is possible to obtain exact color matches between bugles and rocailles, particularly if you're buying from a well-stocked supplier. Bugles are sold by the strand, hank, or weight.

PAILLETTES AND SEQUINS

Although the term paillette includes sequins, it is common to distinguish paillettes as flat metal disks and sequins as fluted plastic disks (see the left photo on the facing page). Both types of beads come in a variety of sizes, have a hole in the center, and possess light-reflective properties. You can attach rows of paillettes or sequins to fabric using the tambour method or couch individual disks with a bead sewn through the center or with decorative hand stitches. Paillettes and sequins are sold by the strand or weight.

Paillettes and sequins are available in a number of sizes and both types reflect light.

DECORATIVE BEADS

More unique than rocailles, decorative beads are available in a range of shapes, sizes, and colors (see the top photo at right). Crystal and cut-glass beads are available in teardrops, cones, bicones, barrels, bells, balls, and cylinders. Molded glass, plastic, and metal beads also come in these shapes and others, including flowers, leaves, hearts, moons, and stars. Metal filigree, enamel, and cloisonné beads round off the cast of decorative beads at your disposal.

Decorative beads tend to be expensive and large and are used primarily as accents for trims, fringe, and beaded buttons. They are sold individually or by the strand.

RONDELLES

Rondelles are disk-shaped beads, with a hole in the center—like a doughnut (see the photo at right). They come in many sizes and are made from a wide variety of materials. Rondelles can be sewn onto fabric with decorative hand stitches or couched on with another bead. Backing a beautiful ornamental bead with a rondelle highlights the bead by lifting it away from the fabric and by framing it with a contrasting ring of color. Rondelles are sold individually and by the strand or weight.

Decorative beads are available in many shapes, sizes, and colors, as well as materials, including glass, plastic, and metal.

Rondelles are disk-shaped beads, with a hole in the center. They also come in many sizes and are made from a variety of materials.

Pendants, drops, and charms have a hole or loop fixture at the top, so the bead dangles when sewn.

Natural pearl and gemstone beads can serve as wonderful accents on a garment.

PENDANTS, DROPS, AND CHARMS

Available in a variety of interesting shapes, the distinguishing feature of these accent beads is that they have a hole or loop fixture at the top, so the bead drops or dangles when sewn. Pendants, drops, and charms (see the photo above) tend to be more expensive than most decorative beads, but the designs are also more detailed, and some are exquisite. You can use these beads as accents on collar tips, pockets, or front bands or incorporate them as the dangles for netted fringe. Pendants, drops, and charms are sold individually and by the strand.

PEARLS AND GEMSTONES

Natural pearl and gemstone beads are available in numerous ball sizes and in a variety of decorative styles (see the photo at left). They are not recommended for extensive embroidery applications but can be used sparingly in designs. For instance, pearls and gemstones are wonderful as accents for picot-edged beaded buttons and beaded fringe. (Simulated pearl beads come in a wide range of sizes, the smaller of which can be treated as rocailles. Larger ones are suitable as accent beads.) Pearls and gemstones are sold individually and by the strand.

Needles

For beading tasks, you have a variety of needles to choose from (see the photo below), including beading needles, milliners needles, delica needles, big-eye needles, beadweaving needles, and tambour hooks, which consist of needle and holder. As with all hand-sewing needles, the larger the size designation, the smaller the diameter of the needle. Tambour needles, however, are sized like machine-sewing needles, in which case larger numbers indicate a larger size needle.

BEADING NEEDLES

Beading needles are designed to pass easily through the hole of a bead. They are longer and thinner than most hand-sewing needles and bend easily, which makes them ideal for picking beads up from a flat surface and enables the needle to accommodate a number of beads on its tip at one time.

Beading needles are produced in England and Japan. To make selection painless, English beading needles have size designations that correspond to standard seed-bead sizes. For example, size 12 beads require an English size 12 needle, and so on. English needles are very thin and flexible. They are available in sizes 10 to 16, as well as in extra longs. Beading needles made in Japan are slightly larger and sturdier than the English variety and are available in sizes 10, 12, 14, and 16. When choosing beading needles, pick a size slightly smaller than the bead size.

MILLINERS NEEDLES

Milliners needles are longer and less rigid than standard hand-sewing needles but are sturdier, slightly shorter, and easier to thread than beading needles. In some ways, they are ideal for beading directly to garments, since they are straight, long, and flexible; don't get bent out of shape easily; and have a sharp, sturdy point that can penetrate several layers of fabric with ease. Unfortunately, even the smallest size (10) is too large to pass readily through the hole of some of the smaller seed beads (sizes 13 and 15).

DELICA NEEDLES

Delica needles were designed for use with delica seed beads. Four lengths are available (1¾ in., 2 in., 3⅝ in., and 4¾ in.). Use the larger two for beadweaving and the shorter two for bead embroidery and beaded edges.

BIG-EYE NEEDLES

Big-eye needles are the easy-threading needles of the beading world, so take note! They have one large eye made from two high-tension steel wires that are soldered together at each end and sharpened. Available in 2½-in. and 5-in. lengths, these needles are suitable for size 11 beads and larger and for a variety of beading applications, including beadweaving. Needless to say, they will accommodate any size thread.

Needles for beading come in a variety of styles and sizes and are designed for specific beading tasks. From the top: delica needle, big-eye needle, beadweaving needle, beading needle, and milliners needle.

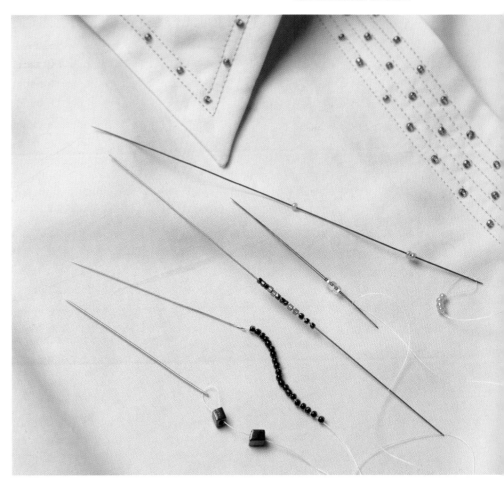

BEADWEAVING NEEDLES

Beadweaving needles have blunt points and are long (5 in. to 7½ in.). They are long enough to pass through the entire length of beads selvage to selvage (referring to the beadwoven area) and thin enough to pass easily through the beads. The blunt point prevents the needle from damaging or hanging up on threads.

TAMBOUR HOOK

The tambour hook is *the* essential tool for tambour embroidery and beadwork (see the drawing below). It consists of two parts: the tambour needle and a separate holder. Tambour needles are shaped like tiny crochet hooks, but unlike crochet hooks, they are designed to pierce fabric and have an extremely sharp point at the working end. Short and long lengths conform to styles of holders (be sure to get the correct length for your holder), while needle sizes correspond to various thread weights and types of fabrics.

Seven needle sizes (#70 to #130) are available. Of these, the finest needle (#70) is used primarily when beading to very fine, sheer fabrics like silk chiffon and organza. Sizes #80 and #90 work well for most other beadwork applications, while the heavier needles are used to embroider heavier fabrics or to work heavier threads.

The tambour holder is designed to hold the tambour needle in place and to provide a comfortable handle to work the stitch by hand.

The holder has a shaft for the needle at one end, which is tightened with an adjustable thumbscrew to keep the needle in place. Holders made from plastic, bone, brass, wood, and ivory are available, with price differentials hinging upon ornate aesthetic qualities of the holder as opposed to its basic performance. Starter sets that include the holder and several needle sizes are a practical option for beginners, since they offer versatility at a reasonable price. If you can't find a local source for a tambour holder and needles, I've included a list of several mail-order suppliers that offer them (see p. 168).

Thread

The thread you choose to attach beads to garments depends on the size of the needle and bead, the color of the garment or the bead, and the degree of stress and wear the garment will receive. Weighty fringe will pose different practical requirements than embroidered surface embellishments. The three types of thread typically used for beadwork include silk, polyester, and Nymo.

LIGHTWEIGHT SILK

Lightweight silk is the thread of choice for standard bead-embroidery applications. It's strong, resilient, and produces the smoothest stitch of any thread. It knots easily when knotting is desired, doesn't kink or twist while being worked, and resists fraying. Fine-gauge

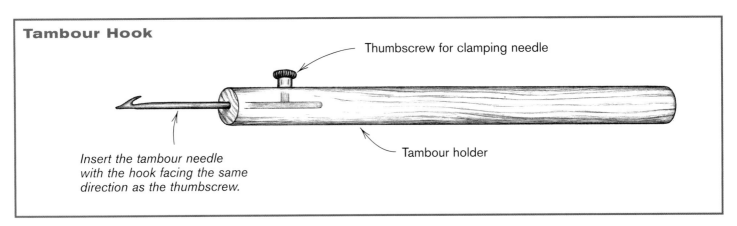

Tambour Hook

Thumbscrew for clamping needle

Tambour holder

Insert the tambour needle with the hook facing the same direction as the thumbscrew.

silk threads for machine sewing and appliqué come in a range of colors. If they're unavailable at your local sewing store, you can get them through a mail-order thread source (see p. 168).

POLYESTER

Polyester is the standard machine-sewing thread, yet it's also a good choice for beading, both in terms of strength and the available range of colors. It tends to be wiry, but running it through beeswax prior to beading makes it more manageable.

NYMO

Nymo, the prestretched, multifilament nylon thread made by Belding Corticelli, is the only beading thread I have found that is soft enough to use on garments, and I use it when tensile strength is the primary consideration. Available by the spool or bobbin, Nymo thread comes in a range of weights designed for use with specific beading needle sizes. Sizes 0 (very fine) and 00 (ultra fine) are suitable for beading to garments and are available in black and white only. Size B medium thread comes in a variety of colors but may be too heavy for some fabrics. Nymo can be purchased from most beading suppliers.

Frames and holders

Frames produce stability by stretching fabric taut, a necessary requirement for certain beading techniques, tambour and beadweaving included. Bead embroidery may also require a frame if the area to be beaded is not already stabilized in some way.

Two types used for beading are ring and scroll frames, and both come in a considerable range of sizes (see the photo on p. 14). Quality hardwood frames are more expensive, but they are less prone to warping and have proven more durable over time. If you are purchasing a frame specifically for beading,

consider buying a versatile size and style that will suit your needs from one project to the next (for a list of suppliers, see p. 168).

RING FRAME

Also known as a hoop, a ring frame consists of inner and outer rings that are used to stretch the fabric. Using a ring frame is fairly simple. Place the fabric on top of the inner ring, then draw the outer ring snug over the fabric and inner ring. Use the wing nut on the outer ring to increase the tension on the fabric and to hold all layers securely in place.

When using a ring frame, the size of bead work is limited to the workable area within the frame, since repositioning the embellished fabric to extend the work area would result in crushing the beads. While this problem can be circumvented by equipping the frame with muslin, which is cut away to produce an open work area, continually having to repin the fabric over this spot can be time-

Waxing thread prior to beading strengthens and lubricates the thread, which makes it easier to sew with and reduces knotting and kinking.

TIP

The three types of thread most commonly used for beadwork are silk, polyester, and Nymo.

Frames stabilize the fabric for bead embroidery or tambour beading.

bars and then scroll it to one side. Baste the other end of the fabric to the tape on the opposite roller bar, with the working length exposed between the extender rods. As the work is completed, scroll it to the opposite roller bars (at the same time you'll be moving a new supply of fabric into the work area). To prevent the beads from crushing, place a layer of batting on top of the newly beaded area prior to scrolling it onto the roller bar.

Tension in the frame is controlled by the knobs attached to the roller bars: Tighten the bar that feeds the fabric first, then scroll the opposite bar forward to remove slack from the fabric in the working area. Secure the second bar once you have reached the desired degree of tension. Overall, the tension on the work area is more consistent on a scroll frame than it is on a ring frame.

While this type of frame is extremely accommodating in terms of the length of fabric that can be mounted for embellishment, the fabric width is limited to the working width of the frame. Most manufacturers, however, sell sets of different length rods and extender bars as accessories.

HOLDERS

Ring and scroll frames are convenient and portable, but there are times when you need to have both hands free, such as with tambour beading, which requires both hands to guide the beads and manipulate the tambour hook. Frame holders—both permanent and adjustable—make this possible. Permanent freestanding frame holders are less expensive than the adjustable models but are not collapsible nor as versatile.

Adjustable frame holders can be freestanding or clamped on a table. (You can even get models that you can sit on while working!) Some are designed for use only with scroll frames, while others feature a clamp assembly that will accommodate a variety of frame styles, including ring frames.

Adjustable frame holders also add control and comfort, allowing you to adjust the height

consuming, and it is difficult to produce and maintain even tension on the fabric.

A disadvantage of using a ring frame is that it does not hold tension well or distribute it evenly, so the fabric is subjected to ring marks and possible distortion. An advantage is that it allows you to hoop a small area on a large—or even completed—segment of the garment.

SCROLL FRAME

A scroll frame is a rectangular needlework frame with roller bars that form the long sides of the frame. A scroll frame is especially useful for working large borders and motifs.

To use a scroll frame, baste the fabric being worked to the twill tape on one of the roller

Creating a Comfortable Work Space

The ideal work space for beading consists of three things: A clean desk or tabletop with ample room to spread out supplies; a sturdy chair with a wide seat and back support to keep you in the comfort zone; good overhead lighting plus a task light that can be positioned to spotlight your work area. I have a task light with incandescent and fluorescent bulbs (though some people prefer halogen lights) and am convinced I could not live without it.

Beading is concentrated, "close" work that intensifies even more when working with small beads or on a large project. To avoid fatigue and muscle strain while beading, work at a comfortable pace, change positions, stretch frequently, and take breaks at regular intervals.

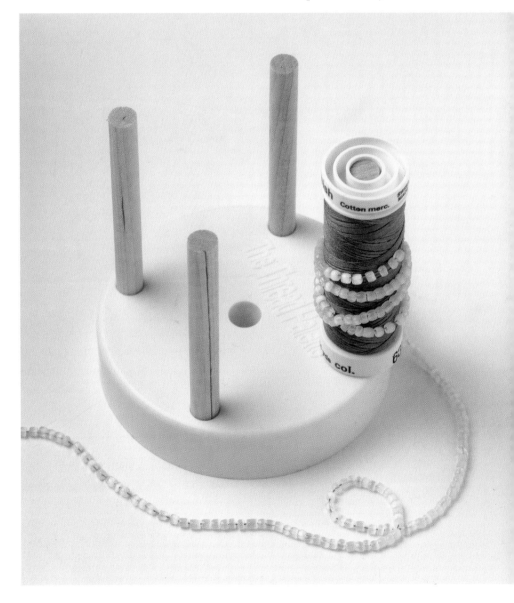

A freestanding spool holder keeps the thread spool in place and allows the thread to feed off the spool smoothly.

and angle of the frame or even rotate it (some frames can rotate 360°, so that the underside of the work can easily be turned for viewing— a necessity for tambour beading). Another nice feature of some adjustable frame holders is that the frame can be removed from the holder, so you always have the option of working in hand.

Spool holder

For projects that require you to have both hands free, such as with tambour beading, you'll need a spool holder (see the photo at right) to hold the spool so that the thread feeds freely as you work the design. Commercial thread palettes, consisting of a plastic base and dowels, work fine. Or you can make a simple spool holder by drilling a hole in a scrap of plywood and gluing a matching 3-in. to 5-in. dowel into the hole.

Boxes and trays

Like all things sewing and craft related, beading presents unique storage requirements. I have both long- and short-term storage arrangements. I use clear plastic boxes with dividers for my permanent (though ever-changing) bead stash and several shallow bead trays with covered compartments for projects

Fabric

While there's probably not a fabric in the world you couldn't bead, there are better and worse choices for beaded garments. For heavily beaded clothes, strength is a primary consideration, since the weight of the beads will stress the base to which they're sewn. Strength is determined by a number of factors, including fiber content and the structure of the weave. These are also factors that influence the longevity of the garment.

A second consideration is related to cleaning and pressing. Because pressing is problematic near beaded portions of the garment, it's worth considering fabrics that have natural wrinkle-resistant characteristics. Rayon, cotton, and linen are more prone to wrinkling than silk and wool. Likewise, plain-weave fabric structures tend to wrinkle more readily than crepes, jacquards, and twills.

Finally, while beading may enhance printed fabrics, it will appear more distinct on a solid color. All fabrics should be preshrunk in the same manner they will be cleaned when the garment is constructed. If you incorporate just a little beadwork on a corner prior to preshrinking, you can pretest the cleaning method you've chosen and switch to another should problems arise.

Design-transfer tools

Tools abound for transferring designs to fabric. Detailed information regarding methods and materials for design transfer are included in the Appendices (see p. 166). Always pretest chosen transfer methods to ensure that they produce distinct lines that will not inadvertently rub off or disappear and that the markings can be satisfactorily removed from the fabric after beading.

Bead trays and containers protect beads and keep them neatly organized and accessible.

in progress (see the photo above). Both arrangements allow me to separate beads by color, transport projects with ease, keep what I immediately need at hand, and work directly from the separate storage compartments and beading tray.

BEADING METHODS

Almost any manner of needlework can be adapted to beadwork and used to embellish garments. This is no great secret, of course. Beads have been used to adorn clothing from time immemorial and in cultures that span the globe. Bead embroidery, beaded buttons, edge, and fringe, tambour beading, and beadweaving into fabric are modes of ornamentation that will feel familiar to anyone with a working knowledge of ordinary needlework techniques. Common as these traditional beading methods might be, the bead-embellished garment is never regarded as such. Part of beadwork's appeal hinges upon its ability to elevate the mundane to the spectacular. The following methods offer simple yet highly effective ways to do just that.

Bead embroidery

Bead embroidery is the art of embellishing fabric with beads (see the photo below). Methods for doing so are as simple as they are innumerable, yet permutations of infinite complexity, depth, and character are possible. Likewise, their applicability to garment design is limited by imagination alone.

Nowhere is this more evident than in the garments embellished by the *paruriers*, or "adornment makers," of the French haute couture embroidery houses. In these houses, artful innovation, consummate craftsmanship, and pure genius remain unhindered by worldly considerations, such as time and money. In these enclaves of unfettered devotion, as many

Bead embroidery can add character to most any garment.

as 400 to 2,500 hours are lavished on *hand-worked* embellishments for a single garment. In all likelihood there's not a home sewer on the planet who'd entertain the possibility of devoting that amount of time to a project. Nevertheless, bead embroidery's many charms are well within the scope of practical application and offer myriad ways to elevate and transform your best sewing efforts.

PLANNING A BEAD-EMBROIDERED GARMENT

A bead-embroidered garment (see the drawing below) can be spontaneous or rigorously planned and precisely executed. The following considerations are offered to help you gauge the level of involvement that various bead-embroidery applications entail.

Beaded Blouse with Jewel Neckline

Bead embroidery offers myriad ways to elevate and transform your best sewing efforts. Here, bugles and flat faceted beads or paillettes accent the neckline and sleeves. Note that at the neckline, the sequence to the left and right of the center beads is decreased by one.

When to transfer the design to fabric

There are three instances in which transferring the design to fabric is called for: when design motifs are elaborate and complex; when the placement is critical in relation to its position on the garment and its wearer; and any time the design is worked in a frame. Designs can be drawn directly to fabric using a water-soluble marking pen or dressmaker marking pencil. They can be transferred using the prick-and-pounce method, dressmaker's transfer paper, and a tracing wheel, or with iron-on embroidery transfer pens (for more on transferring designs, see the Appendices on p. 166).

Complex borders and bands are simple to execute with the aid of a premarked grid. Use a clear ruler and water-soluble pencil or marker to draw grid lines directly to the fabric, or use your sewing machine with a seam-gauge attachment to baste in a grid structure that can be removed once the beading is complete.

When you need a frame

A frame stretches fabric taut, which temporarily stabilizes fabric for beading. It is a necessary tool for beading to noninterfaced, lightweight to medium-weight fabrics; for densely beaded applications; and for beading large areas of fabric that will be incorporated into a garment design. Also, some stitches require more stability than others for their successful execution. The lazy satin stitch, for example, has a tendency to draw the fabric in as it's being worked. The running stitch, on the other hand, works up readily without a frame because it puts little tension on the base fabric. Generally, beading in a frame is done prior to the construction of a garment, but a frame can also be used to add beaded motifs to noninterfaced areas of already constructed clothing.

When to bead in hand

Beading in hand (without a frame) is appropriate for many simple beading applications, including light beading (such as a running stitch) on stable, medium-weight fabrics;

beading interfaced portions of a garment; and beading dense, upholstery-weight fabrics. I love the simplicity of working without a frame because the project is less cumbersome and easier to transport.

For the most part, beading in hand is worked on completed garments. Interfaced areas such as collars, cuffs, facings, and front bands present wonderful opportunities for beading without the use of a frame. Likewise, tucks, pocket welts and flaps, insets, yokes, and plackets offer a stable canvas for bead embellishments. Used to full advantage, the lines, perimeters, and details of a garment provide reference points for simple designs and eliminate the need to premark fabric.

In addition to being easy to work, these interfaced and faced parts of the garment support the weight of the beads without being subject to distortion. Avoid large areas of dense beading without the use of a frame, unless you are working on a highly stable, heavy-weight upholstery fabric or feltlike fabric such as melton.

Consider the weight of the beads

Any time you plan elaborate beading for a garment, the weight of the beads should factor in with other design considerations. For instance, if the garment is unlined and the beaded area is not interfaced, the weight of the beads may have a dramatic impact on the way the garment hangs and the material drapes. In most cases, the weight of the beads should be distributed evenly from back to front and to the right and left side of the garment. Heavy beadwork at the hem of a dress, for example, should be balanced on the front and backside of the garment. On the other hand, the design itself need not be perfectly symmetrical.

Bias is yet another consideration, since any portion of the garment that's cut on the bias will be especially responsive to the weight of the beads. A-line skirts, with the seams cut on the bias, for instance, may be subject to a greater degree of distortion from the weight of beads than would skirts with the side seams cut on the lengthwise grain.

How to position the design

Working with a basted muslin of the garment is the only foolproof way I know to get a true indication of how the placement of a design interacts with the garment's drape on an actual figure. If possible, the muslin should be draped on the person for whom the finished garment is intended. Placement lines can be drawn in with a water-soluble marking pen, which allows you to reposition them until you get the design and placement right. In addition to pinpointing correct design placement relative to aesthetic concerns, be certain to position the design so that it will not be sat upon or rubbed against other beadwork.

Beading is done prior to cutting and construction when elaborate designs are worked directly to large, noninterfaced areas of the garment; when it is desirable to hide the stitches on the wrong side of the garment with a facing, hem, or lining; and when the area to be beaded would be difficult to reach or to work with a needle and thread once the garment was constructed.

Prior to transferring the beading design, pin the pattern piece that is to be beaded to the right side of the fabric and trace around it. When transferring the actual beading design, bear in mind that beadwork can extend to the seamline but not beyond it. When you position beadwork near a seam, that portion of the garment must be sewn by hand or with a zipper foot because a standard presser foot would crush the beads. Also, designs that meet at a seamline must match when the pieces are sewn, so proper placement of the design is critical. Another way you can ensure that the design flow is uninterrupted at the seam is to add beadwork once the seams in question are sewn; however, this is not always an option.

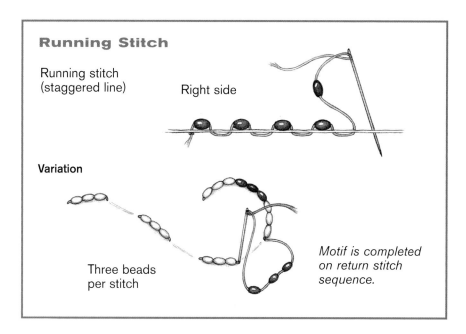

Running Stitch

Running stitch
(staggered line)

Right side

Variation

Three beads
per stitch

*Motif is completed
on return stitch
sequence.*

BASIC STITCHES
FOR BEAD EMBROIDERY

If you've done any type of needlework or
embroidery, working with beads will expand
upon skills you already possess. If not, rest
assured that the techniques are easy to master.
As the diagrams of basic stitches in this section indicate, simple approaches can be effective, and the skills you build embellishing
an easy beaded tunic for everyday wear are
readily transferred to an elaborately designed
dress for a special occasion.

The repertoire of bead-embroidery stitches
falls into two basic classifications: sewing and
couching. Sewn beads are stitched directly
through the hole of the bead to cloth, while
couched beads are prestrung (for more on
couching, see the sidebar on p. 25). Beads are
worked singularly and in sets. The most common stitches used to sew beads to fabric
include the running stitch, lazy stitch (and a
variation called the lazy satin stitch), overlay
stitch, raised stitch, backstitch, and chainstitch. In addition to these, almost any decorative embroidery stitch can be used with beads.
You can couch with a single needle and thread
or with two needles and thread.

Applications for the basic stitches are
numerous, since beads can be combined in an
infinite variety of ways. The stitches described
here can be used alone or in combination to
produce edges, motifs and trims, wide border
designs, or all-over beading on garments. Use
them as well to adorn ribbons, braids, gimps,
and trims, or combine them with other
embellishment techniques to add color, texture, and light. Hand or machine embroidery,
trapunto, channelstitching, traditional or
reverse appliqué, quilting, and any form of surface embellishment can be further enriched
with beadwork.

Running stitch

The running stitch is the simplest bead-
embroidery stitch (see the drawings at left). It
works up exceptionally fast, and the results are
very effective. Because it puts so little stress on
the fabric, this is a good stitch to work in
hand. Use it to create simple motifs on a beaded blouse; to edge a collar, cuffs, or tucks; or
combine with topstitching and stagger beaded
rows for a dappled effect.

1   Thread the needle, knot the thread, and
    bring to the right side of the garment at
    the beginning of the design.

2   Pick up a bead on the tip of the needle.

3   Reinsert the needle a bead length away,
    take a stitch up to ½ in. on the underside,
    and bring the needle to the right side of
    the garment.

4   Pick up a second bead and continue the
    basic stitch along the design line. More
    than one bead can be threaded on the
    needle at one time.

5   To work a solid line, thread several beads
    at a time. When the line is complete,
    work back along the same line from the
    opposite direction. Fill in the spaces be-
    tween beads on the return pass.

Lazy stitch

The lazy stitch is used primarily to produce areas of solid beading (see the drawing at right). Rows of beads are stitched side by side and can be worked vertically or horizontally in any direction. Use this stitch to bead floral motifs, bands, and borders, and to bead over quilted or corded trapunto designs.

1   Stretch the area to be beaded in a ring or frame.

2   Knot the working thread and bring the needle to the right side of the garment.

3   Pick up three to six beads on the tip of the needle.

4   Reinsert the needle three to six bead lengths away.

5   Take a small stitch to the right of the bead row (working the design left to right) and bring the needle to the right side of the garment.

6   Pick up three to six more beads and bring the stitch down, parallel to the first row.

7   Take a stitch to the right, and proceed, laying parallel rows up and down, and working to the right.

Lazy satin stitch

This variation of the lazy stitch works up even more quickly than the previous version. Rather than taking a short stitch at the top and bottom of each beaded row, pass the needle beneath the fabric to the opposite side of the row prior to adding beads for each stitch (see the drawing at right). The stitch is always worked in the same direction, and the thread forms a satin stitch on the wrong side of the fabric. (With the other version, very little thread shows on the back side.)

Overlay stitch

The overlay stitch is an excellent way to produce a solid beaded line. Use this stitch for

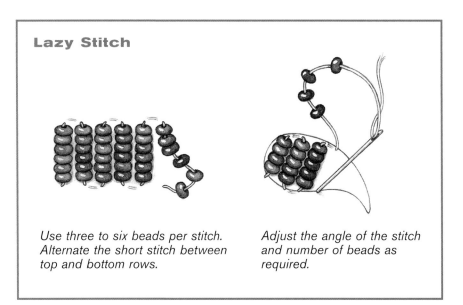

Lazy Stitch

Use three to six beads per stitch. Alternate the short stitch between top and bottom rows.

Adjust the angle of the stitch and number of beads as required.

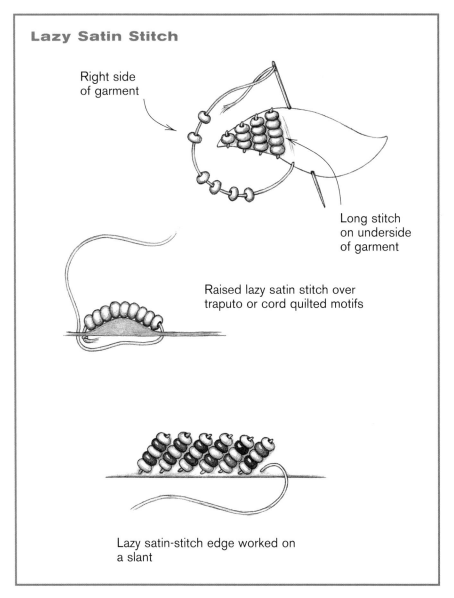

Lazy Satin Stitch

Right side of garment

Long stitch on underside of garment

Raised lazy satin stitch over traputo or cord quilted motifs

Lazy satin-stitch edge worked on a slant

Overlay Stitch

Two-bead overlay stitch

Four-bead overlay stitch

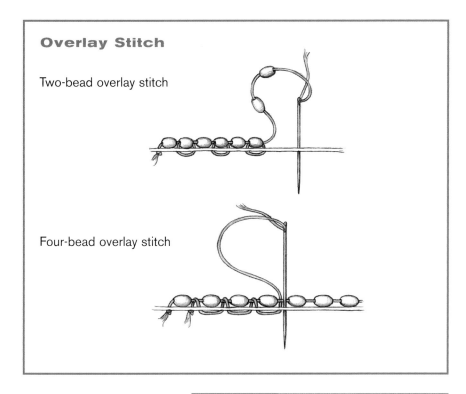

Raised Stitch

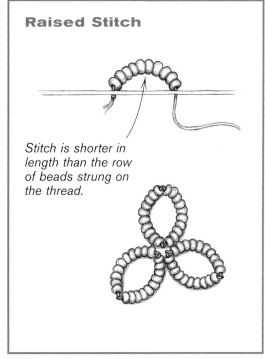

Stitch is shorter in length than the row of beads strung on the thread.

beading large motifs and borders, or work it in consecutive rows to create a sturdy edge on necklines, sleeves, and hems. Simple color and pattern variations work up well. For complex patterns, charting the design on graph paper will help you keep track of the color sequences. This stitch does not work up as quickly as the running stitch or couching, but the stitch is more secure, since the backstitch "locks in" each stitch sequence. The following directions for the two-bead overlay stitch can easily be adapted to the four-bead version (see the drawings at left).

1   Thread the needle, knot the end of the thread, and bring it to the right side of the garment.

2   Pick up two beads on the needle.

3   Take the stitch into the fabric two bead lengths away.

4   Backstitch one bead length and bring the needle to the right side of the fabric, between beads.

5   Insert the needle through the hole of the second bead. Add two more beads to the needle and repeat the stitch, moving forward along the design line.

Raised stitch

A raised stitch arches away from the fabric slightly (see the drawings at left), similar to a bullion stitch in embroidery.

1   Begin with several seed beads on the needle.

2   Take a stitch into the fabric that is shorter that the length of beads on the needle. The short stitch keeps the beads from lying flat.

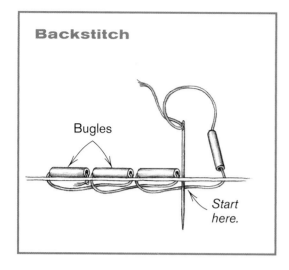

Backstitch

Bugles

Start here.

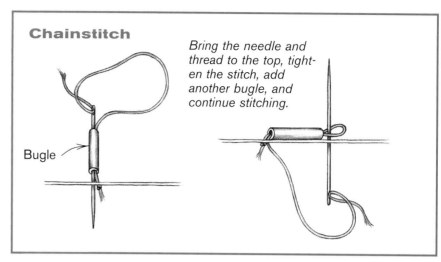

Chainstitch

Bring the needle and thread to the top, tighten the stitch, add another bugle, and continue stitching.

Bugle

Backstitch

The backstitch works well for sewing a solid line of bugles (see the left drawing above). Use it as well for sewing sequins, paillettes, or several seed beads at one time. Paillettes can be worked edge to edge or overlapping, in which case the stitch will be shorter. Either way, the thread will show, so consider using invisible nylon or something suitably decorative.

1   Working away from you, bring the needle and thread to the right side of the fabric, a bugle's length from the beginning of the design line.

2   Pick up a bugle on the needle, backstitch the length of the bugle, and bring the needle to the wrong side of the fabric at the beginning of the design.

3   Bring the needle forward to the right side of the fabric, two bugle lengths along the design line. Add a second bugle with the backstitch, bring the needle forward two bugle lengths, and repeat the sequence.

Chainstitch

I like using the chainstitch (see the right drawing above) because I never have to second-guess the length of the stitch. Also, the back side of the garment is neat, and the short

stitch is not likely to catch on something and pull or break. The chainstitch is great for sewing bugles, but it can also be used to sew a row of seed beads or large decorative beads.

1   Working away from you, bring the needle and thread to the right side of the garment.

2   Add a bugle, and with the bugle perpendicular to the fabric, reinsert the needle into the hole from which it emerged.

3   Lay the bugle along the design line and pull the thread through to the wrong side of the fabric until a small loop remains at the tip of the bugle.

4   Bring the needle through the fabric and the loop on the right side of the garment. As you pull the thread through, it will tighten the stitch and form a chain.

5   Add another bugle, and repeat the stitch sequence.

Couching with a single needle and thread

I recommend this method of couching when working small areas (see the steps and drawing on p. 24). Couching worked in a freestanding frame frees up both of your hands to position the row of beads and to guide the stitch.

Couching with a Single Needle

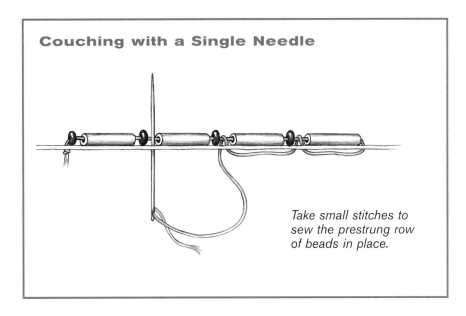

Take small stitches to sew the prestrung row of beads in place.

Couching with Two Needles

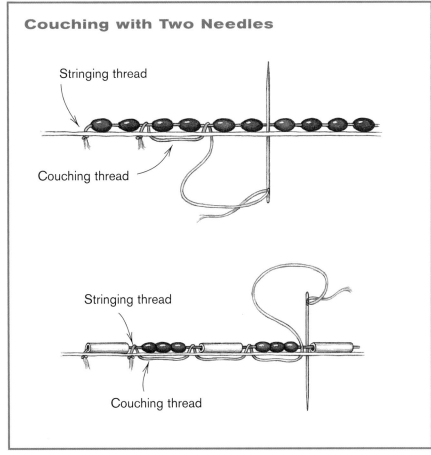

Stringing thread

Couching thread

Stringing thread

Couching thread

1 Knot one end of the thread and bring the needle through to the right side of the fabric.

2 String the beads on the thread. The number of beads will depend upon the line or row that you are beading. The length of beads should equal the length of the line to be beaded.

3 Lay the beads on the fabric along the design line.

4 Backstitch into the fabric at the end of the design and couch back over the row of beads, taking small stitches into the fabric every three beads or so, to keep the string of beads in place.

Couching with two needles and threads

Use this method of couching to attach long rows of prestrung beads (see the drawing at left). If you are working with beads of one color, save stringing time by transferring the beads from the hank directly to your thread.

1 Knot one end of a long length of thread and bring the needle through to the right side of the fabric.

2 String the beads individually to thread or transfer beads from the hank.

3 To transfer beads from the hank, tie thread ends together with a square knot, and transfer the beads from the hank to your thread (see the drawing on p. 27).

4 Rethread the needle and use a backstitch to secure the beaded thread to the fabric along the design line.

5 Thread a second needle and bring it to the right side of the fabric at the beginning of the design. Couch down the beaded thread between beads at regular intervals.

Couched Beads

Unlike beads sewn directly to fabric, couched beads are prestrung. The beading string is stitched to the fabric between beads at regular intervals, which hold the row of beads in place. Couching works up faster than sewing beads individually. It is an especially quick way to fill in large design areas and rows of beading. Couching can be done with one needle and thread or two. Some of the basic couching stitches are shown below.

Basic couching stitches

Couching to fill in design, or for borders

Attaching decorative bead, doughnut, or sequin with a smaller (seed) bead or crystal

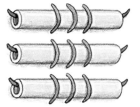

Couched fringe or zigzag motif

Couched bugles

Row of paillettes couched with bugles and seed beads

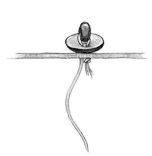

Sewing paillettes with beads and stitches

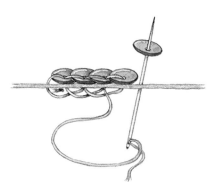

Overlapping sequins sewn with backstitch

Tambour beading

Tambour beading is an offshoot of tambour embroidery and is an eminently practical method of producing beaded motifs, bands, and overall designs. Speedier than most handwork, it's widely used in ethnic textiles, fashion garments, and haute couture. Worked with the fabric in a frame, and a specially designed needle or hook, tambour beading is an extremely versatile and efficient way to embellish clothing and accessories. Like knitting or crochet, the technique is simple, but it does initially take practice, time, and patience to develop a feel for guiding the tambour hook and for attaching beads to the underside of the fabric. (For tambour beading, the right side of the work is positioned to the underside of the frame.)

For best results, allow time to sample the basic methods and develop a consistent stitch before you embark on a major project. As you master the technique and pick up speed, you'll develop a feel for how long it takes to bead a design. This will help in planning designs and will ensure that your project does not demand substantially more time and energy than you expected to devote to it.

PREPARING FOR TAMBOUR BEADING

To prepare for tambour beading, you must first choose a basic design and determine the placement of the beadwork in relation to the finished garment. Then you transfer the design to fabric and stretch it in a frame. You can then string the beads or transfer them to the working thread and begin beading.

Transferring the design

Tambour beading is worked with the wrong side of the fabric facing up, which virtually eliminates concerns about removing transfer lines once the work is complete. Removing the marking material is still desirable, of course, but a slight residue on the fabric is bound to be less of an issue when it's invisible from the outside of the garment. What is problematic about transferring the design to the wrong side of the garment is that it reverses the direction of the beaded image seen from the right side.

To correct this problem, you need to reverse the image prior to transfer. A simple way to do this is to tape the image to a window or light table, with the image toward the table and the wrong side facing you. The light will shine through the image, which you will now see in reverse. You can tape a piece of tracing paper to the window over the reversed image and trace the design as accurately as possible with a pencil. The traced design can then be transferred to the wrong side of your fabric using the prick-and-pounce method, transfer paper, or with an embroidery transfer pen (see the Appendices on p. 166).

Framing

Tambour beading and embroidery demands that the working surface be stretched tight as a drum, which is how the technique originally got its name. A properly stretched fabric resists the tension of needle and thread and allows a perfect stitch to form on the surface of the fabric.

If you use a ring frame, you can stretch fabric—wrong-side up—directly to the frame. Wrapping the inner ring of the frame with flat bias tape will increase the holding power of the frame and reduce slippage. For fine fabrics that may distort easily, baste the fashion fabric to muslin that's already stretched in the frame. Then simply cut the muslin away from beneath to provide an open area for beading to the fashion fabric. In this manner, you can reposition the fabric (basted or pinned) for beading a large motif or for beading more than one motif on a large piece of fabric. While it is conceivable to bead a large area in this manner, it is far more expedient to use a rectangular frame to bead large sections of fabric. In the best of all possible worlds, this frame would be large enough to accommodate pattern pieces that are to be embellished for the garment. That way, the entire pattern piece could be drawn onto the fabric and beaded prior to cutting out the garment. This method is frequently used in haute couture.

Transferring beads to the working thread

Buying beads by the hank eliminates the need to prestring them prior to beading and is a great time-saver. To transfer prestrung beads, tie the thread from the bead strand to the working thread with a weaver's knot (see the drawing at right) and slide the beads over the knot onto the working thread. Of course, there will inevitably be loose beads that appeal to you for reasons other than mere convenience, and you'll have to string these beads on the working thread.

No more than a yard of beads should be added to the spool at one time to minimize the length of repair should a portion of the chain come loose. Working bead lengths shorter than 36 in. are fine, but tie-offs will be more frequent. For practical purposes, that means when the beads on the working thread are exhausted, it will be necessary to fasten off and secure the working thread, restring or transfer a new strand of beads, fasten on the working thread, and proceed with beading.

Tambour-beading methods

The foundation for tambour beading is the chainstitch. Worked with bead-strung thread, the tambour hook draws the beaded thread from front (bottom facing) to back (top facing). A chain is formed on the wrong (top) side, which is pulled forward to form a stitch that secures the bead to the right side of the garment. Sequential stitches are worked in lines or motifs using this basic stitch.

Since the addition of beads involves coordinating yet another element into the stitch formation, it is a good idea to master the basic chainstitch using thread only. When you

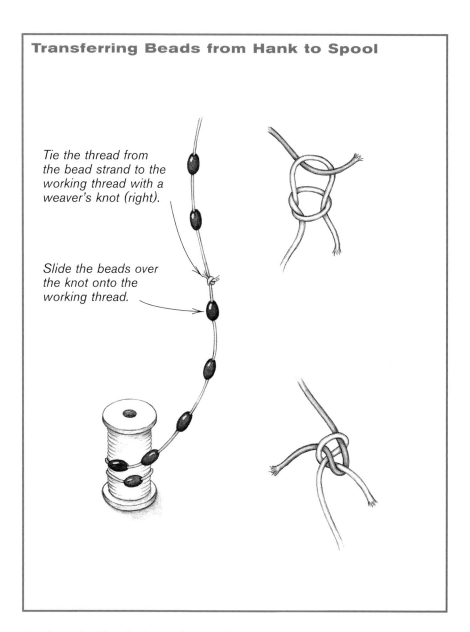

Transferring Beads from Hank to Spool

Tie the thread from the bead strand to the working thread with a weaver's knot (right).

Slide the beads over the knot onto the working thread.

develop a feel for the basic chainstitch, move on to beading. Try working your first samples on a sheer fabric, such as silk organdy or even nylon net. When you can see where your hands are positioned, see where to put the thread around the needle, and see what's going on with the beads that you're attempting to find and hold in place while you work the stitch, you will learn faster and fumble less.

Working the basic chainstitch

The chainstitch can be used for embroidery. Once you perfect it, you will have mastered a major component of tambour beading (see the steps on p. 28).

1   Insert the needle into the tambour holder. Check to see that the hook side of the needle aligns with the thumbscrew.

2   With your left hand, pick up the working thread approximately 10 in. to 15 in. from its end. Fold this length in half to form a loop. Insert your thumb and forefinger into the loop and stretch taut, holding the remainder of the thread tight in your fist. Hold the stretched thread beneath the tambour frame, just below the start of your design.

3   Insert the hook into the fabric at the beginning of a row or design. The thumbscrew will face away from you and will indicate the direction of the stitch.

4   Slide the taut thread onto the tambour hook from the underside of the frame (see drawing 1 on the facing page). You can actually hear a faint "pop" as it engages with the hook. Turn the hook to the left and bring the thread loop through the fabric to the topside of the frame (see drawing 2 on the facing page).

5   Bring the loop forward along the pre-marked stitching line; turn the hook 90° to its original, forward-facing position and reinsert into the fabric.

6   This time, slide the loose tail end of the thread onto the hook beneath the frame. Twist the hook to the left and pull the tail of the thread completely through the fabric so that it lies on the top of the frame (see drawing 3 on the facing page). With a hand-sewing needle, thread the tail end, take a tiny stitch through the fabric, wrap the thread under and around the first loop of the chain, and knot off. This secures the beginning of the chain.

7   Reinsert the tambour hook into the first thread loop. The needle must completely penetrate the fabric but should lie just below the fabric's surface (see drawing 4 on the facing page).

8   Slide the working thread onto the hook, beneath the frame, rotate the hook 90° left, and pull the working thread through the fabric. Reduce tension on the working thread to allow it to feed easily and form a loop. (Tension on the thread is controlled by the hand below the frame.)

9   Draw this loop through the first and bring it forward along the stitching line to form a chain. Subsequent stitches are formed in the same manner (see drawing 5 on the facing page).

10   Rotating the needle so that it draws up a loop and enters and exits the fabric without snagging is the key to developing a consistent stitch. Penetrating the fabric at a slight angle and exerting light pressure on the needle by pulling it toward you as you pull the working thread to the top side enlarges the needle hole and provides clearance for the reemerging hook and thread. Likewise, twisting the hook to the right or left prior to raising the needle minimizes the opportunity to snag the fabric or the previous loop.

11   Work the stitch sequence loosely, allowing enough thread to feed into the working loop, and draw through the previous chain. While working the needle, the hand should remain directly on the frame. As with handwriting, or typing, the motion is in the fingers, not in the arm.

12   To change directions, simply rotate the hook in the direction of the design. The thumbscrew will indicate the direction of the next stitch. Since the thumbscrew is always visible from the top side of the frame and is in alignment with the hook side of the needle, it also serves as a guide for placing the thread into the hook from beneath the frame.

Tambour Beading

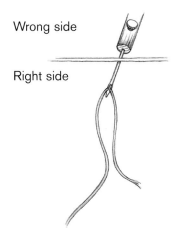

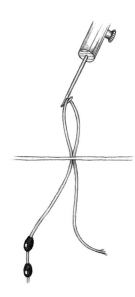

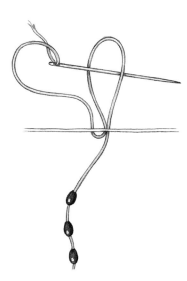

Wrong side

Right side

1. Insert the hook through the fabric. Lay the thread into the hook.

2. Rotate the hook 90° to the left and pull the thread tail to the top side of the fabric.

3. Thread the tail end with a hand-sewing needle. Backstitch through the fabric and tie off in a knot.

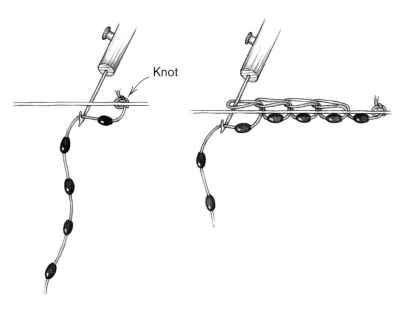

Knot

4. Reinsert the hook and pull the working thread to the top, forming a chain or loop. Twist the hook to the left prior to drawing the working thread to the top.

5. Bring the chain forward, reinsert the hook into the fabric. Draw the working thread through the fabric and the previous chain and bring the next loop forward along the stitching line once more.

Working the beaded chain

Now that you can work the basic chainstitch comfortably, it is time to add beads.

1 Place spool on spool holder, and transfer the beads to the working thread (see the drawing on p. 27).

2 Insert the needle, draw up the thread, and begin the row with two or three small chainstitches prior to adding beads.

3 When the third chainstitch loop is pulled to the surface, push one bead snug against the underside of the fabric, close to the previous stitch.

4 To keep beads from dropping away from the work area, keep the drop from the frame to the spool holder short and the angle parallel rather than perpendicular to the frame.

5 Pull the chain forward. Insert the hook from the top side and latch onto the thread below to secure the bead and produce the next stitch.

6 Again, bring the thread to the top through the previous loop. Add a bead directly beneath it on the underside, move the chain forward to secure the next bead, and so on.

Securing the beaded chain

This method will result in a clean and strong finish.

1 When a beading sequence has been completed, finish the row with two small chainstitches.

2 Break the thread underneath the frame, leaving a tail.

3 Thread the tail through the last chain to the top side of the frame.

4 Work the thread tail into the surrounding threads and tie off. If the chain is worked as embroidery on the right side of the garment, bring the loose tail through and

over the loop. Pull or thread it to the underside of the frame and tie off. Knotting on the top side of the frame is appropriate for beading applications only, since the wrong side of the garment faces up.

Beaded edges and fringe

Beaded edges and fringe are finishing touches added to a garment or accessory once it has been sewn (see the top drawing on the facing page). Faggotting, on the other hand, is a method of construction that, when worked in beads, also functions as ornamentation. Of these methods, edges are likely to prove most versatile, and they're simple, fast, and fun to do. Use them on collars, cuffs, borders, and hems of garments. Fringe runs the gamut in terms of complexity and adds elements of flamboyance, romanticism, and mystique to whatever it adorns. Try my method for netted fringe on a cut-velvet scarf or even at the hem of a tunic or shell.

BEADED-EDGE METHODS

The following beaded edges are stitched directly to the garment but extend beyond it like a tiny ruffle or fringe. Used to trim collars, cuffs, necklines, and hems, they impart delicacy and charm to whatever they adorn. Have fun experimenting with color combinations, various bead sizes, and the addition of small crystals, gems, or other accent beads for that perfect look.

Running-stitch edge

This edge is easy and makes up very quickly (see the bottom drawing on the facing page). The running stitch is worked between two layers of fabric (upper and under collar, for example), so the thread is completely hidden.

1 Knot one end of thread and bring the needle between layers through the seamed edge or hem of the area to be embellished.

Simple Beaded Tunic with Beaded Edges

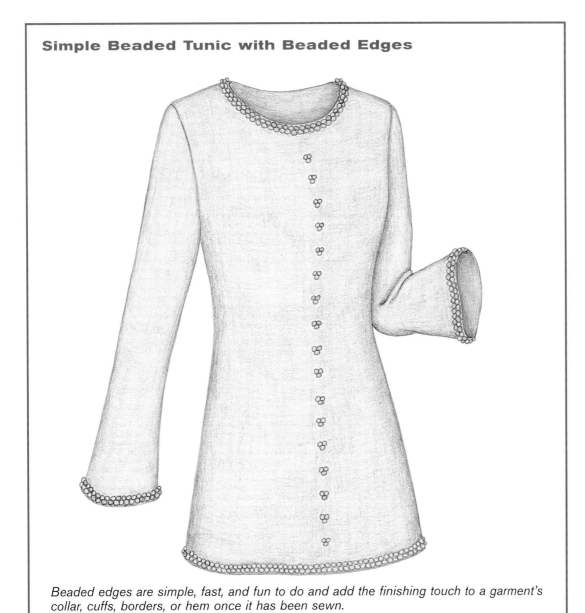

Beaded edges are simple, fast, and fun to do and add the finishing touch to a garment's collar, cuffs, borders, or hem once it has been sewn.

2   Pick up three beads on the needle.

3   Reinsert the needle into the same hole and take a running stitch ⅛ in. to ¼ in. away from the previous stitch.

4   Draw the thread through. The three beads will form a triangular shape.

5   Pick up three more beads and repeat the sequence around the entire edge.

Running-Stitch Edge

Take stitches between fabric layers at the garment's edge.

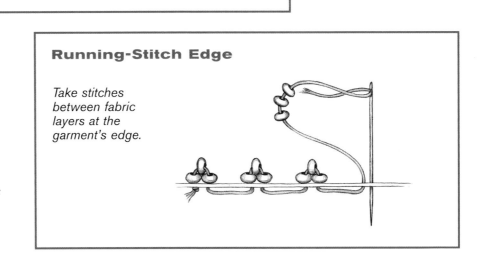

Zigzag bugle-bead variation

This is a variation of the running-stitch edge described previously (see the drawing below).

1 Bring the needle through to the edge of the area to be embellished.

2 Pick up a seed bead, bugle, seed bead, bugle and seed bead, in that order.

3 Reinsert the needle into the fabric edge, one bugle and one seed-bead length from the original stitch. The strung bead sequence will form a V.

4 Take a tiny running stitch through the fabric layers and pick up the next sequence of beads.

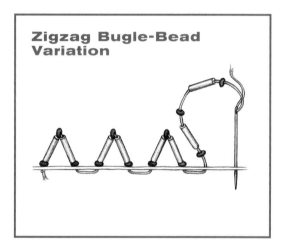

Zigzag Bugle-Bead Variation

Outline edge

This stitch produces a solid line of beading around an edge (see the drawing below). Directions are for a single bead edge, but up to four beads per stitch can be used. If desired, loops and picots can be added by weaving back through the foundation rows.

1 Knot the end of the thread and bring the needle through the fabric from back to front.

2 Pick up a single bead and secure it to the fabric with a tiny stitch from back to front.

3 Bring the needle through the hole of the bead. (If you've picked up more than one bead, thread back through the entire sequence of beads. The thread will emerge from the outermost bead. Proceed to step four, picking up the next sequence of beads.)

4 Pick up a second bead and take a stitch into the edge of the fabric from back to front, next to the first bead.

5 Bring the needle through the hole of the second bead and repeat the sequence. The beads should touch and will form a solid line.

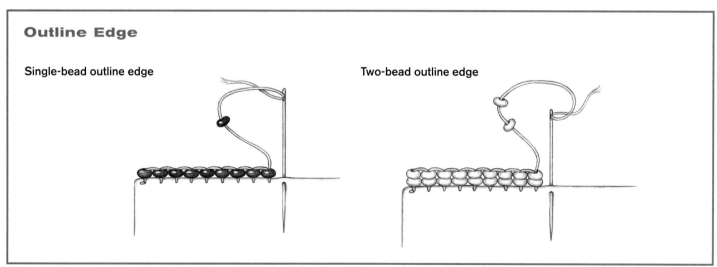

Outline Edge

Single-bead outline edge

Two-bead outline edge

Bead-laced edges

Bead-laced edges are sturdier than those worked with the running stitch, but they look every bit as delicate, especially if done with small, uniform beads (variations are shown in the drawings at right). For a more compact look, eliminate the space between the stitches. To vary the basic stitch, increase the number of beads picked up in each sequence; alternate the number of beads picked up every other stitch sequence; or pass the needle through more than one bead on the return.

1   At the edge of the fabric, take a small stitch from back to front.

2   Pick up a single bead on the needle.

3   Again, bring the needle from back to front, securing the bead.

4   Bring the needle through the hole of the bead, and pick up two more beads.

5   Insert the needle from back to front, one bead width from the first bead in the row.

6   Pick up two more beads and continue the sequence.

NETTED FRINGE

This two-step fringe (see the photo on p. 34) incorporates two basic elements: a closely netted border and a loose netted fringe that dangles from the border at regular intervals (see the drawings on p. 35). The border is worked horizontally; the loose netted fringe is worked vertically. The effect is lush. You can make the length of both the border and the fringe longer or shorter to produce a range of effects and to suit your project.

Seed beads of uniform size are used for the border and netted fringe. Larger beads and crystals can be used at the bottom of the fringe and where the net intersects. This fringe can be worked in one or many colors. Play with color variations as you work up your initial sample, or chart a pleasing pattern in advance. Cut beads yield good results and

Bead-Laced Edges

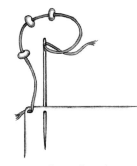

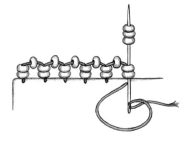

Stitches spaced one bead width apart

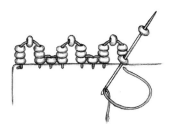

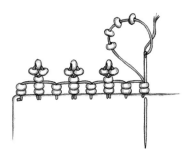

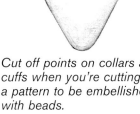

Cut off points on collars and cuffs when you're cutting out a pattern to be embellished with beads.

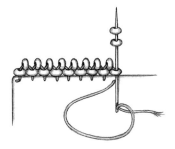

Same stitch pattern—spacing between beads eliminated

Beading around the tip of a collar may require adding a few more beads and altering the spacing.

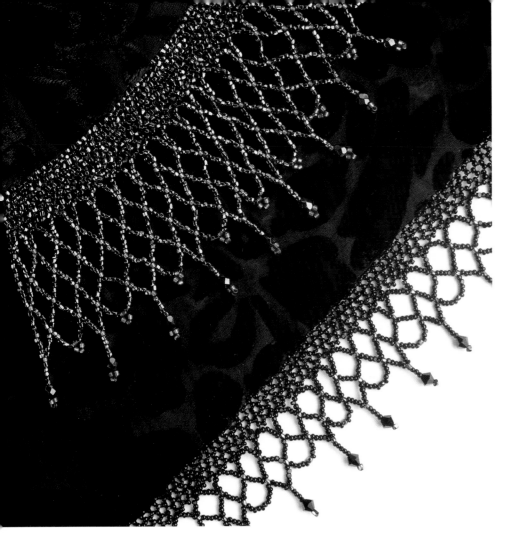

This two-step fringe incorporates a closely netted border (worked horizontally) and a loose netted fringe (worked vertically) that dangles from the border.

provide sparkle due to the way that faceted beads catch the light. I've had excellent results with size 13 charlottes and size 11 tricuts, but there are numerous other beads worthy of experimentation.

Horizontal netted fringe
This stitch serves as a foundation for the looser fringe. You can vary the tension for a dense or more airy effect.

1   Knot a length of thread and take a stitch in the fabric from back to front. Secure with a small backstitch. To begin the first row of beading, pick up one bead only. Secure with a stitch from back to front and pick up two beads for each subsequent stitch. Work from left to right, with the edge of the garment pointing away from you, as shown in drawing 1 on the facing page.

2   With two beads threaded, reinsert the needle from back to front and draw the entire length of thread through the cloth, as shown in drawing 2 on the facing page. As you pull the stitch tight, the first bead will "pop" out, producing a picot effect.

3   With the needle pointing away from you, bring it through the center of the last bead in the row. Complete the stitch and pick up two more beads. Repeat until the row is complete. At least one row of the foundation netting is necessary.

4   Add more rows as desired. To continue working additional rows of foundation netting, turn the edge to the reverse side, and work the subsequent row in the same direction as you did the first: left to right, if you're right-handed, right to left if your left-handed.

Vertical netted fringe
The fringe can be as dramatic or as restrained as you want, depending on the length and the bead combinations you choose.

1   Begin the fringe by beading through the first bead in the last row of the foundational border. Work left to right if you're right-handed; right to left if you're left-handed. For this portion of the beading, the edge of the fabric should face you.

2   The first length of beads establishes the pattern for the net portion of the fringe. Any number of equal bead groupings can be used for the net, but the total number of sequences must be odd (3, 5, 7). Separate each sequence with a larger bead or contrasting color to add visual interest and to make counting easier (see the bottom drawing on the facing page).

3   The "dangle" portion of the fringe can also be any length. Unlike the net portion—which requires a consistent number of beads for each length—the length of the dangles can be varied. Dangles of alternate or graduated lengths can be used for visually stunning results.

Horizontal Netted Fringe

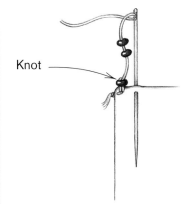

Knot

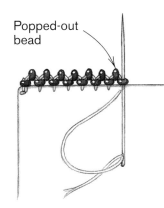

Popped-out bead

1. Knot the thread, take a stitch from back to front, and secure with a small backstitch. Pick up one bead and secure it with a stitch from back to front.

2. Thread two beads, reinsert needle from back to front, and draw the length of thread through. As you pull the stitch tight, the first bead will "pop" out.

3. Add more rows as desired.

Vertical Netted Fringe

When back at the top, pass the needle through the third or fourth bead in the last row of close border (or space as desired), and begin new row of fringe. Alternating the dangle designs adds interest.

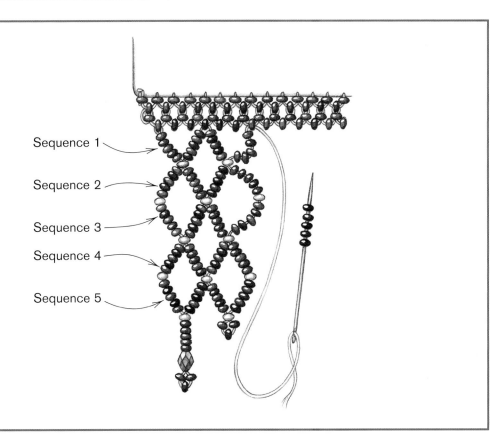

Sequence 1

Sequence 2

Sequence 3

Sequence 4

Sequence 5

Beadweaving into fabric provides a stunning accent suitable for a variety of blouse and jacket styles.

Beadweaving into fabric

Traditional beadweaving is produced on small looms warped lengthwise with an odd number of threads. Beads are strung on a weft (cross-grain) thread, passed under the loom selvage to selvage, and held in place from beneath so that a single bead fills each space between the threads. The direction of the weft is then reversed and passed over the top of the warp (lengthwise grain) directly through the entire row of beads.

Rows worked back and forth in this manner create a fabriclike structure from beads, with the weft passing under and over the warp to secure them. Like needlepoint or cross-stitch, motifs for beadweaving are rich and varied. Any design that can be graphed or charted can be worked in this manner. Beadweaving that's done on a loom is used for a variety of applications, including appliquéd surface design for garments.

In the following beadweaving variation, weft threads are removed from fabric to simulate a loom structure. The fabric is stretched in a ring or frame to keep the threads taut for working. The beads are then secured to the exposed warp with a weft thread. The beauty of this technique is that the beading is fully integrated into the structure of the fabric (see the photo at left). It sinks into the garment, rather than sitting on top of it. Even in small doses, this method of embellishment produces a wonderful, mysterious effect.

COORDINATING AND PRETESTING MATERIALS

The range of fabrics suitable for beadweaving applications for garments is narrow compared to other techniques. It is essential to coordinate and pretest fabrics for general suitability in relation to the technique and compatibility with appropriate beads.

Beadweaving tends to work best on firm, even-weave fabrics such linen, cotton, and linenlike silk. It is critical that the fabric be stable and strong enough to support the bead-work. Loosely woven fabrics with a low thread count are ideal. Weft-faced fabrics may also work, since the warp is set farther apart and, when exposed, may readily accommodate beads without alterations. Depending on the thread count, some fabrics may require some warp—as well as the standard weft threads—to be removed to make room for the beads.

To determine whether a fabric is suitable for beadweaving applications, take a small swatch of the fabric, remove a few threads from the lengthwise edge, then pull out the crosswise threads to expose the warp. Gauge the distance between warp threads to determine if a bead is likely to fit between two threads. If not, determine how many warp threads would need to be removed for a size 13, 14, or 15 bead to fit. If more than every other thread would need to be removed, consider looking for another fabric.

Beads should be chosen after an appropriate fabric selection has been made. Take your fabric sample with you when you shop for beads so that you can select the right size beads and make good color choices. The bead should fit between warp threads. If the beads you are considering appear to be too large, try removing every other warp thread to create more room, or find another appropriate style bead in a different size.

Beadweaving requires beads that are smooth and uniform in shape and size. Delica beads are designed specifically for beadweaving applications. Their square shape allows the beads to snug up to one another, with little space between, and the large hole of the bead readily accommodates needle and thread. Small seed beads (sizes 12, 13, and 15) can also be used for beadweaving but may not be as uniform as delicas, and the holes are generally smaller. Test the beads you select with the long needle you intend to use to be sure that the needle fits through the hole.

SELECTING A DESIGN

Your beadweaving design will no doubt be worked out in relation to a host of other considerations, including pattern and fabric selection, the type of beads available, etc. Keep in mind that even very simple graphic motifs will have a powerful impact.

Design sources for beadweaving are numerous. Any charted needlework design can be transposed. Beadweaving patterns are available by the sheet, pamphlet, and book from bead suppliers. One of the most exciting design tools available to beaders are computer programs such as Bead Plan II (see p. 168), which allow you to chart bead designs in color using a bead graph. The programs allow you to plan a design and color scheme true to the shape and size of your beads and print it out for easy reference. Alternatively, graphing paper specifically for charting bead designs is available through bead suppliers.

PLACING THE DESIGN

Placement of the beadwoven design must be determined in relation to the garment. The possibilities are limitless. Picture bright, beaded squares on the lapel of a jacket; a beaded band near the hem of sleeve; a rectangular window of light on the front of a vest.

Although it's conceivable to chart the design in alternative shapes, the most straightforward approach assumes that the beadweaving will be done in rectangles or squares and will be aligned with the lengthwise and crosswise grain of the fabric. It is therefore necessary to consult the grainline indicators on the pattern prior to placing the design. Designs can also be placed on the bias for a different effect. This is an inherent possibility if a beadwoven design is worked into a lapel, for example, or a bias inset.

Once you have determined how large the finished designs will be and where they are to be arranged, take the following steps to ensure their proper placement on the finished garment.

Blouse with Bead-Woven Insets

1. Trace the outline of each garment piece that will be embellished directly to the fabric. Do not cut these pieces out prior to beading.

2. Once you've determined the exact size of the beaded areas, mark their exact size and placement on the outlined garment piece (the fabric) and the paper pattern using a water-soluble fabric marker or other appropriate marking device.

3. Double-check the placement by pin-fitting the pattern, then make any necessary adjustments. Once you are satisfied with the placement, you're ready to prepare the warp.

(see p. 168)

BEADWEAVING INTO FABRIC

Delica seed beads, or other uniform rocailles (sizes 12 to 15)

Beadweaving, delica, or big-eye needles (longer than the width of the area to be woven)

Lightweight silk, polyester, or Nymo 0 or B thread

Embroidery ring or scroll frame

Water-soluble fabric marker

M A T E R I A L S   L I S T

37

PREPARING THE WARP

The fabric "loom" for beadweaving is prepared in the following manner.

1 Locate the areas of your fabric that are marked for beadwork. Cut weft threads from top to bottom down the center of these marked areas, parallel to the warp. For precise results and control, use small, sharp embroidery scissors. Be very careful not to cut the surrounding warp threads (see drawing 1 on the facing page).

2 With a needle or awl, coax the weft threads out of the warp until you reach the outer border of the design. The first few threads will be resistant, but as you withdraw consecutive threads, this chore will become easier.

3 When the weft threads are completely withdrawn, the warp will be exposed. If alternate threads are to be removed from the warp, clip them in the middle.

4 All threads that are clipped must be turned away from the opening and woven back into the surrounding fabric. If the area cut was small and the threads are short, a tiny crochet hook will prove more useful than a needle for this task. Once you've woven them in to the point of being secure, draw in all loose threads to the wrong side of the garment. Or carefully press the loose threads back, away from the window, and secure in place with fusible interfacing.

5 Place the fabric in an embroidery ring or freestanding frame and stretch it taut to produce an even tension on the exposed warp threads. Check to see that the fabric grain runs straight from edge to edge and that it's not distorted in the hoop.

ADDING THE WEFT THREAD

Beadweaving into fabric consists of replacing the actual weft threads with a combination of beads and a working weft thread that secures the beads to the warp. The working thread must be attached to the fabric at the left cor-

ner, where the first beaded row begins. Tie a knot at the end of the thread, and work a small backstitch into the fabric to secure it prior to weaving (see drawing 2 on the facing page).

It is possible to work a small beadwoven design with a single length of thread. For larger designs, more than one length of thread may be required. Use a square knot to tie the new length to the end of the working thread, prior to weaving the thread through a row of beads. That way, the knot will be hidden inside the beads.

STRINGING THE BEADS

String beads to the working (weft) thread one row at time. Read the graph from left to right, as you would a book, to determine the order in which beads should be strung. The design can be worked from the bottom up, or vice versa; whichever proves easier for you. I work from the bottom up, which seems natural to me, since it is the way that weavings progress on a loom.

WEAVING THE BEADS

When you have the first row strung, pass the bead-laden weft thread below the warp threads from left to right. Take a tiny stitch into the right edge of the fabric and draw the thread tight. Align the beads between warp threads and hold them in place with your left forefinger. Then pass the needle back from right to left over the top of the warp and through the hole of each bead in the row. This pass locks the beads into place between the warp threads (see drawing 3 on the facing page).

Again, take a small stitch into the fabric after the needle exits the first bead in the row and move up or down one bead length to begin the second row. The appropriate beads for that row are strung in accordance with the bead graph; work the thread under and over the warp from left to right and back again to secure the second row of beads. Work subsequent rows until the entire design is beaded (see drawing 4 on the facing page).

Weaving Beads into Fabric

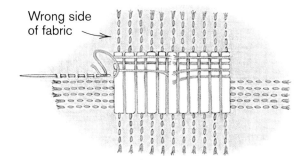

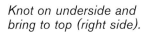

Wrong side of fabric

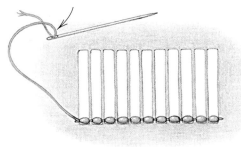

1. To prepare the warp, cut carefully through center of the marked area between warp threads.

Knot on underside and bring to top (right side).

3. Take a small stitch into the fabric on the right. Pull the weft (needle) thread tight. Pass the needle and thread right to left; over the warp thread and through the center of each bead.

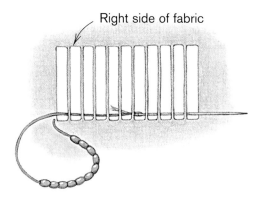

Right side of fabric

2. With fabric stretched in a hoop or frame, pass the needle and beaded thread beneath the warp, from left to right.

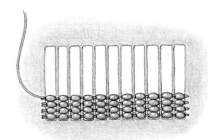

4. Work subsequent rows in the same manner as row 1 until the design is complete.

FINISHING

When the beadweaving is finished, the garment is cut out, interfaced (if not done previous to bead weaving), and assembled. A few simple steps are required to protect your work.

1 Interfacing adds support to the fabric surrounding the beadwork, but prior to fusing, it should be cut away from beadwoven areas. Apply interfacing with a handheld iron rather than with a press, and press carefully so that the hot iron does not come into contact with the beads.

2 Line the garment to protect the beadwork from wear and abrasion.

3 If beaded areas are hazardously close to seamlines, sew the seam by hand or use a zipper foot to sew by machine.

BEADED BUTTONS

Two- or four-hole buttons (⅝ in. to 1¼ in.) sewn to garment

Large decorative beads or baubles with holes for sewing (large enough to cover the holes of the button when sewn in place)

Beading needle

Polyester thread, color to match garment

BEAD-LACED BUTTONS

Four-hole buttons (½ in. to ¾ in.), sewn to garment

Round rocailles (sizes 12 and 15)

Small glass and crystal beads for the center of the button

Polyester thread, color to match button (may show slightly)

Beading needles

Beaded buttons and buttons made from beads can add sparkle to most any garment.

Beaded buttons

Buttons are an integral part of clothing design. Small as they may be, they possess the power to make or break a garment. The following methods for adding beads to buttons and creating buttons from beads offer exciting alternatives to ho-hum and not-quite-right button solutions. Whether you use them to produce continuity in a beaded garment or as the singular mode of ornamentation, they're sure to add the perfect finishing touch.

TWO- AND FOUR-HOLE BEADED BUTTONS

Adding beads to two- and four-hole buttons is a beautiful way to embellish a garment. Since the only requirement for beading is that the button already be sewn in place, this technique lends itself to ready-to-wear and vintage clothes as well as to those you sew yourself.

If you are embellishing something ready made, make a sample button to determine whether the height of the beaded button is compatible with the existing buttonhole. If you are making a garment, simply sew the buttons to the garment first and leave the buttonholes for last.

Beading a button can be as simple as stacking a large decorative bead on top of the button and sewing it in place. This method is as easy as it sounds and can be used on buttons large and small. It's also a great way to highlight fantastic beads, particularly if you select a button in a contrasting color.

Beading the button

The button should already be sewn to the garment. Use it to jazz up any outfit, but test that the button will still fit through the buttonhole.

1   Thread the beading needle, knot the end of the thread, and bring the needle from the wrong side to the right side of the garment through any hole in the button (see the top drawing on the facing page).

2   Slide the decorative bead onto the needle and bring the needle to the wrong side of

the garment through the opposite hole of the button. Repeat this sequence several times to ensure that the bead is firmly attached to the button.

BEAD-LACED BUTTON

Bead-laced buttons rely on seed beads to produce a delicate, lacy effect. Worked in one or more colors and possibly in more than one size bead, these buttons make up quickly and add a distinctive touch wherever they're used. I especially like to pair bead-laced buttons with soft solids and neutral-colored silks. Think of this method as well when you have a beaded garment that calls upon the buttons to provide cohesion for the overall design, since seed beads used to embellish the garment can be worked into the button as well.

Beading the button

This is another technique for which the button should already be sewn to the garment.

1   Sew a bead into each hole of the button, attaching the bead to fabric as you would a button (see drawing 1 below).

Two- and Four-Hole Beaded Buttons

Sew directly through a two-hole button to attach a large, decorative bead.

Secure a bead to a four-hole button with a diagonal stitch between two holes.

Bead-Laced Button

1. Sew one seed bead into each hole. After sewing the fourth bead, bring the needle to the right side of the garment, between the top two beads.

2. Add a bead and sew through the attached bead to the left. Pick up second, third, and fourth beads as you draw the thread through the holes of the remaining attached beads.

3. Attach a center bead, using a figure-eight stitch worked through the top, center, and bottom beads on the button.

4. Add more beads by working them into the existing pattern. When beading is complete, bring the thread to the wrong side of the garment through one of the buttonholes and secure it.

Design Ideas for Picot-Edged Beaded Buttons

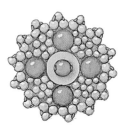

Stacked rondelle and decorative beads

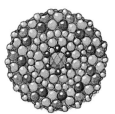

Pearls and seed beads

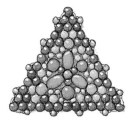

Seed beads with crystal in center

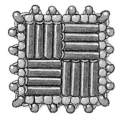

Bugles

PICOT-EDGED BEADED BUTTONS

Rubberized flannel (hospital sheeting) or craft felt interfaced with Armo-Weft

Ultrasuede, Ultra-leather, or Facile (1/8 yd.), to match garment and/or to complement beads

Permanent fine-point felt-tip pen

Round rocailles (sizes 12 and 13 or sizes 12 and 15 combined)

Accent beads (to complement design): crystal, pony beads, gemstone, cut glass

Nymo beading thread, to correspond with bead size

Silk or polyester thread

Beading needle, to correspond with bead size

Embroidery hoop or scroll frame (optional)

Washable fabric glue or fusible web

2 When the four beads are sewn in place, bring the needle through the hole of the fourth bead to the right side of the garment.

3 Add a bead to the needle (this can be a contrasting color, if desired) and bring the needle counterclockwise through the hole of the neighboring bead (see drawing 2 on p. 41). Add another bead and proceed through the next attached bead. Continue around the circle, adding two more beads. When the circle is complete, run the needle and thread through the entire beaded circle a second time to tighten the stitch. This will align the beads.

4 Bring the thread to your left through the top bead. Pick up the center bead on the tip of your needle. (This can be a cut glass or crystal bead, if space allows.) Thread through the bottom bead, working right to left. The center bead will now be in place. Thread the needle through the hole of the center bead (left to right) and through the top bead to complete the figure-eight pattern. Repeat the figure eight through the center bead to secure the stitch (see drawing 3 on p. 41).

5 At this point, the beaded design forms a circular motif. You can bring the thread to the back and tie it off, or, if a floral motif is desired, continue beading, as shown in drawing 4 on p. 41.

6 When you're finished beading, bring the needle to the wrong side of the garment and secure the working thread.

PICOT-EDGED BEADED BUTTON

These exquisite buttons are like tiny jewels. Whatever their shape or size, the garments they adorn become undeniably special. As you'll soon see, they're also fun to make—and easier than they look.

The beading technique remains the same for buttons large and small (see the drawings above). Seed beads are stitched around a center seed or decorative bead to form consecutive rows that radiate from the center. Bugle beads are worked somewhat differently for square and rectangular buttons, but the edge and finishing techniques are the same as for other shapes.

Make matching suit buttons in two sizes for the front and sleeves on jackets and coats; small buttons of uniform size for vests, dresses, and button-down shirts. If you're not up to beading an entire set, consider incorporating a hidden front placket into your garment design and showcase one or two spectacular beaded buttons in an eye-catching location.

In addition to using these buttons for my own garments, I like to make them as gifts. Although they look delicate, they're actually quite sturdy. If you use the materials recommended here, they're hand-washable as well. As with any button, it's a good idea to bead an extra button when making your set, just in case a replacement is required.

Preparing for beading

You can make a uniform set of buttons if you take the time to lay out a grid.

1 Decide on a basic shape and size for your button. Buttons can be round, oval, triangular, or square. Button sizes suitable for this technique should be at least ½ in. (finished), but this is an excellent method for making large buttons as well.

2 Determine how many finished buttons are required. Add at least one extra button to have on hand in case of potential loss or damage to the original.

3 For each button you plan to make, mark a square area on the flannel or felt. Leave ½-in. margins around the area to be beaded. The beaded area will be approximately ⅟₁₆ in. to ½ in. smaller than the finished size of your button.

4 If several buttons are required for your project and you plan to bead the buttons "in hand" rather than using a frame, the entire set can be worked side by side off a large grid (see the drawing at right). This is a very efficient way to mark, bead, and finish a set of buttons. Use a permanent felt-tip marking pen to mark squares for the total number of buttons you plan to bead directly to the flannel or felt.

5 Inside each square, draw in grid lines for the shape and size button desired. Regardless of the button's shape and size, beading always begins in the center of the button, so be sure to mark the center.

6 If you prefer beading to a taut surface, stretch the flannel or felt in an embroidery ring or frame. You'll need larger margins around beaded areas to accommodate the hoop.

Beading the button

Once the grid has been established, these beads work up quickly and can even be a portable project.

1 Thread the beading needle, knot the end, and bring the thread from back to front through the center of the button base. Take an additional stitch through the felt to anchor the thread.

Grids for Picot-Edged Beaded Buttons

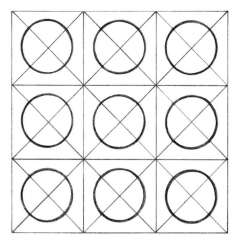

Grid for nine round buttons

The area marked for beading is ⅛ in. to ¼ in. smaller than the finished size of the button.

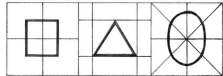

Grids for square, triangular, and oval buttons

2 To begin beading, attach a large bead or crystal to the felt in the center of the circle. Secure the bead with an additional stitch. If other large beads are called for in the design, sew them in place as well.

3 Bring the needle from back to front directly next to the center bead. Pick up two seed beads and move forward around the center bead. Reinsert the needle two bead lengths away. Draw the needle to the wrong side of the felt. Backstitch between beads, bring the needle to the right side of the felt, and draw the thread through the second bead in the row (see drawing 1 on p. 44).

4 Pick up two additional seed beads and repeat the basic stitch. Move forward along the design line using the seed bead to outline the center bead. When you've completed the first circle of beads, run the needle and thread through the entire row. Draw the thread in to tighten the circle (see drawing 2 on p. 44).

5 Bring the needle to the wrong side and come up directly next to first row to be-

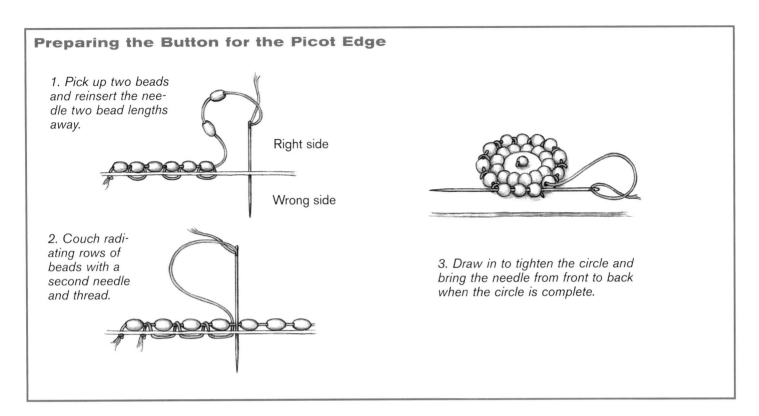

1. Pick up two beads and reinsert the needle two bead lengths away.

Right side

Wrong side

2. Couch radiating rows of beads with a second needle and thread.

3. Draw in to tighten the circle and bring the needle from front to back when the circle is complete.

gin the second. Work consecutive rows in the same manner. If larger beads were sewn in place, simply work around them in a logical fashion. At times, it may be necessary to pack beads in or spread them out to accommodate the design.

6 When the outermost row is complete, bring the needle and thread to the wrong side, take a stitch into the felt, and knot off securely.

7 You can couch radiating rows of beads with a second needle and thread. I like the measure of security this provides, since the buttons will be subjected to the repeated stress of passing through the buttonhole (see drawing 3 above).

Finishing the button

By gluing or fusing on an Ultrasuede back and finishing it with a picot edge, you cover all of the stitching and add a final decorative touch.

1 Cut a square of Ultrasuede or Facile the same size as the beaded felt. Glue the two pieces, wrong sides together, using a washable fabric glue. Check the labels to be sure the glue you use will bond to the button base and backing materials. Leave overnight to dry. (An alternative is to use fusible web, such as Wonder-under or Heat 'N Bond.)

2 If a set of buttons was beaded to one large piece of felt, cut the large piece into individual squares. Cut around each beaded button, leaving a ⅛-in. margin.

3 Carefully trim the margin flush with the beaded edge of the button.

4 With the right side of the button facing you, work the picot edge around the circumference of the button (see the bottom drawing on the facing page). Stitches into the button base must go through both the felt and the Ultrasuede backing, as it joins the two together and neatens the appearance of the button.

5 Sew the shank to the back of the button using silk or polyester thread (see the top drawing on the facing page).

Making a Shank

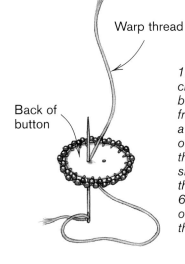

Warp thread

Back of button

1. Using a single thread to create a two-thread warp, bring the thread from back to front, leaving a 6-in. tail. Take a small stitch on the right side of the button and bring the thread through to the back side. Match this end of the thread to the other and cut a 6-in. tail. These two threads on the hank form the ways for the button shank.

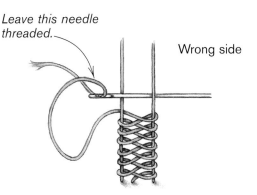

Leave this needle threaded.

Wrong side

2. Knot the end of a separate thread and thread from front to back, so the knot is well hidden between beads. Use a needle to weave the weft thread back and forth between the two warp threads.

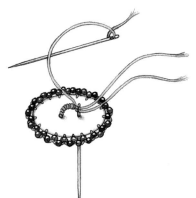

3. Bring the two warp threads to the front side. Tie close to the surface (the knot should be hidden between beads). Rethread to the back side, stitch into the fabric and cut away loose ends.

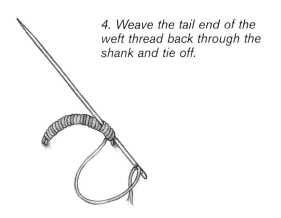

4. Weave the tail end of the weft thread back through the shank and tie off.

Adding the Picot Edge

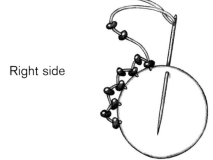

Right side

Insert the needle from back to front, one bead width away.

Draw the needle through the last bead in the row, pick up two beads, and repeat the sequence to complete the row.

45

Threadwork

Exquisite threads are the fine wines of the sewing world. When well chosen and worked to creative perfection, they complement, balance, and finish a garment as no other embellishment can. Moreover, their application frequently constitutes an integral part of clothing construction. A beautiful thread used for topstitching adds color and contrast and accentuates the lines of the garment. Yet its intrinsic function is to stabilize and reduce bulk at the edge of a collar or at the top of a seam. Likewise, a pickstitched lapel boasts a couture signature that looks lovely, even as it tames an otherwise unruly turn of the cloth.

No wonder high-end designer garments, quality vintage wear, ethnic clothing, and haute couture maximize the embellishment possibilities inherent in threadwork. Here, attention to detail is everything, as form and function combine to create the hallmark of a well-made garment. Yet threadwork is hardly limited to practical applications. As a purely decorative element of clothing design, threadwork presents numerous avenues for creative expression.

As you explore and master individual techniques throughout this chapter, contemplate ways to elaborate upon and combine them. A world of embellishment awaits!

MATERIALS AND EQUIPMENT

Many of the threadwork techniques used to produce pure and functional embellishments in the vintage and ready-to-wear clothing we so admire are easy to reproduce. Even in simple form, they can dramatically enhance a garment. To obtain professional results, however, it is essential to realize that not just any thread, needle, or presser foot will do.

Making the beautiful garments you envision requires mastery of the tools, materials, and techniques at your disposal. If this task seems daunting, keep in mind that excellent tools are a sewer's best friend, designed not only to do a job well but also to make it easier.

The only prerequisite to incorporating new tools and techniques into your sewing repertoire is the willingness to experiment with fresh options. As you learn how to use new and familiar tools effectively and explore their range of applications, your efforts will reward you with workmanship that increasingly meets your greatest expectations.

Threads

Choosing from the vast array of threads available can make you feel like a kid in a candy store. There are rayon, cotton, acrylic, metallic, and silk threads; cords, braids, and ribbons; flat, round, and textured threads; variegated and solids. Threads come thick and thin, on spools, on cards, and in skeins. Classified by characteristics that include fiber content, color, texture, size, degree of twist, and sheen, the specifications for sewing each weight and type of thread varies, as does the price.

I have yet to buy a spool that comes packaged with directions for sewing, however, and will make no bones about it: My first attempts at using decorative threads in my machine were a disaster. If you've ever experienced frustration working with decorative threads because they fray, break easily, don't offer enough impact, cause puckering, or refuse to feed smoothly through the needle, you're not alone. Working with decorative threads should be a creative challenge, not a technical one (for information about specific thread types, see the chart on p. 162). Though I've had best results with silk thread, I've had success with the following thread types: machine embroidery, fine metallic, topstitching (or buttonhole twist), pearl, thin braids and cord, many needlepoint threads and knitting yarns (experiment to determine their compatibility with machine work), fine monofilament (or invisible) nylon, lightweight bobbin, and water-soluble basting thread (it dissolves when exposed to water or steam).

Machine-embroidery threads come in a variety of fibers, weights, and colors.

Presser feet

Presser feet are designed to make specific sewing tasks easy, accurate, and efficient (see the photo on p. 50). If you already use a variety of presser feet for various sewing applications, you know how they streamline your efforts. If you are not yet acquainted with the range of presser feet available and what they can do for your sewing, make friends with the presser feet discussed here.

To obtain presser feet for your machine, contact your local sewing-machine dealer. Brand-specific feet are available for some types of machines, while generic presser feet are available for others. When purchasing generic feet, it is essential to know what type of shank is on your machine. Presser feet are generally available in high, low, slant shank, and snap-on styles. Some feet require the use of an adapter, which may have to be purchased separately. The following presser feet work well for threadwork embellishments.

- An **edgestitch foot** has a metal or plastic guide in the center of the foot. When positioned against the edge of the fabric or middle of a seam, the guide is used in conjunction with needle positions on the machine to produce perfectly aligned edgestitching to the right or left of the guide. Used with the needle in the center position, the guide is also useful for "stitching in the ditch" (stitching directly between two seam allowances) as well as for pintucks or rows of corded satin stitch.

- The **patchwork, or ¼-in., foot** is tremendously useful for decorative topstitching as well as for garment construction. The distance from the edge of the presser foot to the center needle measures exactly ¼ in. (which is why it's known as the ¼-in. foot). Additional notches on the foot indicate ¼-in. placement directly in front of and behind the center needle, and ⅛-in. placement from mid-toe to center.

Metallic threads enrich the color palette and add sparkle and flair to any project.

Storing Thread

A top priority when it comes to storage is to protect thread from light and dust, since both are detrimental to the color properties, performance, and longevity of thread. I use clear containers with lids and drawer-style cabinets. Boxes contain a particular thread type—60-wt. cotton, for example—and if I have a lot of one thread type, it is further classified by color.

Boxes that contain spindles for individual spools are also available. Threadracks are useful to keep threads organized and displayed for a project that is underway. But if you use the racks for long-term storage, either cover or store them where they are protected from dust and light.

A second priority is to keep threads tangle free. Some spools have thread locks at one or both ends, but for those that don't, wrapping the spool in acid-free paper or cellophane secured with tape will keep loose threads in place. A commercially available product called Thread-Wrap works well and consists of a precut plastic film that sticks to itself when wrapped around the spool.

The patchwork foot is a straight-stitch type designed to be used with the needle in the center position only. The small needle hole and solid base of the foot lend greater stability to the fabric as the stitches are being formed, resulting in superior stitch quality on a range of fabrics. The patchwork foot is brand-specific for some machines and is also available as a generic foot. A jeans foot or basic straight-stitch foot offer similar stitch quality without the ¼-in. and ⅛-in. guides.

- The standard **embroidery foot** is similar in appearance to the basic zigzag foot, except that its toes are shorter, which improves visibility. The base of the embroidery foot has an indentation to accommodate thread bulk produced by compact embroidery stitches. This fan-shaped groove facilitates proper satin-stitch formation by allowing the presser foot to ride smoothly over the stitches without hanging up on thread beneath the foot. A standard embroidery foot may also have a hole in the center of the "bridge" that connects the toes of the foot, which can be threaded with thick threads for couching and corded satin stitch.

- The **open-toe embroidery foot** (unlike the standard embroidery foot) has no bridge between the toes of the foot, which allows greater visibility for appliqué and decorative machine stitching. The inside edges of the toe can also be used as a guide. This foot is an excellent candidate for twin-needle topstitching and for application of flat braids and trims.

- The **pintuck foot** is a versatile foot used for pintucking and a variety of other embellishment applications, including corded satin stitch, corded topstitching, and the application of narrow ribbons, soutache, and corded trims. Available in three-, five-, seven-, and nine-groove variations, the grooves are designed to produce different pintuck widths when used with the appropriate twin needle. This foot performs best with straight lines of stitching, distinct angles, and gentle curves. It is not suited to complex motifs or close curves.

- A **walking foot** (also called an "even-feed" foot) is indispensable in certain topstitching and embroidery applications. It is especially appropriate for hard-to-sew fabrics such as velvet, corduroy, satin, leather, lace, and slippery silk, which tend to shift, slide, stretch, or pucker when sewn.

- The **leather roller foot** is one of my personal favorites. It's ideal for decorative topstitching, outlining, and bobbinwork, and is exceptionally fun and easy to use. Designed for maneuverability on leather, suede, vinyl, and quilted fabrics, the roller foot virtually glides over the surface of the fabric, offering

Presser feet commonly used for threadwork embellishments include (clockwise from upper left): leather roller, edgestitch, patchwork, walking, pintuck, and open-toe embroidery.

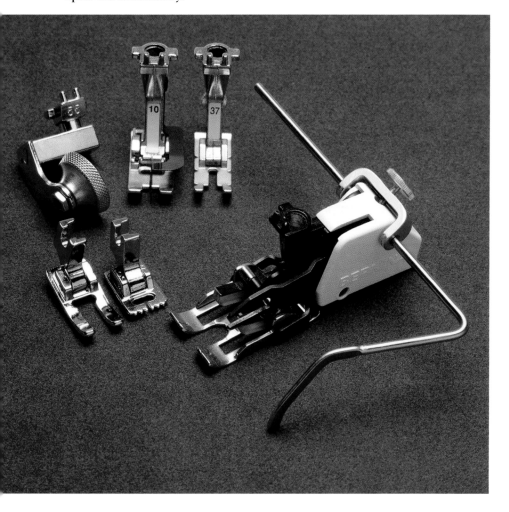

the path of least resistance for curves, angles, and motifs of all kinds. The roller foot can be used with single or double needles.

Stabilizers

Most threadwork applications require the use of stabilizers to support the base fabric for decorative stitching (see the photo at right). Properly selected for the technique and materials at hand, a stabilizer will prevent skipped stitches, puckering, and thread breakage. Since the added support allows basic machine stitches to form with minimal distortion, the end results are uniform and professional. Numerous stabilizers are currently available on the market. The following categories offer a range of options to suit various sewing needs. Stabilizers deemed to give superior results for specific techniques are listed in the techniques sections (guidelines for choosing a stabilizer are listed in the sidebar on p. 52).

- **Iron-on interfacings** lend sufficient stability for many light threadwork applications. Available in a variety of weights, the stabilizing properties of interfacings used in garment construction should always be taken into account.

- **Tear-away stabilizers** made from paper or other nonwoven fibers are pinned, basted, and, in some cases, ironed to the wrong side of the cloth prior to stitching. Excess stabilizer is torn away once the threadwork is complete. Available in a range of weights, tear-away stabilizers can be used in single or multiple layers to suit various sewing needs, but keep in mind that the stabilizer that remains beneath the actual stitching will stiffen the area being embellished.

    Tear Easy, Jiffy Tear, Tear Away Soft, ArmoTear Away, Stitch-n-Tear, and Stitch 'n' Ditch from Thread-Pro are excellent for firm wovens and for knits. Iron-on varieties such as Totally Stable, Press-n-Tear Soft, and Press-n-Tear Crisp offer a greater de-

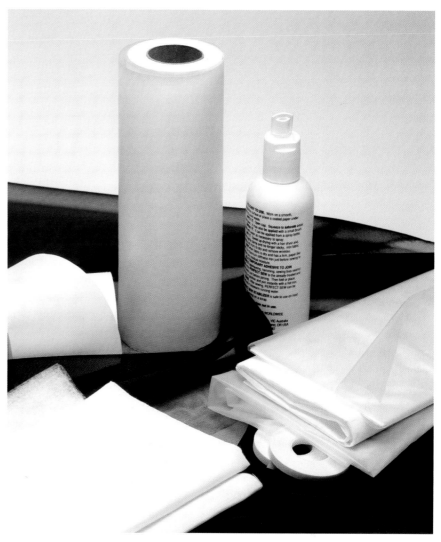

gree of stability for fluid fabrics that tend to shift when pinned or basted and for long rows or large areas of embellishment.

- **Wash-away stabilizers** are water soluble. Once they have served the purpose of stabilizing a fabric for decorative stitching, excess stabilizer is torn away. The residue can be completely removed with water, so the original hand of the fabric is retained. Fabrics and threads used with wash-away stabilizers must be washable as well. Prior to embarking on a major project, preshrink all yardage and test threads and fabric in advance to determine that they are colorfast.

    Wash-away stabilizers come in spray, liquid, and sheet forms. Spray-on stabilizers include spray starch (available in the laun-

Stabilizers lend essential support for a variety of threadwork techniques. Clockwise from upper left: tearaway, liquid, wash-away, and heat-disintegrating stabilizers.

Guidelines for Choosing a Stabilizer

Availability of certain stabilizer products may vary from store to store, and new products continually enter the marketplace. I don't believe it's critical to keep abreast of every product on the market, but general knowledge of existing options will always give you an advantage. When selecting a stabilizer, you should consider the following:

• The stabilizer, thread, and fabric choice must be compatible in terms of weight, removal, and cleaning methods. A wash-away stabilizer may be appealing in terms of retaining the hand of the fabric, but it's not an appropriate choice for threads and fabrics that are not colorfast or those you do not wish to wash for other reasons. Likewise, heat-disintegrating stabilizers would be a discouraging choice for threads and fabrics that cannot withstand a high heat setting.

• For finished results that are consistent with the characteristics of the fabric, use the lightest stabilizer that provides adequate stability for your project.

• Lightweight stabilizers can be strengthened with additional layers. Stabilizers can also be combined (for example, use a lightweight tear-away stabilizer on the bottom of the fabric, with Solvy on top).

• Fluid rayons and silks may require a stabilizer that temporarily alters the characteristics of the fabric so it doesn't shift, fall away, buckle, or stretch as it's being stitched. Liquid stabilizers such as Perfect Sew and iron-on stabilizers such as Totally Stable make decorative sewing a pleasure on fabrics that are difficult to keep in one place.

• Test for compatibility of materials and techniques in a sample, prior to working on the actual garment. When feasible, sample more than one option and select the best.

• If you foresee incorporating a lot of threadwork into your sewing, maintain a small supply of several stabilizers to have on hand for samples and for small, spontaneous projects. Larger projects may require greater amounts, but samples on hand will help you determine in advance which product to buy when you go to the store.

dry section of any grocery store) and specialty products such as Stitch 'n Spray and Sullivan's Spray Fabric Stiffener. These stabilizers offer sufficient stability for topstitching interfaced portions of a garment and for some threadwork applications on lightweight or extremely stable fabrics. They do not offer adequate support for decorative machine stitches unless used with a hoop.

Liquid stabilizers like Perfect Sew and Sew Stable come in gellike liquid form, which is applied directly to the fabric in the area to be embellished. The liquid saturates the fabric and dries to a stiff, paperlike consistency that makes embellishing a breeze. Liquid stabilizers are an excellent solution for working with fluid rayons, silks, and any other fabric that is difficult to stabilize for the purpose of embellishing.

Solvy, Avalon, Aqua-Solv, and YLI Solv-It are sheets of clear plastic film that can be basted or pinned in place. Unlike paper or nonwoven tear-away stabilizers, they can be used from the right as well as from the wrong side of the fabric. One advantage of these stabilizers is that motifs or designs can be traced directly to the film, which acts as a template for the stitch design. Solvy is now available in two weights; the heavier version is two times the weight of the original. Rins-Away from Handler is similar in appearance and texture to heavy tear-away stabilizers but dissolves in three to four launderings.

- **Heat-disintegrating stabilizers** such as Vanish-a-Way, Heat and Brush, and Heat-Away, offer a degree of stability that is comparable to lightweight tear-away stabilizers. Like a wash-away stabilizer, heat-disintegrating muslin preserves the characteristic hand of the fabric. Since high iron temperatures are required to reduce the muslin to ashes once the stitching is complete, these stabilizers are incompatible with fabrics and threads that cannot withstand high heat settings. One vanishing muslin product—Hot Stuff—disintegrates in the heat of the sun or with steam from an iron, making it appropriate for use with a broader range of decorative threads and fabrics.

Machine needles

To take advantage of the best stitch quality your machine can deliver, select a machine needle (see the photo at right) that suits the type of sewing you intend to do and correlate the size of the needle with the fabric and thread you plan to use. It's not unusual to use a variety of needle types while incorporating threadwork embellishments into a garment.

Machine needles are available in sizes 60/8 to 120/19; however, needles designed for specific sewing applications are typically manufactured in a limited size range. Size designations correspond to the thickness of the original wire used to make the needle: the larger the number, the larger the needle.

As a general rule, larger thread and heavier fabrics require larger needles, while lightweight fabrics and fine threads require smaller needles. Needles that are too small for the type of thread being used can cause fraying and skipped stitches. Needles that are too large may mar the fabric with holes larger than the thread requires.

Variables such as thread, fabric, and technique combine to create unique requirements for every project. In some instances, it may be necessary to experiment to determine which

needle type and size delivers the best results. I keep a full range of needle types and sizes on hand at all times. Stocking up on needles does require an initial investment, but if you sew frequently, as I do, having needles on hand in the sewing room is as essential as having pots and pans in the kitchen. The following Schmetz and Lammertz brand needles are recommended for threadwork techniques presented in this chapter.

- **Topstitching needles (N)** have a larger eye, longer groove, and sharper point than standard sewing needles. The increased size of the groove and eye allow the needles to accommodate thick threads, while the sharper point aids in proper stitch formation. Topstitching needles produce an even, straight

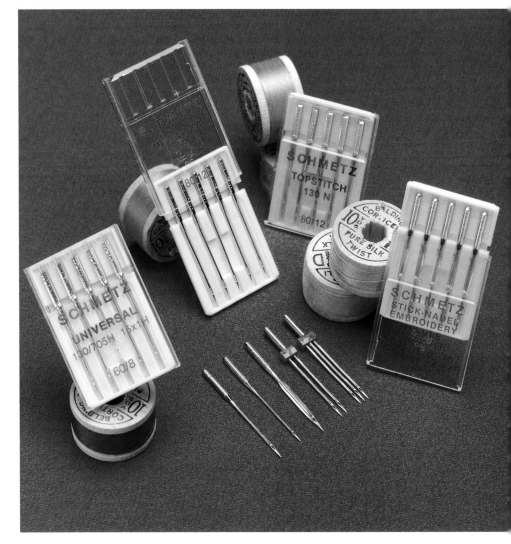

Machine needles (clockwise from left): universal, metallica, topstitch, embroidery, triple or drilling, twin, wing, Microtex, and jeans/denim.

stitch on woven fabrics. Regardless of the type thread used in the needle, a standard weight sewing thread is typically used in the bobbin. Topstitching needles are available in sizes 80/12 to 110/18.

- **Microtex Sharp (H-M) needles** are designed to penetrate densely woven microfiber fabrics. Use them as well for topstitching, particularly on microfiber and other similarly dense woven fabrics.

- **Machine-embroidery needles (H-E)** are designed to handle light- to medium-weight machine embroidery and metallic threads in a range of decorative stitching applications. The needles have a scarf, eye, and groove formation especially designed to reduce thread breakage (to find out how to deal with thread breakage, see the sidebar below) and skipped stitches and allow the thread to feed through the needle with minimal resistance.

- **Metafil (H-M) and Metallica (H-Met) needles** have a long eye and groove to accommodate lightweight metallic threads that tend to fray and break easily. Both needles can withstand the heat and friction associated with metallic threads, which produce more wear and tear on a needle than any other thread. One thing to note: Switch to a new needle when the thread frays and breaks repeatedly. The problem most likely is the result of a burr in the needle, which will continue to plague your efforts.

- **Denim needles (H-J)** feature an extremely sharp point that penetrates directly through the fabric to produce a straight, even stitch. Designed for use on tightly woven twills, which resist uniform stitch formation due to the fabric's directional weave, they tend to improve stitch quality on a variety of wovens, making them a favorite for basic construction as well as for topstitching. Once available only for heavyweight fabrics, denim needles are now available in sizes 70/10 to 110/18.

- **Wing needles** are wide with metal extensions, or "wings," on either side of the needle shaft. As the needle penetrates the fabric, the wings push aside threads to create the characteristic holes in hemstitching. Wing needles can be used with plain or decorative thread in the needle. Unthreaded, they can also be used to produce evenly spaced holes for handworked saddle-, blanket-, and running-stitch variations.

- **Universal needles (H)** are the most versatile of all machine needles. They can be used on just about any woven or knit fabric and come in a complete range of sizes, from 60/8 to 120/19. Universal needles are used widely for garment construction, but they also work well for decorative applications and topstitching on knits, textured woolens, and velvets.

What to Do When the Thread Runs Out or Breaks

Decorative threadwork depletes thread rapidly—more so than with garment construction. When a thread breaks or runs out midway through a line of stitching, you can still finish the work in a seamless fashion. Here's how:

1. Work the last few inches of stitching back out of the fabric so that top and bottom thread tails are at least 3 in. long.
2. Pull lightly on the thread tail on the wrong side of the fabric. This will bring the top thread through the cloth and form a loop, which can be pulled to the underside.
3. If the thread on the underside is weak and risks breaking, bring the top thread to the underside with a needle. To work with a short thread, insert the needle through the fabric midway. Thread the eye of the needle and draw it through to the underside.
4. Knot and tie off thread tails and work into stitching on the underside of the garment.
5. Rethread the machine and resume stitching directly at the point where the break occurred.

- **Twin needles (H-ZWI)** produce two evenly spaced rows of stitching at one time. They are used for decorative topstitching, machine embroidery, plain and corded pintucking, hemming, and applying flat ribbon to fabric. Universal twin and triple needles are accessible in a variety of sizes, ranging from 1.6/70 to 8.0/90. Specialty twin needles—stretch (H-S ZWI), wing (ZWI-HO), denim (H-J ZWI), metallica (H-METZWI), and machine embroidery (H-E ZWI)—are available in a limited size range.

  Please note that not all twin needles are compatible with every machine. The 6.0 and 8.0 needles require stitch-width settings that exceed the maximum settings on many machines. Also, some machines require a brand-specific twin needle. Others, including straight-stitch-only machines and zigzag machines with a side-loading bobbin, are incompatible with twin needles. Consult your machine manual or local dealer if you have doubts about which needles are appropriate for your machine.

- **Drilling or triple needles (H-DRI)** are special needles that can produce three rows of decorative stitching or two rows of pintucking at once. They come in two sizes: 2.5 and 3.0.

Hand-sewing needles

The hand-sewing needles best suited for decorative threadwork include embroidery/crewel, chenille, tapestry, and calyx (also known as self-threading) needles (see the photo at right). Sizing for these needles is opposite from machine needles: the larger the number, the smaller the needle. For handworked decorative stitches, select a medium-length needle with a large-enough eye for the thread. The needle itself should be as thick as the thread, so the resulting hole does not cause friction that could fray or break the thread.

Machine accessories

When embellishing garments with special threadwork, you may need a few accessories for your machine, such as an extra bobbin case, a straight-stitch needle plate, and an adjustable seam guide (see the photo on p. 56).

- An **extra bobbin case,** designated for use with heavy threads only, is a good idea to save wear and tear on the bobbin. Using decorative threads in the bobbin requires frequent adjustments to the bobbin tension, and frequent tension adjustments made to the bobbin case can damage the tension spring and cause problems for normal sewing. Additionally, having a bobbin case specifically for decorative threadwork allows you to alternate quickly and smoothly between decorative work and actual garment construction.

Hand-sewing needles (clockwise from upper left in fabric): self-threading (or calyx), tapestry, chenille, and embroidery/crewel.

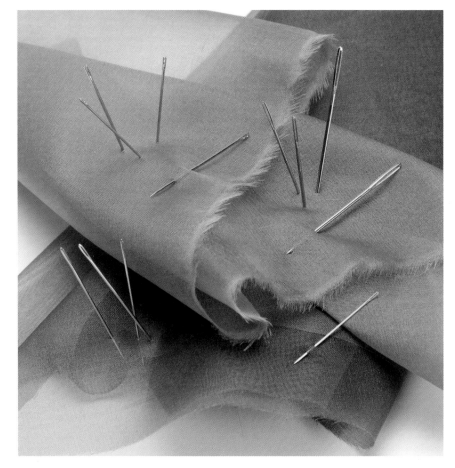

A bobbin case is not a generic accessory, since it is an actual part for a specific machine. To obtain an extra bobbin case, contact a reputable dealer that carries parts for your make and model sewing machine. It is important to distinguish the extra bobbin case from the one you use for normal sewing so that you don't accidentally adjust the tension on the wrong case. I mark my extra case with a permanent-ink pen for easy identification. Some brands market a bobbin case that is color coded, but this type is typically more expensive than a standard bobbin case.

- A **straight-stitch needle plate** can dramatically improve the stitch quality of straight-stitch seaming and topstitching on a variety of fabrics. With its small, circular hole, the straight-stitch needle plate provides more surface area beneath the fabric, which yields greater stability as the fabric feeds through the machine and the stitches are formed. It

is especially useful for sewing sheer, lightweight, or soft fabrics that tend to get pushed into the large, rectangular hole of the standard zigzag needle plate. Straight-stitch needle plates are brand specific and must be purchased for the make and model of your machine.

- An **adjustable seam guide** (also called a quilting bar) is especially useful for parallel topstitching, when the space between rows is farther than the width of a standard presser foot. A long, metal bar with a guide on one end, this tool can be used with a variety of presser feet, including most walking feet. Additionally, left and right guides are available that allow for directional stitching on both sides of a garment. Other types of guides include snap-on and screw-in styles, adhesive guides that can be applied to the machine, magnetic guides, and makeshift guides, such as a piece of tape spaced the appropriate distance from the needle.

Machine accessories (clockwise from top center): magnetic seam guide (for wide rows of parallel stitching), extra bobbin case (for bobbin work), and straight-stitch needle plate (for topstitching).

THREADWORK EMBELLISHMENTS BY HAND

Handwork is a signature of sorts and, in a garment, the most personal evidence of its maker. When the work is impeccable, its discovery is always a happy one. Delicately whipstitched collars; pickstitched side seams on pants; running-stitch motifs at the hem of a dress—details such as these were once ubiquitous among vintage garments. Now rarely seen in ready to wear, they remain versatile, easy embellishments for today's home sewer. The pickstitch, whipstitch, and running stitches are kindergarten stitches—the ones we learned to sew doll clothes by hand. As you will see, they've lost neither relevance nor charm (for some simple guidelines, see the sidebar on p. 58).

Pickstitch

The pickstitch is a classic hand topstitching method used to finish and accentuate collars, cuffs, jacket lapels, pockets, waistbands, and seams (see the drawing on p. 58). A variation of the sturdy backstitch, it is extremely strong and durable and suited for use with multiple layers only. Unlike the backstitch and its offshoots—half-backstitch and prickstitch—the pickstitch is not worked through the bottom layer of fabric. Meticulous topstitching shows from the right side of the garment only, while the bottom portion of the stitch catches and remains hidden within the seam.

A variety of needlework threads are compatible with this technique, but for exceptional luster and sewing ease, try silk topstitching thread or buttonhole twist. If you like metallic accents, Kreinik's fine (#8) braid holds up well without twisting or shredding and resembles a row of tiny beads when sewn. Stitched in a lightweight thread, it is also possible to incorporate real seed beads that are held in place with the tiny backstitches.

The pickstitch is always worked in hand on portions of the garment that are already interfaced, faced, turned, and pressed. Depending on the garment, the stitching may be done during various phases of construction or after the garment is complete. The appearance will vary according to the size of the stitch taken, the thread used, and the distance between each stitch. Generally, thicker threads are spaced farther apart while fine threads on delicate fabrics are worked closer together.

In this method, the length between stitches is roughly equal to the stitch itself.

1 Mark the stitching line, using one of the methods in the sidebar on p. 62. As with machine topstitching, the row is typically situated ⅛ in. to ⅜ in. from the garment's edge.

HANDWORKED STITCHES

MATERIALS LIST

Hand-sewing needles (medium length and as thick as the thread)

Silk, cotton, wool, linen, rayon, and metallic threads for hand needlework

Marking tools (vary with method used)

Tiger Tape or wing needles

Machine and handworked stitches embellish the cuffs and collar band of this silk dupioni blouse, while a sprinkling of beads and set of picot-edged beaded buttons complete the picture.

Guidelines for Threadwork Embellishments by Hand

For lovely results when handworking thread embellishments, follow these guidelines:

- Select a method to obtain evenly spaced stitches (see the sidebar on p. 62).

- Practice the stitches you plan to use and perfect your technique. Experiment with variables such as thread type, number of strands used, stitch length and placement, stitch variety, and unique combinations.

- Recognize the role of proper materials. Threads vary in terms of decorative impact and sewing ease. Natural fibers are most manageable for hand sewing, and among these, silk is the most trouble free. Synthetic and blended threads are prone to kinks and knots and are not recommended unless specifically manufactured for handwork.

- Utilize the functional aspects of hand stitches, which can be a practical solution to working with slippery, springy, and napped fabrics, such as wool gabardine or velvet. Hand stitches also solve the dilemma of topstitching fabrics too bulky to fit beneath the presser foot and are routinely used to keep a lining from "falling away," to flatten turned or pressed seams, to understitch a facing, and to apply zippers.

- Needle size should roughly correspond to the diameter of the thread and the length of stitches.

- Cut thread at an angle and, to minimize twisting, thread the needle with the end from the spool.

- Regardless of the thread you use, work with no more than an arm's length at one time. For fragile threads, or those that twist or knot, a shorter working length of 12 in. to 15 in. may be required.

- Work the stitching line from right to left if you're right handed; left to right if you're left handed.

- Kinks and knots result from too much twist in the thread. To resolve this problem, turn the work upside down, let the thread unwind, then resume normal stitching. Waxing thread increases its manageability for standard hand-sewing applications but is not recommended for decorative threads.

- A tiny backstitch at the beginning and end of every row performs a securing function and can be used in place of a knot. Knots and tail ends of threads should remain inconspicuous from the right side of the garment.

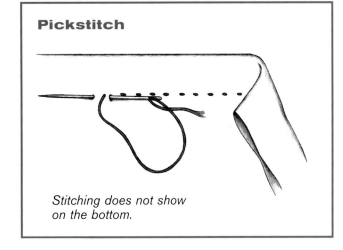

Pickstitch

Stitching does not show on the bottom.

2 Knot one end of the thread. Bring the needle from the bottom to top through all of the layers near the edge or seam to be embellished.

3 Insert the needle one stitch length behind the thread's point of origin.

4 Catching the seam allowance, if desired, but not the bottom layer of fabric, move the needle forward two or more stitch lengths beyond the previous stitch approximately ⅛ in. to ⅜ in.

5 Draw the needle through to the top, pull the stitch taut, and repeat the sequence along the stitching line, as shown in the drawing on the facing page.

Whipstitched edgestitching

I had never given thought to the decorative potential of the whipstitch until I came across an exquisite vintage dress that forever altered my thinking. Made from smoky taupe georgette, its shaped collar was rendered all the more distinct by an intricate, two-tone edge treatment echoed in the cuffs and hem of the dress, as well as in the slender, hand-sewn tucks that graced its front. At first glance, I was sure I was looking at an interesting antique trim, but careful inspection revealed the to-die-for embellishment to be no more than the simple whipstitch. Worked in silk thread the color of cappuccino foam, the perfect stitching added warmth and light to create an irresistible garment.

Illustrating that less is indeed sometimes more, the whipstitched collar, cuff, or hem makes any garment special. Almost any thread for handwork is suitable, providing it's heavy enough for the fabric. Silk twist or floss are pretty, but I am also partial to cotton threads for this technique and love the soft matte sheen of DMC Flower thread, as well as other pearl cottons and various hand-dyed threads from the Caron Collection. Also favored are the Kreinik metallic ribbons. The $1/16$ in. is ideal for light- to medium-weight fabrics, while the $1/8$-in. ribbon is useful where more impact is desired. These ribbons are easy to sew, lie flat against the edge, and integrate well with most garments. And, while my personal preference for whipstitched edgestitching is the delicate type described above, the same technique translates well to casual, even rugged wear. Ribbon, cording, turned fabric tubes, and flat leather lacing can be worked on jacket collars and lapels, yokes, and sleeves.

Use a tailor's awl to make holes to prepare the fabric for these heavier embellishments.

Yet another application for this stitch is to whip it around other hand- and machine-worked stitches, including pickstitch, running stitch, and decorative bobbinwork, or over pintucks or piping.

Bear in mind that the whipstitch is a directional stitch (see the drawing below). If you want stitches on opposite sides of a collar to "lean" in opposite directions, you'll have to change direction midway around the collar. Here are the basic steps.

1 Use Tiger Tape (narrow flexible tape used as a stitching guide), or use the edgestitch presser foot to sew in water-soluble basting thread close to the garment's edge.

2 Thread the appropriately sized hand-sewing needle, knot the end of the thread, and draw through to the right side of the fabric along the edgestitch line.

3 "Whip" the thread over the finished edge and reinsert the needle from the underside of the garment one or more full stitches beyond the needle thread's point of origin.

4 Repeat the stitch sequence along the edge, using the basted line as the spacing guide. The stitches will slant in one direction, which may vary, depending upon the length of the stitch and the width of the overcast from the garment's edge.

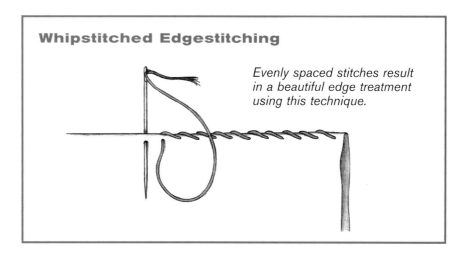

Whipstitched Edgestitching

Evenly spaced stitches result in a beautiful edge treatment using this technique.

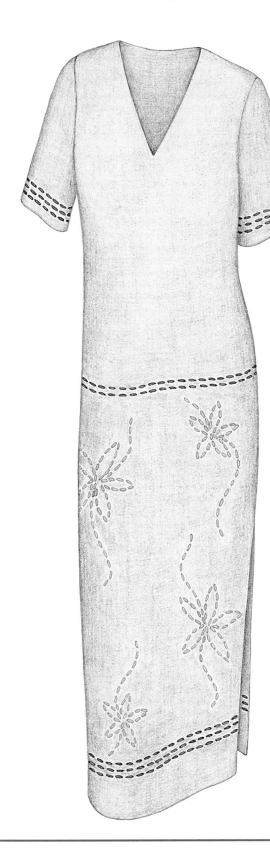

Dress with Running-Stitch Embellishment

The running stitch is the most basic hand-sewing stitch, but it can be used to apply a variety of embellishments to a garment.

Running stitches

The running stitch (see the drawing on the facing page) is the most basic hand-sewing stitch and is used for a variety of practical and decorative applications, including gathering, seaming, basting, traditional quilting, sashiko, appliqué, pintucking, and—the focus of our attention—hand topstitching. Topstitching with the running stitch is bolder, more casual, and works up more rapidly than the pickstitch. In addition, it is not limited to the perimeters of the garment and can be used to produce all-over embellishments and simple motifs.

When applying the running stitch to a non-interfaced area, spray starch or a lightweight spray-on stabilizer is recommended, unless the fabric is sufficiently stable. Of the marking methods, the wing needle is advantageous, since the holes created by the needle form a direct path for the running stitch and minimize stress on the thread. For a less controlled look, premark the basic line with a water-soluble marker and work the stitch freely, gauging stitch intervals by sight.

Because this stitch shows off thread to a greater extent than the pickstitch, the running stitch provides ample opportunity to play with thread—combining unique space-dyed and variegated threads and the strategic use of color. More than one color can be introduced by combining threads treated as one to produce the running stitch; alternating thread colors along the stitching line; or working a second row of stitching into the stitch intervals provided by the initial row. Also, the running stitch can be combined with the pickstitch and whipstitch to produce unique color and pattern combinations. Instructions follow for the basic running stitch and four variations of it: the saddle stitch, double running stitch, twisted running stitch, and threaded running stitch (see the drawings on p. 64).

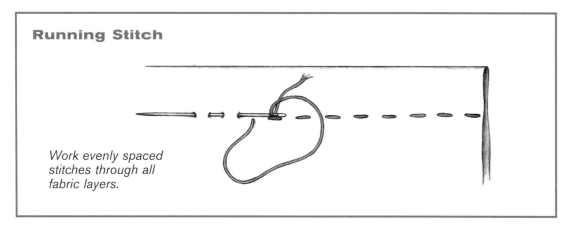

Running Stitch

Work evenly spaced stitches through all fabric layers.

BASIC RUNNING STITCH

Attention to detail can turn one of the world's most basic stitches into a beautiful embellishment. Here's how.

1 Premark the line of stitching using the wing-needle method, or for straight lines of stitching, place Tiger Tape along the stitching line as a guide. For motifs or for stitching lines on the body of the garment, draw in lines with a water-soluble marker and follow with unthreaded wing-needle stitching.

2 Knot the thread, thread a long needle, and bring it through all layers at the beginning of the stitching line.

3 Weave the thread in and out of subsequent holes along the stitching line. Take several stitches onto the needle before pulling the needle and thread through.

4 Since the running stitch is also used to gather, take care to keep the work flat. Straighten any gathers that do occur by smoothing them along the working thread, toward the needle.

SADDLE STITCH

Used for high-impact topstitching on casual, sporty garments, the saddle stitch is worked with a thick thread in a contrasting color. Work as for the basic running stitch but increase the stitch length to between ¼ in. and ½ in. long. Work the stitch evenly so that the distance between stitches is equal to the stitch itself. You can work thread through all of the layers or hide the underside of the stitch within the seam. A simple variation on this stitch incorporates a second pass along the line, in which a tiny pickstitch is taken between each of the original stitches in the row.

DOUBLE RUNNING STITCH

This variation is worked in two passes of the thread to form a solid line. Work the basic running or saddle stitch along the stitching line and, when the row is complete, work the original thread back. Or you can introduce a new color to fill in the stitch intervals on the second pass of the thread.

TWISTED RUNNING STITCH

This rendition combines the double running stitch and whipstitch. Work the row of double running stitch first along the stitching line. With a contrasting thread, add the whipstitch, whipping the thread beneath each stitch, working forward along the row. The whipstitch does not pass through the fabric, except for at the beginning and the end of the row.

THREADED RUNNING STITCH

To make this variation, work one or more rows of the running stitch parallel to one another so that individual stitches in equidistant rows are aligned, or staggered. Lace additional threads through the lines of stitching. The lacing is worked beneath the decorative surface threads only, not through the fabric.

Four Ways to Obtain Evenly Spaced, Handworked Stitches

One of the primary challenges of handwork is achieving evenly spaced stitches aligned with the garment's edge. The handworked stitches in this chapter are generally worked in ⅛-in. to ⅜-in. intervals. To achieve accurate spacing, premark intervals along the stitching line by machine basting, using an unthreaded wing needle, using a water- or air-soluble marking pen, or using tape.

With any of these methods, always create a sample using the fabric, interfacing, and number of layers planned for your actual project, as this is the only way to determine accurately the proper stitch-length setting on your machine.

Machine basting

This method requires basting a line of stitching that then serves as a guide for placement of handworked stitches. The basting thread is removed once handwork is complete, so use thread that removes easily and does not mar fabric. Thread choices include water-soluble basting thread—which dissolves when exposed to steam from an iron—or 50- to 100-wt. silk. If you're using silk, decrease the needle tension slightly, which will make the bobbin thread easy to remove from the fabric once the hand stitching is complete. Choose a color that contrasts with both the fabric and thread used for handwork, and keep in mind that long stitches are easier to rip out once the basting has served its purpose.

1. Determine the placement of handworked embellishments on the garment and machine baste (topstitch) along these lines. Use presser feet, an adjustable seam guide, or predrawn lines/motifs to guide your stitches. Experiment to determine the stitch length that will enable you to achieve the desired effect. Some machines have long stitch and basting stitch settings that will be especially welcome for marking long stitch intervals.
2. Work hand stitches over water-soluble basting thread, or directly beside silk thread, following the machine-basted placement line. Use the length of the basting stitches as a guide to achieve accurately spaced handwork.
3. Secure handworked stitches on the wrong side of the fabric and remove all traces of basting thread.

Using an unthreaded wing needle

This is the fastest, easiest way to mark in lines for the running stitch and pickstitch. It is best suited to loose-weave, natural-fiber fabrics such as linen and cotton, which retain the holes produced by the wing needle. Test the fabric in advance to determine suitability of this method.

1. Determine the design and placement of stitching lines on the fabric.
2. Apply spray starch to the area to be embellished. If additional stability is required, consult the list of stabilizers on pp. 51-52 and test to determine an appropriate choice.
3. Preset the machine or test to determine the desired stitch length.
4. Run the fabric through a machine fitted with an unthreaded wing or large universal needle. Use presser feet, an adjustable seam guide, or predrawn lines/motifs to guide stitching. As the needle penetrates the fabric, visible holes will appear to designate the stitching line for handwork. Create lines to embellish along the edge or across the body of the garment—anywhere handwork is desired.
5. Loose-weave, natural-fiber fabrics will retain the needle hole, making the stitching line and spacing between stitches readily visible. Synthetic fibers and certain fabric weaves will cause some fabrics to spring back into place after the needle has penetrated, making it difficult to determine the placement of the hole. When this happens, it is often feasible to hold the fabric to a light source and mark the holes with a contrasting-color fabric marker immediately after the fabric has been run through the machine. In this way, a fabric with short-term retention can be used with this method.
6. Work hand stitches directly into the holes produced by the wing needle and secure the stitches as required.

Using a water- or air-soluble marking pen

This method takes more time and is no more accurate than the previous methods, but it may be appropriate for applications that are difficult to gauge or maneuver directly on the machine. Motifs, tight curves, long, asymmetric, or uneven stitch intervals call for this method, which can also be used in conjunction with the previous two.

1. Use a water- or air-soluble marker with a clear, gridded ruler to mark long, asymmetric, or uneven stitch intervals; a French curve, protractor, or flexible ruler to indicate curves; or simply draw freehand motifs of any shape or size, wherever embellishment is desired.
2. If regular spacing along a stitching line is desired, mark intervals using increments on a straight or flexible ruler. Or, combine with either of the previous methods to create even spacing where feasible.
3. Work hand stitches directly over the markings and remove the pen marks as per the manufacturer's instructions.

Using tape

Tiger Tape, ¼-in.-wide tape, and flexible tape can be adhered directly to your garment wherever you plan to hand stitch. The nonadhesive side of the Tiger Tape is marked at nine lines per inch, or roughly ⅛ in. apart. The ¼-in.-wide tape would be a good choice for guiding parallel rows of running stitch, since you could sew to either side of the tape. At a narrow width of 1/16 in., flexible tape is a good choice for any of the stitches, including whipstitching along a garment's edge. More flexible than its counterpart, flexible tape is also suitable for marking gentle curves.

1. Use the edges of the garment as a placement guide, or, if desired, premark lines the desired distance from the edge using a clear, gridded ruler and a water- or air-soluble marking pen.
2. Position the adhesive side of the tape to the fabric directly next to the stitching line.
3. Work hand stitches directly next to the tape, using the evenly spaced marks on the tape to determine consistent stitch length.

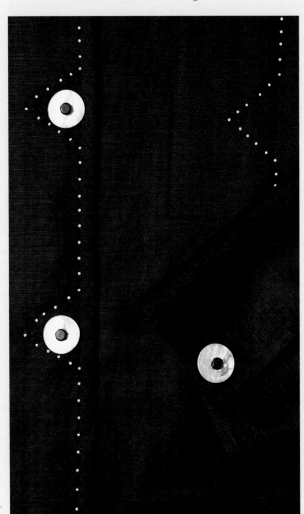

Though time-consuming, using a water- or air-soluble pen is the best method for marking a pickstitched motif like this one. (Photo by Sloan Howard.)

Running-Stitch Variations

Saddle stitch (one pass)

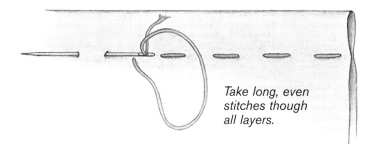

Take long, even stitches though all layers.

Double running stitch (two passes)

Work two parallel rows of evenly spaced stitches through all layers.

Threaded running stitch (two passes)

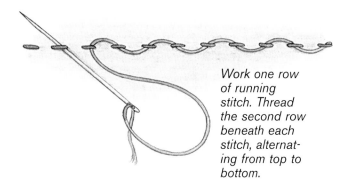

Work one row of running stitch. Thread the second row beneath each stitch, alternating from top to bottom.

Twisted running stitch (two passes)

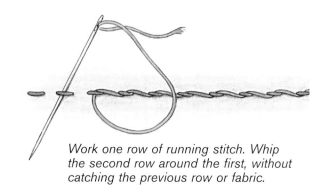

Work one row of running stitch. Whip the second row around the first, without catching the previous row or fabric.

Threaded running stitch (four passes)

Work two parallel rows of running stitch close together. Thread from left to right, then right to left.

Stepped running stitch (two passes)

Work two parallel rows of running stitch. Step the second row so that the under/over pattern alternates with the first.

Stepped and threaded running stitch (three passes)

Work two rows of running stitch. Zigzag over and under alternate rows.

Saddle stitch and pickstitch (two passes)

Work one row of saddle stitch. Work the pickstitch along the same row.

Threaded running stitch and pickstitch (six passes)

Work three parallel rows of running stitch. Thread all three rows from right to left, then left to right. Work one row of pickstitch in the center of each oval.

THREADWORK EMBELLISHMENTS BY MACHINE

The topstitch, channelstitch, bobbinwork, and corded satin stitch are uncomplicated techniques at their fundamental best. They demand quality materials and workmanship, but successful results can be achieved with even the most basic machine. They are all machine-worked techniques that can add designer details to any garment. Learning how and when to use them will put at your disposal embellishments that once seemed outside the realm of possibility. The garments you make will appear more finished and professional, not to mention more intriguing.

Apart from "just right" materials and a fabulous design, mastery of threadwork embellishment relies on the sewer's knowledge of how to obtain consistent, satisfactory results from the sewing machine. Understanding tension and stitch quality and being able to recognize and control these factors on your machine are vitally linked to achieving your creative visions with utmost success.

Tension adjustments

Decorative threadwork by machine requires adjustments to the needle and/or bobbin tension settings used for standard sewing applications. It is important to know how and why to make adjustments to achieve the look you desire for the stitches you select.

NEEDLE TENSION

The needle tension affects the degree of tension on the needle thread and the rate at which it passes through the tension disk to the eye of the needle. Ultimately, it controls the amount of thread that is fed into the top side of the stitch. Most machines have a dial for controlling needle tension on the front or at the top of the machine. The dial may be numbered, from one to ten, or simply indicate plus

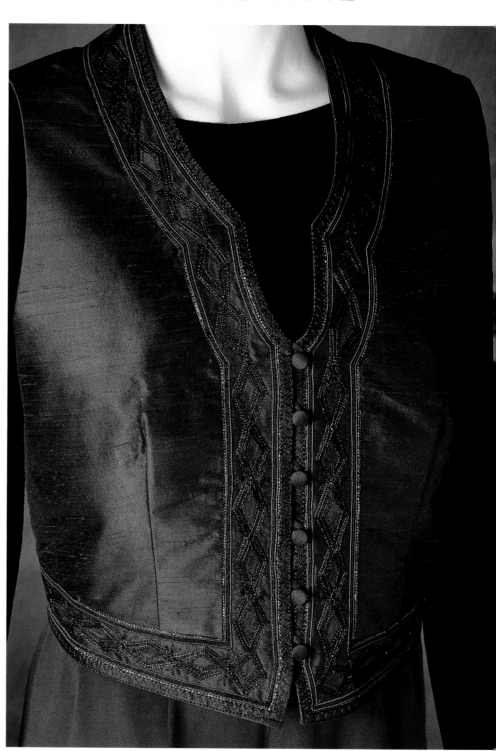

Decorative machine stitches are featured in the ornate border design of this vest.

or minus for more or less tension. "Normal" tension is generally at or near the center of the dial. When the needle and bobbin tension are appropriately set for standard sewing, the result is a perfectly balanced stitch.

Most decorative threadwork requires *loosening* the needle tension slightly, which feeds more thread into the top side of the stitch and allows the embellishment threads to "relax" and lie flat, without puckering or distorting the fabric. For satin stitching and compact embroidery stitches, loosening the needle tension draws the top thread to the underside of the fabric, where the loop is formed. This prevents the bobbin thread from showing on the right side of the garment. When a looser tension setting is called for, begin by reducing the tension by one to two settings, then fine-tune the setting from there.

In some instances, it may be desirable to tighten the needle tension. A contrasting thread in the bobbin can produce unique topstitching effects when tension is increased enough to draw the bobbin thread to the right side of the garment. Decorative bobbinwork is yet another place to experiment with tension, as unique effects can be achieved by loosening or tightening the needle tension.

BOBBIN TENSION

The bobbin tension controls the amount of thread fed into the underside of the stitch. When a decorative thread is used in the needle, tension adjustments are generally made to the needle or top tension only. However, some machines have a "finger" or extension of the bobbin case, which increases tension (without altering the setting of the bobbin case) when the thread is routed through. This draws the top thread to the underside of the fabric. Also, lightweight bobbin threads benefit from increased tension, since normal bobbin tension is set for thicker, standard-weight sewing thread. If your bobbin case has this feature, use it in conjunction with reduced needle tension for decorative stitches.

Negative adjustments to the bobbin tension may be required for decorative bobbinwork so that the heavier thread can pass readily through the bobbin case. This is done by loosening the tension screw on the bobbin case, or on some machines, bypassing tension completely. (For specific instructions on adjusting the bobbin-case tension, see p. 77.)

Stitch quality

With threadwork embellishments, stitch quality (the overall performance and appearance of stitches produced on a sewing machine) determines aesthetic appeal and, ultimately, the success of the project.

Poor stitch quality refers to a stitch that does not perform its basic function well, appears unattractive, or both. Indications of poor stitch quality include uneven tension, a poorly balanced stitch, puckering, stitches that are wobbly or uneven, and "skipped stitches" that unravel from the fabric or ball up beneath it. Poor stitch quality detracts from both the appearance and basic performance of a garment. Good stitch quality refers to properly formed stitches that function appropriately and are generally pleasing to the eye.

OBTAINING GOOD STITCH QUALITY

While overall stitch quality corresponds directly to the basic performance characteristics of a sewing machine, a variety of factors combine to produce the stitch quality evident in any given situation. By paying attention to these factors, it is possible to obtain consistent, good stitch quality with your machine.

- Keep the machine clean, well oiled, and maintained.

- Always begin a project with a fresh needle, appropriately chosen for the application at hand. In some cases, more than one type of needle may be a candidate for the task. If the first needle you select produces less-than-satisfactory results, try an alternate needle type or size.

- Change the needle whenever stitch quality deteriorates, as a bad needle is often the culprit. Decorative threadwork puts more stress on the needle than general sewing and requires frequent needle changes.

- Fraying thread and skipped stitches can be the result of lint buildup in the machine; an improper needle point or size too small; an improperly inserted, dirty, or damaged needle; or the type of thread used in the machine. A silicone lubricant such as Sewer's Aid is frequently helpful for touchy threads, including metallics. Try this directly on the thread or in the eye of the needle if cleaning the machine and changing the needle fail to produce desired results (do not use lubricants with tinsel threads.)

- Most decorative threadwork applications require tension adjustments to the needle and frequently to the bobbin. If you are not well acquainted with how tension is controlled on your machine, consult your machine manual.

- Adjust stitch length and width settings for different threads, as well as the materials being sewn. In general, compact stitches and short stitch length settings are appropriate for lightweight threads, while heavier threads in the needle require longer settings for proper stitch formation. Heavier fabric utilizes more thread to form a basic stitch and may require additional length to produce the same visual result as a shorter stitch length on a finer-weight fabric.

- Stabilizers enhance stitch quality. The degree of support required varies according to the stitch, application, and materials selected for embellishment. Lightweight thread in the bobbin facilitates proper formation of decorative and compact stitches.

- Thread quality is critical. Don't be tempted by bargain-basement thread unless you're willing to pay its true price: frustration.

- Select a needle that best corresponds to the thread, fabric, and task at hand. A single garment may require using a variety of needles for various phases of construction and finishing.

- Proper presser-foot selection improves stitch quality. The foot secures the fabric for insertion of the needle and keeps it stable as the feed dogs move it forward for the stitch. In addition to performing specialized embellishment and sewing tasks, the presser foot is designed to keep the basic function of the foot intact by accommodating surface variations produced by such embellishments. An embroidery foot, for example, has a deep, wide groove to accommodate the added bulk of compact decorative stitches without hanging up beneath the presser foot.

- Reduce speed when sewing decorative and compact embroidery stitches! Sewing slowly allows the thread to feed through the needle properly and the machine to deliver its best stitch formation.

Topstitching

Topstitching—defined as visible stitching on the right, or top side, of the garment—is so routine to sewing that its decorative potential is easy to overlook. Yet, all it takes to elevate this ordinary sewing task is selecting the appropriate needle, thread, and presser foot, and making a few simple adjustments to the sewing machine. Add this to the generic prescription for excellent stitch quality, and the result is an elegant embellishment that delivers all of the functional benefits of topstitching: a finished, professional look, crisp lines and edges, increased body, and shape that holds fast through repeated cleaning and wearing.

MATERIALS LIST

TOPSTITCHING

Needles for lightweight threads: topstitch (70/10 to 90/14); Microtex sharp (60/8 to 90/14); wing (100/16 to 120/19); double hemstitch, embroidery twin (2.0/75 to 3.0/75); twin/double (3.0/90 to 4.0/90); drilling/triple (2.5 to 3.0)

Needles for heavy topstitch threads: topstitch (90/14 to 110/18); jeans/denim (100/16 to 110/18); universal (100/16 to 120/19); Microtex sharp (100/16); twin jeans/denim (4.0/100); twin/double (4.0/100 to 8.0/100)

Needles for knits: twin/double (3.0/90 to 8.0/100); twin/stretch (2.5/75 to 4.0/75); universal (80/12 to 120/19); stretch (75/11 to 90/14)

Presser feet: ¼-in. (patchwork) foot, jeans foot, walking foot, Cordonnet (topstitch foot), edgestitch foot

Straight-stitch plate (for single needle)

Adjustable seam guide

Sewer's Aid (optional)

Seam gauge

Fabric marker

Perhaps you've tried decorative topstitching in the past and experienced difficulty achieving straight, uniform stitches; gauging the appropriate distance from the edge; or getting stitches to form properly and remain consistent. The information here will help you side-step problems such as these and achieve the results you're after.

WHERE TO TOPSTITCH

Topstitching is frequently use to accentuate seamlines and to embellish the edge of a garment, such as collars, cuffs, facings, yokes, front bands, seams, pockets, welts, belts, and waistbands (see the photo below). Unlike many other forms of embellishment, topstitching thrives on complex or unusual piecing and can be used to draw attention to the structure of an intriguing garment. Yet topstitching need not be lavish to have an effect. Typically even light touches create substantial impact.

COLOR CONSIDERATIONS

Decorative topstitching relies heavily on color and is especially well suited to solid fabrics, as prints tend to diminish its impact.

High-contrast fabrics and thread, such as black on a cream ground or white thread on navy, are eternally popular since the result is so vivid, but subtle combinations can also be compelling.

Tone on tone works best when the light-reflective properties of the thread and fabric differ. The luster of a heavy silk thread against the matte appearance of wool crepe, for example, imparts low-key elegance that enriches the appearance of the garment without being showy or dramatic.

Yet another approach is to use topstitching to introduce more than one color, by way of consecutive rows worked in alternate colors or with a variegated thread. High or low contrast, classic or innovative, colors used for topstitching can integrate various components of a wardrobe and draw attention to—or away from—a particular aspect of a garment or ensemble.

FABRIC CONSIDERATIONS

Topstitching is compatible with most wovens and knits; however, some fabrics do not show off topstitching well, while others require special accommodations. In general, topstitching is at its best wedded to a smooth, even surface. Heavily textured fabrics and dense, heavy twills often skew the stitches, making the result less attractive.

Possible solutions include changing the needle and thread and making alterations to the stitch. For heavy tweeds or textured boucles, try a size 110/18 or 120/19 universal needle. For twill, try a 16/110 topstitch needle, or 16/110 Microtex sharp. In both instances, topstitching with silk thread and/or lubricating the needle, tightening the tension slightly, and lengthening the stitch may make a positive difference. Be sure to press the topstitched row prior to assessing the stitch, as the silk thread will actually sink into the fabric.

The topstitched details on the collar, cuff, and pocket flap take this casual brown wool shirt out of the realm of the ordinary. Simple handworked stitches accent the cuffs and the back yoke.

PREPARATION FOR TOPSTITCHING

Topstitching must be done on stabilized areas of the garment. Because this technique is typically applied to portions of the garment that are already interfaced, faced, turned, and pressed, use of additional stabilizers may not be necessary. For lightweight and slippery fabrics, and in other instances when additional stability is desired, spray starch is recommended.

Topstitching sequences correspond to the making up of the garment and must be thought out logically in advance. As a general rule, topstitch as soon as possible in the construction of the garment. Working small and reducing bulk as you sew keeps you in control and makes it easier to guide garment sections through the machine.

Frequently, patterns include topstitching in the general sewing directions for that garment. If not, determine what portions of the garment you wish to embellish, read through the construction sequence advised in the pattern directions, and determine where, in the sequence, topstitching must be done. Write these notations directly in the pattern instructions so that you don't overlook topstitching the collar, for example, before it's already sewn to the rest of the garment (general topstitching guidelines are listed below).

USE OF GUIDES AND GUIDING TECHNIQUES

One of the hallmarks of attractive topstitching is that consecutive rows are uniformly distant from one another as well as from the seam or edge. Achieving consistent spacing is not a matter of luck. Here, the notion of skill is tied not to the ability to gauge distance but to proper selection of a presser foot or guide that helps accomplish that task.

A presser foot is the best choice for guiding widths of up to ⅜ in. (this distance may vary,

Topstitching Guidelines

The following techniques emphasize methods and materials that perform well on a variety of machines. Regardless of the machine you own or the type of topstitching you elect to do, the following guidelines apply.

- Hold on to thread tails when you begin to stitch to keep the thread from balling up, or jamming, on the underside.

- Stitch slowly, with the outside of the garment right side up. If your machine has a reduced speed setting, use it.

- Follow general recommendations for stitch quality (see pp. 66-67).

- For heavy threads, tighten the top tension, lengthen the stitch, and lubricate the needle.

- For fine fabrics, use fine thread and a short stitch length to reduce puckering.

- Topstitching adds body and crispness that increases with the number of rows stitched. The stitch length also corresponds to the degree of stiffness, with shorter stitches adding more body.

- Prior to topstitching, all seams should be pressed open, even if they are to be pressed to one side before sewing. A final pressing once the row of topstitching is complete will "set" the threads and give that portion of the garment a finished look that will remain evident once the garment is complete.

- Long rows of topstitching—such as those that extend from around the neck, down the front, and around the hem—can be broken up and completed in more than one pass. Begin at a midpoint, such as at the back neckline, and sew opposite sides in a parallel direction. Be sure to stop and start in a seamless fashion.

TIP

To topstitch with a heavy thread in the needle, pair it with a standard or light-weight thread in the bobbin. Use a machine needle with an eye large enough to accommodate the thickness of your thread, such as a size 14-18 topstitch needle. Finally, to produce a great-looking stitch, lengthen the stitch to 3mm-5mm and increase the needle tension, which will control the amount of thread fed into the top portion of the stitch and prevent it from balling up or knotting on the underside of the fabric. Increased needle tension is also called for when topstitching with a heavy thread in the bobbin (see pp. 76-79).

depending on the presser foot used and on the maximum stitch width of the machine). Which presser foot to use will depend on the topstitching method used and on other factors, including materials selection. (For more on the presser foot, see pp. 49-50.)

My favorite foot for topstitching is the ¼-in. foot because the markings front and back of center, as well as the perfect ¼ in. to each side, make it so easy to use. Likewise, the edgestitch foot used in conjunction with the needle positions on my machine is ideal for edgestitching on the outside of a garment and allows for directional stitching on either side of a seam. Favorites aside, I routinely use all of the presser feet indicated in the materials list, when they conform more precisely to the particulars of whatever task I am trying to achieve.

A presser foot designed for straight stitching only offers the greatest degree of stability and produces the straightest possible stitch, especially if used with a straight-stitch sole plate and a Microtex sharp, jeans/denim, or topstitch needle. A presser foot designed for use with zigzag stitches, on the other hand, accommodates the various needle positions on the machine but may not provide enough support for a quality stitch on some fabrics or with particular threads. Every project is unique, and some experimentation will be required to determine which foot works best in a given situation. When you use accessories designed for straight stitching only, always check to see that the needle is in the center position before stitching, and remember to change the presser foot and switch back to the standard sole plate prior to altering the needle position or using a zigzag stitch. Failure to do so will cause the needle to break.

For distances wider than ⅜ in., use a seam guide attached to the presser foot or use consecutive markings on the sole plate of the machine. If additional markings are required to gauge the distance between rows of topstitching, tape a clear adhesive ruler to the bed of the machine.

Temporary guides can also be used to mark a specific distance from center needle to any point on the bed of the machine. Frequent solutions include magnetic seam guides (be sure they can be used with your machine), drafting or Sewer's Fix It Tape, or a rubber band wrapped around the free arm of the machine.

Perfect corners result from determining the exact pivot point, and not overriding or stopping short of that location. You can achieve precise results with a ¼-in. presser foot, or you can mark the pivot point directly on the fabric using an air-soluble pen.

Use a tailor's awl or sew a thread tail to the corner to provide a secure hold as you pivot the fabric and to prevent the presser foot from hanging up on the corner as you stitch away from it. Use silk thread for the tail, since it doesn't mar the fabric.

If you reach the pivot point and the needle is midway through a stitch, it is still possible to pivot at the appropriate point. The following method results in a shorter stitch to one side of the corner, but this is preferable to overriding the correct location for the pivot point. To complete the stitch immediately where the needle is located, follow these steps.

1 Drop the feed dogs.

2 Sink the needle into the fabric.

3 Raise the presser foot and pivot the fabric, bringing the perpendicular edge into alignment with the guide or presser foot.

4 Drop the presser foot, raise the feed dogs, and continue stitching along the new edge.

To guide topstitching around curves, gauge a point equidistant to the needle and to the end of the presser foot and directly to the right of the fabric. To guide edgestitching, keep a midway point on the inside of the presser foot in view. For topstitching or edgestitching, keep the edge of the fabric aligned with this point as it feeds beneath the presser foot. Stitch slowly, stopping, if necessary, to check alignment or to reposition the fabric. In some instances, successfully negotiating tight curves may also require shortening the stitch just enough to round the curve smoothly, and resume regular stitch length once the turn is complete.

TRADITIONAL TOPSTITCHING

Traditional topstitching consists of rows of straight stitching worked at the seams and at the edge of the garment. Rows are typically ⅛ in. to ⅜ in. from the edge, and the stitching is guided by use of a standard or ¼-in. presser foot. Edgestitching may run parallel to these rows and is guided with an edgestitch foot, the blindhem foot, or the inner toe of a standard presser foot, with adjustments to the needle position made as required. The stitch length is determined by the weight of the fabric: Short stitches (2mm to 2.5mm) are appropriate for lightweight threads and fabrics, while a longer stitch (3mm to 6mm) produces a desirable look for heavier fabrics and threads.

In general, for topstitching to be considered an embellishment, it must be decorative in some way. Typically, topstitching derives impact through repetition (as with channelstitching) or the bold use of line and color. Use the following methods to produce high-impact topstitching for a classic look with timeless appeal.

- **Double up machine embroidery threads** in a single 90/14 topstitch or embroidery needle. Use lightweight bobbin thread or 60-wt. cotton in the bobbin.

- **Use buttonhole twist or topstitching thread** with a heavy topstitching needle. Use standard thread in the bobbin.

- **Sew with a triple straight stitch,** if you have that option on your machine, or a feather stitch with the stitch width adjusted to zero.

This produces the look of heavy topstitching but allows you to use lightweight, decorative thread in the needle. Use a topstitch or embroidery needle 75/10 to 90/14 (select the size to match thread). Use lightweight cotton or bobbin thread in the bobbin.

- **Sew with a heavy, decorative thread** in the bobbin and with lightweight decorative thread in the needle. (See pp. 76-78 for bobbinwork instructions.) Select the needle size to match the thread in the needle.

TOPSTITCHED MOTIFS

Curved and geometric motifs can be easily worked into topstitching treatments. For best results, select simple designs that consist of one continuous line. The easiest way to transfer the design is to trace it to a piece of water-soluble stabilizer and pin or baste the stabilizer in place on the area of the garment to be embellished. Stitch directly on top of the stabilizer along the design line. Use an appliqué or leather roller foot if the design calls for negotiating curves. Sew slowly and adjust stitch length as required to work the motif.

Parallel topstitching

Parallel topstitching refers to rows of topstitching spaced parallel to one another at regular or uneven intervals. The topstitching may consist of single rows or groupings of two to three closely spaced rows set apart by larger interludes. The overall effect and the use of space is more dramatic than traditional topstitching and not as uniform, closely spaced, or repetitive as channelstitching. Parallel topstitching is well suited to cuffs, hems, and lapels and is equally effective on knits or wovens. It looks especially elegant on fabrics with some loft, since they produce texture variations that show off the stitching. To further dramatize this effect, work the topstitching in a shade or two darker than the fabric. Or, if time and inspiration allow, embellish the larger channels with simple geometric motifs or zigzags,

TIP

Don't backstitch to secure the beginning or end of a topstitched row. For rows that are not enclosed within a seam, leave long thread tails and tie them securely on the wrong side of the garment after sewing the line of stitching. Use an easy threading calyx needle to draw both threads through the fabric layers, reemerging on the underside. Clip tails close to the garment.

Accenting with the Topstitch

Topstitch details and accents highlight and play off the cut of the garment.

using the method for topstitched motifs described previously.

To work parallel topstitching, use a medium-weight thread, such as 30-wt. three-ply silk, or two lightweight threads doubled up in the needle. An adjustable seam guide will help to gauge large intervals, while a presser foot remains the most practical way to produce closely spaced rows. A walking foot is also useful for long lines of stitching or for fabrics that tend to pucker or shift, as it feeds the top layer at a rate consistent with the bottom.

Double topstitched seams

Double topstitching worked on each side of a pressed seam always adds a couture touch. Worked in increments more typical of edgestitching than traditional topstitching, the farthest row is generally spaced no more than ⅛ in. to either side of the seam. It is especially lovely worked in silk thread on gourmet woolens, but try it as well on linen or three-ply silk. Garments that feature this detail do take more time to make, but the results are usually well worth the effort, as the top-stitched seams add shape and body, accentuate the lines of the garment, and contribute to its beauty and longevity. Typically, topstitched seams are worked throughout the garment rather than selectively. Topstitching is completed as individual parts of the garment are put together, as it is impossible to get good results once the garment is sewn.

The preferred foot for this technique is the edgestitch foot, but the inside toe of an alternate foot can also be used. To topstitch using the edgestitch foot, guide the blade of the foot directly in the middle, or "ditch," formed by the sewn seam. Work only on seams that have been pressed open. Always begin at the top of the seam (the portion that will be uppermost on the body) and stitch toward the bottom. Each seam will involve four passes. Use a thread similar in weight to what you would use for garment construction, but for decorative effect, choose a thread with luster. Again, because of its light-reflective properties, strength, and resilience, silk is the ultimate thread of choice. To produce a double-topstitched seam, follow these steps.

1   Position the fabric right side up, with the top of the seam beneath the edgestitch foot.

2   Select a needle position directly to the right of the seam and sew, guiding the blade of the presser foot directly in the middle of the seam.

3 Reposition the fabric at the top of the seam and alter the needle position to the left of the seam.

4 Repeat steps two and three but move the needle position to the far right and far left, respectively, prior to stitching the seam.

5 When all rows are finished, use a press cloth, and press the seam.

Multiple-needle topstitching

Double and triple needles offer a convenient and quick solution to producing two—or even three—evenly spaced rows of topstitching with just one pass of the machine. Two or three threads are threaded through individual needles attached to the same shank for insertion in the machine. A single bobbin thread forms a zigzag stitch on the underside of the fabric when the stitch is sewn, so use this method only when the zigzag on the underside is acceptable, or work the topstitching on garment pieces prior to facing them, so the underside will be hidden from view. As usual, thread weights correspond to the needle size, so be sure that thread, needle, and fabric are compatible. Thread colors can be combined for added interest.

Presser feet suitable for a traditional top-stitched look with twin needles include the standard zigzag presser foot, the standard embroidery foot, and the preferred open embroidery foot. Reduced needle tension will be required, in most cases, to get the parallel rows of stitching to lie flat.

If a pintuck effect is desired, use a pintuck foot that corresponds to the needle width you plan to use. To enhance the pintucked effect, tighten the needle tension and, if desired, cord the pintuck with pearl cotton, crochet cotton, or gimp.

Threading two threads through the machine is necessary to use a twin needle. To use a triple needle, three threads must be threaded through the machine. Also, when sewing with twin and triple needles, predetermine the maximum stitch width that the needle can accommodate. Set the machine for that width prior to sewing; otherwise, the needle may break.

To calculate the maximum stitch width of a needle, subtract the needle width (indicated by the first number designation on the package) from the widest width setting on your machine. Be sure to reset the width if you move to a wider needle or select a different stitch. Some machines have a double needle limiting function that automatically limits the width of the stitch. Consult your manual to see if your machine has this function.

To begin sewing, hold on to all thread tails. Manually turn the hand wheel through the first stitch sequence to ensure that the needle clears the presser foot. Then sew a few more stitches and assess the needle tension and stitch length. Loosen the tension if you want a flatter stitch, tighten for a raised effect, and adjust stitch length as required. In addition to straight-stitch topstitching, the double needle can be used with other decorative stitches and practical stitches that produce a decorative effect. Again, check the stitch width prior to sewing to prevent needle breakage.

Turning corners with a double or triple needle requires manually walking the outside needle around the pivot point for a couple of stitches. The inner needle continues to strike the same location until the outer needle has rounded the corner. When the stitching is complete, the inner corner will form a sharp right angle, while the outer corner will be less severe. If you take care when pivoting, the difference between the two will be barely noticeable.

To turn corners gracefully, stitch along the stitching line until the inner needle reaches the pivot point or inside corner. Sink the double needle at this point, dropping the feed dogs if you reach this point midway through a stitch. For the next two or three stitches, the inner needle will penetrate the same corner location. Here's how to turn a corner.

1 With the needle down in the fabric, lower the feed dogs, and lift the presser foot.

2 Turn the fabric approximately 45° so that the outer needle rounds the corner halfway. Check the location of the inner needle to see that it will reenter the same corner hole when the needle is lowered.

3 When the needle is properly positioned, lower the presser foot and turn the flywheel forward manually to sink the needle, taking a single stitch.

4 Repeat the process to complete the turn, raise the feed dogs, and finish sewing.

5 When using a wide double needle, you can make a less-conspicuous turn by taking additional, shorter stitches as you complete the turn.

Channelstitching

Channelstitching is an extremely versatile and effective embellishment that can be used to adorn sandwashed silk blouses, wool melton coats, and everything in between (see the photo below left). Channelstitching consists of multiple rows of topstitching, generally worked from 1/8 in. to 3/8 in. apart. The closely worked rows have a stabilizing—even stiffening—effect that must be considered in advance but can be used to advantage on facings, applied welts, waistbands, cuffs collars, and the like.

In general, channelstitching is worked with a slightly shorter stitch length than decorative topstitching. A variety of light- to medium-weight threads are appropriate for cottons, linens, and rayons, but for silks and woolens, silk thread is especially recommended. Avoid heavy topstitching threads for this application, as the results will be too stiff.

A variety of feet can be used for channelstitching, but my personal favorite is the 1/4-in. foot, when I can get away with it, since it provides guides for perfect 1/8-in. and 1/4-in. intervals. However, in some instances—such as large groupings of long rows—a walking foot is a necessity. In this case, I use the outside and inside of the presser-foot toe, along with the needle positions on the machine, to gauge the distance accurately between consecutive rows.

Although the traditional use of channelstitching is lovely in its own right, the decorative potential of this technique is underused and far richer than one would first assume. To pique your imagination, here are some ways to use channelstitching to create elegant embellishments.

Channelstitching lends body, texture, and guidelines for beading to the collar, frontband, and cuffs of this blouse.

CHANNELSTITCHED MOTIFS

Channelstitching doesn't have to consist of straight lines only, nor is it wed to the shapes that define the edge of the garment. Anywhere that channelstitching can be worked, the opportunity exists to introduce simple, geometric motifs that radiate out in consecutive lines to whatever border confines them, including the edge of the garment. To further accentuate motifs, add a layer of cotton flannel beneath the areas to be embellished. This will create a quilted texture and make the motifs even more distinct.

Channelstitching offers the perfect opportunity to combine thread colors or use unique variegated threads to optimum effect. Combinations are endless and can be subtle or bold. Sometimes using colors that are close to one another but a slight shade off enriches the overall effect in an intriguing way.

Beaded channelstitching

Once rows of channelstitching are in place, they can be used as a basic grid for working beaded motifs or regularly spaced beaded rows (see the drawing above). Use the basic running stitch to attach individual beads, taking stitches ½ in. to ⅝ in. apart (for more on beading, see Chapter 1) and staggering bead placement from one row to the next. Select beads and thread that are complementary.

Corded channelstitching

Corded channelstitching is also known as Italian quilting, or trapunto. The traditional technique is to stitch the top fabric to an underlining. Cording is then drawn through the channels with a ball-point bodkin, which "raises" the channels and gives dimension to the design. Wide bands of corded channelstitching can broken up with rows of decorative stitching to create additional texture, variety, and interest. The embellishments are worked prior to construction, and the garment is typically lined. Garments of exceptional beauty can be created using this method, and

Beaded Channelstitching

Parallel rows of beads can be staggered and combined with topstitching.

the underlining and the cording add desirable weight and drape to the garment.

Corded channelstitching can be worked on a variety of natural fiber fabrics, although twills and highly textured fabrics are not recommended. Wool crepe, wool doubleknit, silk dupioni, and linen are among the best choices.

To produce embellishments using this method, follow these steps.

1 Interface areas to be embellished and baste the underlining to the fashion fabric.

2 Mark the first row of stitching, if necessary, and channelstitch consecutive rows from edge to edge, wherever the corded embellishment is desired. Stitch directly through the seamlines to create channels for cording. Pretest the width to be sure they'll readily accommodate the bodkin.

3 Thread cording through channels (I prefer baby yarn to cording). Leave long tails at the beginning and end. Stitch the ends in place along the seamline once all channels are corded for that garment piece.

4 Trim away the yarn or cord ends, press using a press cloth, and construct the garment as directed.

Decorative threads: pearl cotton/rayon, silk buttonhole twist, gimp, wool yarn, metallic braid, narrow ribbon

Needle threads: rayon, cotton, silk, metallic machine-embroidery thread, invisible nylon

Machine needles (12/80 to 14/90): embroidery, topstitching, or Metallica/Metafil

Extra bobbin case

Presser feet: ¼-in. foot, edgestitch foot, pintuck foot, embroidery foot, open-toe embroidery foot, leather roller foot, clear appliqué foot

Iron-on interfacing: tricot knit or weft insertion

Stabilizer: iron-on or lightweight tear-away

Water-soluble pen (with a fine tip)

Tiger Tape

Bobbinwork

If you've ever admired the array of gorgeous threads for handwork and wished there were a way to use them in your machine, take heart! Beautiful threads too heavy to use in the needle can often be incorporated into a garment design by feeding them through the bobbin. The result is a highly textured surface embellishment that shows off thread like no other (see the photo below).

Use straight-stitch bobbinwork for topstitching, for laying in couched threads, and for producing accents, motifs, or all-over designs anywhere on the garment: The effect is outstanding. Decorative machine stitches produce intriguing results as well and can be worked into bands and borders or used to make custom ribbons. Allow ample time for experimentation and, to economize, reserve expensive threads (or those in limited supply) for actual projects.

PREPARATION

Bobbinwork requires you to stabilize the areas to be embellished; to transfer the motifs for stitching; to wind the thread on the bobbin; and to adjust the bobbin tension so that the decorative thread feeds evenly.

Stabilizing areas

Which stabilizer will work best and how much to use depend on the fabric, thread, type of stitches used, and the degree of embellishment. Areas that already call for interfacing may be sufficiently stable or may require little added support. Iron-on tear-aways provide stability and can be used several layers at one time, if need be, but some experimentation will be required to determine appropriate solutions for each project. The stabilizer is applied to the wrong side of the garment.

Transferring motifs

To transfer bobbinwork motifs for stitching, draw or trace the design on the top layer of stabilizer. (This can be done before the stabi-

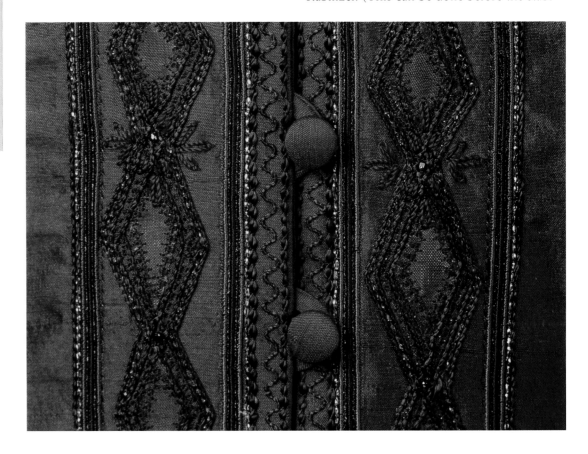

In the border design here, rayon and metallic threads were fed through the bobbin to outline the appliquéd motifs, to lay threads between rows of corded satin stitch, and to create the decorative serpentine stitch.

lizer is placed on the fabric.) All stitching is done with the wrong side of the garment facing up, which means that directional or asymmetrical designs will appear in reverse on the right side of the garment. If you want a directional motif to appear one way on the right side, flip the stitching template to sew its mirror image from the wrong side of the garment.

Winding threads on the bobbin

Wind decorative threads onto the bobbin slowly, by hand or machine. Generally, threads that are already on a spool or card are easy to wind by machine. Skeins of yarn or embroidery thread should be placed around an umbrella swift or the back of a chair and monitored for even feeding. Threads that create undue stress on the tension disk are too heavy for it. When this occurs, bypass the disk normally used to wind the bobbin and guide the thread by hand or manually wind the bobbin. If you plan to do extensive work, wind several bobbins at once. Do not overfill bobbins, as surplus thread diminishes even feeding.

Adjusting bobbin tension

Sewing heavy threads in the bobbin requires loosening or bypassing the bobbin thread tension completely, depending upon your machine. For machines with drop-in (or wind-in-place) bobbins, the tension must be bypassed. This is best done according to instructions included in the manual for that machine. On machines with a removable bobbin case, the bobbin tension is adjusted by way of the tension screw on the outside of the bobbin case. I recommend you purchase a separate bobbin case for use with decorative threads, since constant adjustments to the bobbin tension, as well as the stress of heavy threads, can damage the spring and create difficulties for normal sewing. Here's how to adjust tension on a removable bobbin case.

1   Locate the tension screw. This is a very small screw on the outside of the bobbin case. (Consult your machine manual to double-check the location of this screw.)

The threading on the screw is short, so when you make adjustments, take precautions in case it falls out. Work over a table or put a towel in your lap.

2   Insert the bobbin with decorative thread into the bobbin case. Pull on the thread and compare tension to that of a standard bobbin thread. If the thread resists feeding, loosen the tension on the bobbin case with a tiny screwdriver. Adjust the screw slightly to the left, in increments of no more than a quarter turn. Pull on the bobbin thread after each small adjustment to gauge improvement.

3   If the thread feeds out rapidly, the tension is too loose. To tighten the tension, turn the screw to the right. When the thread pulls with a smooth, even tension, try sewing with the thread in the bobbin. If the stitch forms, adjust the needle tension up or down to fine-tune the stitch before making additional alterations to the bobbin tension.

4   The degree of tension required is determined by the weight of thread in the bobbin. Adjust for specific threads rather than making blind adjustments. If you wish to make adjustments to the bobbin case you use for normal sewing, mark the original tension setting by drawing a thin line from the top edge of the screw onto the bobbin case with an ultra-fine-point permanent-ink pen. When bobbinwork is complete, realign the marks for normal tension. You can add markings in different colors to indicate settings for frequently used threads, if desired.

BOBBINWORK METHOD

Once you've adjusted the bobbin case for the threads you plan to use, you're set to sew. Here are the steps.

1   Install an embroidery or topstitching needle in the machine.

2   Thread the needle with a decorative rayon, silk, cotton, or metallic machine-embroidery thread, or invisible nylon.

TIP

For bobbinwork, an edgestitch foot or pintuck foot works well for placing lines of straight stitching next to each other, between rows of corded satin stitch, and for stitching in the ditch. The embroidery, appliqué, leather roller foot, and circular sewing attachment offer the best options for working motifs, flourishes, circles, and curves. Decorative stitches will perform best with an open-toe or standard embroidery foot.

TIP

For bobbinwork topstitching, sew individual garment sections in the order you would for any topstitched garment. Trim, turn, and press seams and facings prior to stitching. No additional stabilizer will be necessary for most topstitching applications.

3 Use heavy decorative thread in the bobbin. Insert the bobbin case in the machine and sink the needle to draw the thread up through the stitch plate, as you would for normal sewing.

4 Select the stitch. Arrange the fabric beneath the presser foot and sink—then raise—the needle. Pull on the needle thread to draw the bobbin thread to the top through the fabric.

5 Lower the presser foot, hold the thread tails, and sew several inches with the wrong side of the garment facing up.

6 Check the right side of the sample to assess the stitch, and make adjustments to the needle tension as necessary.

7 Experiment with various thread combinations, as well as with practical and decorative stitches. When first trying a new stitch, sew a long row that includes various combinations of stitch width and length settings, as well as tension adjustments to the needle. If you have a computerized machine with mirror image, stitch elongation, directional stitching, or other specialized stitch functions, by all means try them! Use a permanent-ink pen to write down machine specifications directly on the sample (or on tape adhered to the sample) immediately after you've altered the machine settings. Be sure to identify the name or number of the stitch (it may not be recognizable when worked in heavy thread), as well as length, width, and tension settings. Later you can sort through and catalog the best results.

8 When you've completed a motif or row of stitching, *do not backstitch!* Lift the presser foot and cut the thread, leaving a thread tail of 4 in. to 5 in. Pull on the needle thread from the wrong side of the fabric to draw the top thread through. Knot the thread on back side of the garment and work thread tails into the stitched row (or a seam).

Corded satin stitch

Corded satin stitch consists of a very narrow row of satin stitch worked over cording. The resulting stitch is slightly raised and has the appearance of silk or rayon gimp. Single rows can be worked with a standard embroidery foot—or any foot with a guide for narrow cording. Consecutive rows worked with a seven- or nine-groove pintuck foot leave room for inlaid bobbinworked threads, which produce an outstanding decorative band effect (see the photo on the facing page).

Corded satin stitch can be worked on a variety of woven fabrics, but they must be adequately stabilized prior to sewing. The need for stability increases with the number of rows being stitched. When using this technique to embellish a single layer of fabric, the fabric should first be backed with an iron-on interfacing, followed by one or more layers of an iron-on stabilizer. On portions of the garment that consist of two layers and an interfacing—such as collars and cuffs—additional stabilizer may not be necessary. If the bobbin thread will be visible on an underlayer of the garment, use 60-wt. cotton embroidery thread in the bobbin, in a color to match the fabric.

WORKING THE CORDED SATIN STITCH

Once the fabric has been stabilized, proceed as follows.

1 Thread the machine needle with embroidery thread, and the bobbin with lingerie thread or 60-wt. cotton. If your bobbin case has a finger to increase bobbin tension, thread it.

2 Loosen the needle tension and select the zigzag stitch. Set the stitch length to the satin-stitch setting, and the stitch width to 1mm. (If you use a cord larger or smaller than #10 Cebelia crochet cotton from DMC, the width of the zigzag stitch may vary. Increase the width slightly to accommodate a larger cord.)

3 Place the fabric under the presser foot and guide the cord through the cording hole in the embroidery foot or beneath the center groove of the pintuck foot.

4 Hold on to the thread tails and sew slowly along the stitching line. The foot will guide the cord as the row of satin stitch is sewn over it. The satin stitch should appear uniform and adequately cover the cord beneath it. The bobbin thread should not appear on the top side of the fabric, nor should the stitching on top appear loose. Adjust the stitch width or length and tension, if necessary.

5 Sew from edge to edge, mindful of any matching that will be required when the garment is constructed.

6 When the row of stitching is complete, lift the presser foot, leave a thread tail, and cut all thread, including the cording.

7 If you are using the pintuck foot, you can work parallel rows of stitching by placing the original line of stitching in the groove to the left or right of center. Work the second row exactly as the first, with the cording held in the center groove of the presser foot. Work as many rows as desired in this fashion, always placing the previous row in the groove next to center.

LAYING IN BOBBIN THREADS

Once the consecutive rows of corded satin stitch are complete, add decorative threads by using the edgestitch foot to guide straight-stitched bobbin threads between the rows of corded satin stitch. This is done with the wrong side of the garment facing up. A variety of beautiful threads can be used in the bobbin. Experiment to see which you like best.

To work decorative bobbin threads between rows of corded satin stitch, follow these steps.

1 Use a heavy thread in the bobbin and lightweight decorative thread or invisible nylon in the needle. (See p. 77 for complete directions on preparing the bobbin case for stitching.)

2 Set the machine for straight stitching and center the needle position. Start with a stitch length of about 3mm and reduce or lengthen as necessary.

3 Place the wrong side of the garment face-up. The space between rows of corded satin stitch will be visible from this side of the garment.

4 Center the blade of the edgestitch foot directly between the visible underside of the rows of corded satin stitch.

5 Straight stitch along this line, using the blade of the edgestitch foot as a guide.

6 The bobbin thread will be visible from the right side of the garment and will appear to be couched between rows of corded satin stitch.

(See p. 77 for complete directions on preparing the bobbin case for stitching.)

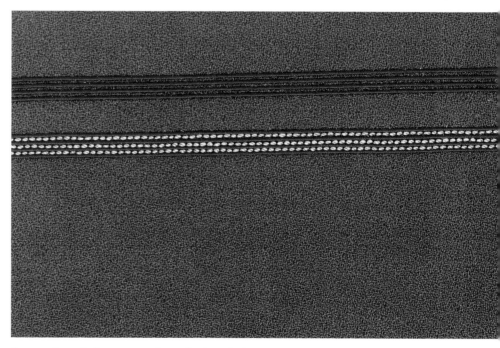

Rows of corded satin stitch worked with the pintuck foot were used here to create elegant bands of color.

CORDED SATIN STITCH

Machine-embroidery thread: rayon or silk

Bobbin thread: lingerie or 60-wt. cotton

Embroidery needles (75/11 to 90/14)

#10 Cebelia crochet cotton or cotton gimp

Presser feet: nine-groove pintuck foot (for evenly spaced consecutive rows) or embroidery foot with guide for cord

Iron-on interfacing: tricot knit or weft insertion

Stabilizer: iron-on or lightweight tear-away

MATERIALS LIST

Trims

Beautiful trims tempt the design-conscious sewer with potent ways to outline the edges of collars and cuffs, to create borders and designs that emphasize the parameters of the garment, and to introduce compelling design within the garment body. Among embellishment methods, trims have the potential to produce maximum impact with minimal effort.

Yet despite their apparent simplicity, incorporating trims into effective garment design is often a challenge, which is why it's not uncommon to leave trim that looked so gorgeous on the bolt off the project for which it was destined.

If you're looking for new and better ways to incorporate trims into your garment sewing, the information in this chapter will enhance your skills. Methods for making custom trims, designing with trims, as well as placing and sewing them on garments put a palette of techniques at your creative disposal. Whether you opt for a "less-is-more" approach or indulge passementerie's traditional association with opulence, the techniques presented in this chapter will help you define and achieve your vision. Inspiration and techniques emphasize the use of braids and cords to create low-key, elegant day wear and special-occasion garments, but with a little ingenuity, these and other trims can be adapted to lavish interpretations—even costume design.

MATERIALS AND EQUIPMENT

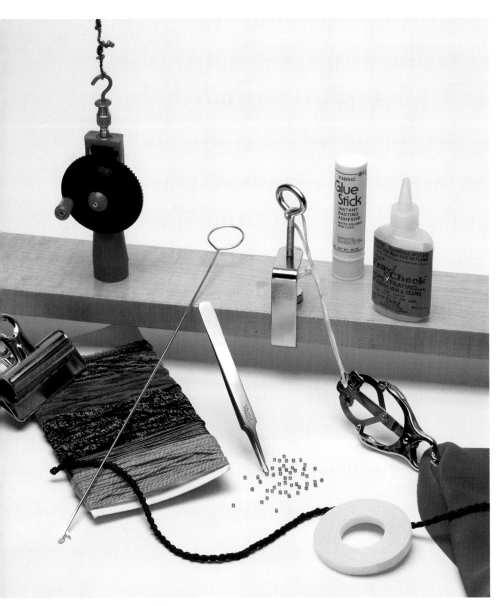

Equipment needed for trimwork includes (clockwise from upper left): Spinster, tube turner, third hand, water-soluble fabric, glue stick, seam sealant, Wonder Tape, and beading tweezers.

Happily, both making custom trims and applying them requires little in the way of equipment (see the photo above). If you elect to make your own trims from self-fabric, you'll see that it's an especially economical way to embellish a garment as well, since it frequently requires nothing more than rearranging a few pattern pieces prior to cutting out the garment.

Purchased trims, in comparison, vary greatly in price and quality. By familiarizing yourself with the basic types of ready-made trims available and by recognizing their attributes, potential uses, and limitations, you will avoid costly mistakes and, better yet, end up with a trim that is perfect for your project.

Trims

Whether you envision using purchased trims or making your own, a general knowledge of the varieties of trim available is an asset in planning your garment. Like all venues of adornment, the selection of trims is astonishing. Consider this: There are flat braids, star braids, scroll braids, military braids, French braids, president braids, foldover braids, and middy braids; there are cords, inserts, cord edges, sheer ribbon, jacquard ribbon, grosgrain ribbon, satin-face ribbon, and velvet ribbon; there are woven trims, knit trims, metal mesh trims, beaded trims, rickrack, fringe, gimp, soutache, and a seemingly endless variety of laces (see the photo on the facing page).

While it is by no means necessary to know all but a few of these trims by name, it is useful to recognize the properties that make particular kinds of trim desirable for garment embellishment. Those properties include flexibility, sewing and handling ease, sturdiness—including the ability to withstand repeated cleaning—and aesthetic properties such as degree of texture, color, and sheen. All relate to the overall look you wish to achieve for your project.

Let's say you had a design that included a wide band of curvaceous designs at the hem of the garment. The success of the project would rely upon finding a pliable trim in an appropriate color. Some pliable trims include petersham, soutache, star braid, president braid, and flexible braid. Each of these trims can be shaped to a curve, but not all are appropriate for the project in mind. Among those that are, some take a great deal of steaming, shaping, and coaxing, while others practically dance into formation. For ornate designs, loops, and curves, only the trims that dance will produce the professional look you're after. If you have to fight, coax, or sway your design into shape, the result will disappoint your expectations. And nothing looks worse than a homemade garment with a trim that scrunches, bunches, or appears otherwise ill applied—except, perhaps, cheap department-store variety clothing of the same ilk.

Depending upon the selection of trims available in local stores, mail-order sources may be the best option for purchasing trims that meet your needs in terms of color, quality, and style. Fabric stores generally carry some trims, but for understandable reasons, selection is limited to the most generic styles and a basic selection of colors. Soutache and Chinese braid may be available in black and white at a local store, for example, but a mail-order supplier may stock 10 to 20 times as many colors and introduce you to a variety of other available trims you never knew existed.

Always check local sources first, however, as they may just have precisely what you need or, at the very least, basic types of trim that you can use for sewing samples to determine how well a particular type of trim works for the application you have in mind. That way, even if you do end up purchasing mail-order trim, you will have fine-tuned your decision based on predictable results. Like fabric yardage, trims are measured goods that cannot be exchanged or returned once cut.

For the most part, the techniques depicted in the next few pages use simple trims that are easy to obtain and come in a wide variety of colors. I am a huge fan of ornate, elegant trims to embellish presents and pillows but rarely use them for garment design.

Use ready-made trims to add color and character to garments.

What I favor in a trim for a garment varies with the project. In general, I tend to work with quality natural-fiber trims that are soft, responsive to shaping, have a rich, uniform appearance, and are relatively small in scale (both width and height). I have found small-scale trims to be the most versatile and the easiest to control. They can be used extensively throughout the garment while maintaining a look that is not too heavy or overdone. I also look for trims that are easy to sew, will hold up well, and maintain an attractive appearance for the life of the garment.

Presser feet

For fast, easy, clean application of trims, machine application is the way to go. Certainly there are instances when hand application is desirable, but, thankfully, they are the exception, not the rule. For ease of application by machine, the key to success is, once again, choosing the correct presser foot (see the photo on p. 84).

Depending upon the make and model of your machine, a variety of brand-specific or generic presser feet are designed to suit your needs in any given situation. Not all of the feet listed here will work with all trims or for all applications. Because the trim and the design dictate which presser foot will be appropriate, select your trim in advance, then buy the presser foot best suited to your needs—unless, of course, you already have a variety of presser feet at your disposal.

FEET FOR APPLYING CORDS AND NARROW TRIMS

The defining feature of a presser foot that will be useful for sewing narrow cords and trims is that the foot has either a hole, slot, or groove that secures the trim as it feeds beneath the presser foot. The location of the hole, slot, or groove varies. It may be on the front bridge of the foot, between the toes of the presser foot, or on the underside of the presser foot, or it may be an attachment that lies in front of a presser foot. In every instance, its purpose is the same: to guide the passage of the trim, to ensure accurate placement, and to maintain uniformity as the needle thread couches the trim to fabric.

Presser feet (clockwise from upper left): edgestitch, zigzag, open-toe embroidery, pintuck, Sequins 'N Ribbon, Pearls 'N Piping, and adjustable zipper.

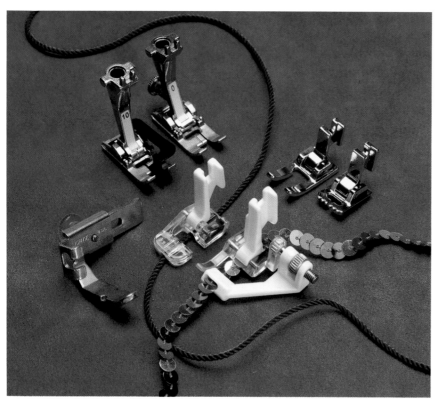

To ensure even feeding and obtain professional, uniform results, the size of the hole, slot, or groove should match the size of the trim as accurately as possible. Rather than second-guessing, try the trim in the hole, slot, or groove to see if it fits. The trim should fill, and thus lie securely in the hole, slot, or groove but should not exceed it in height or width, or feeding of the trim will be impaired.

For stitching narrow cords, potentially useful candidates include the standard embroidery, pintuck, cording, and appliqué presser feet. Larger cords will require a larger hole, slot, or groove, such as those found in presser feet designed to accommodate round piping. For guiding and stitching directly through the center of soutache and narrow, flat braids, the appliqué foot, three- and five-groove pintuck feet, and braiding foot are likely choices. Of these, the appliqué and braiding feet work best for guiding the braid around loops, curves, and scrolls associated with passementerie embellishment and provide adequate visibility, which is imperative for the accurate rendering of designs created with the trims.

A pintuck foot, on the other hand, works well for placement of consecutive, evenly spaced rows of braid and will suffice for working gentle curves and geometric designs. Narrow ribbons can be applied with ease by using a double needle of the appropriate width with the appliqué, pintuck, braiding, or open-toe embroidery foot.

FEET FOR APPLYING WIDE TRIMS

If you cannot obtain any of the above presser feet specifically designed for your brand of machine, generic feet are commercially available. In addition to the feet styles listed previously, the Sequins 'N Ribbon and Pearls 'N Piping feet from Creative Feet can be used for narrow cord and trim applications and include adapters that render the feet usable with any make or model machine.

For applying wide trims, the foot of choice is likely to be an adjustable zipper foot, edgestitch foot, or a standard zigzag foot, which has an indentation at the center of the foot that can be used as a guide. Each of these feet can be used in conjunction with the needle positions on the machine to guide stitching accurately along the edge of the trim with the needle positioned to the left or right of the guide, as required.

Fasturn tube turner

Although there are numerous tools on the market for turning fabric tubes, the Fasturn tube turner takes the cake for ease of use. Nothing brings this home like turning the long lengths required for the bias rouleau (turned fabric tubes) for self-fabric trims, closures, bias appliqué, and faggotted rouleau embellishments. I use it as well for turning straight grain tubes for pinweaving applications.

Sold in sets of three or six tubes, this is one tool worth every penny it costs. Use it in conjunction with the Fastube presser foot, and you'll see that sewing and turning uniform fabric tubes just doesn't get any easier.

Spinster

The Spinster looks something like a hand drill with a cup hook at the end. It is used to make plied cords that can be applied directly to a garment as an edging, used to outline appliqués, or sewn to flat tapes to make cord-edge trim. Although similar cords can be made using the bobbin winder of your sewing machine (providing the winder is on the top end of the machine), this tool is easier to use when long lengths of cord are required and allows you to skip the gymnastics of balancing on top of a table or chair.

Third Hand & Clamp

There is no good substitute for this invaluable tool. It consists of a clamp that attaches to a firm, stable surface and a clamp that grips fabric or threads tightly to provide tension on the item that is being worked, leaving both of your hands free. It is exceptionally useful for working long lengths of braid to make custom trims and can be used in combination with the Spinster for making cords as well.

Fabric glue stick and Wonder Tape

A water-soluble fabric glue stick is used for positioning trims in place prior to sewing. Faster, easier, and in many cases more accurate than basting, it has excellent tacking qualities, yet it won't gum up your needle, doesn't add stiffness, and is removed from the fabric upon cleaning. Wonder Tape is a ¼-in. double-sided tape that's water soluble and won't gum up the needle when sewn through. It is very useful for placing trims prior to sewing.

Seam sealant

Using a seam sealant such as Fray Check or Fray Stoppa on trims prior to cutting the ends will help prevent raveling that could compromise the appearance of your work. Use these sealants with care, keeping the ends clear of your garment fabric as they dry, since these sealants do darken as well as stiffen the fibers they come in contact with.

Beading tweezers

Beading tweezers have very sharp, narrow points that meet precisely at the tip. This is a very useful tool for positioning cords and braids as they're being sewn. The point can be used in a fashion similar to a sewing stiletto, while the tweezers can actually be used to lift and pull the cords in or out of place.

TIP

When making custom braids, individual strands must be firmly secured, as they will be subject to tension as the braid is being worked. Use a clamp or the cheaper alternative–a metal clip with a firm bite commonly available from office, stationery, and art suppliers (see the drawings on p. 89).

MAKING CUSTOM TRIMS

Custom braids, cords, and reembellished trims make for some of the most beautiful embellishments that can be used on a garment (see the photo at left). I love making and using them because I can create a trim in pure accord with the garment. This effect is especially enhanced when the trim is constructed from either bias tubes of the fabric itself or threads pulled from the warp or weft of the fabric.

As the following methods demonstrate, there are other exciting ways to make custom trims as well. Many of them are utterly simple, yet the resulting trims deepen the complexity and character of the garments they adorn.

Monkscord

Monkscord is a simple twisted cord suitable for a variety of garment applications (see the photo below left). I especially like to use it as a trim, since the cord produces a piped effect without added bulk. The cord works up quite quickly and is extremely simple to make.

Any type of yarn or decorative thread can be used for making monkscord: Experimenting with various color and fiber combinations is a great deal of fun. One of my favorite tricks for making a monkscord trim is to incorporate warp and weft threads from the fabric used to make the garment, which results in a perfect color match every time. I especially like to employ this technique when working with wools, which have more substantial yarns than many wovens and often feature a variety of individually colored yarns worked into the warp and weft. Silk ribbon is another favored trim for monkscord, as the resulting cord has a lovely sheen and provides a soft accent for linens, cottons, and silks of all kinds.

Although monkscord can be twisted manually, it works up much faster with the aid of

A three-strand braid made from bias rouleau emphasizes the neckline, shoulder seam, and sleeves of this rayon dress.

Unique Materials for Custom Trims

Master a few basic braid and cord structures, and the world of trims for embellishment is, quite literally, at your fingertips! Custom trims can be created from a variety of beautiful and unique materials. Their selection and preparation is integral to the creative process and at least half of the fun of making trims exclusively your own. Use the suggestions here as a genesis for your own creative exploration.

Braids and cords from bias rouleau

Bias rouleau—or turned fabric tubes—make wonderful braids for embellishing garments. Make them from self- or contrasting fabric, and use them corded with a filler or ironed flat. I especially like using the wrong side of fabrics for making these trims and always keep an eye open for fabrics that are beautiful on both sides.

Warp and weft threads

In the same vein as using the wrong side of the fabric to create contrasting trims, the actual warp and weft threads that make up a fabric can be removed individually and used to create custom trims. This technique works especially well with high-quality woolens, as the individual strands that make up the fabric are often quite beautiful on their own. Multicolored fabrics are fun to experiment with, as several colors of yarn may be available to select from and can be isolated or combined to make the cord. The beauty of this technique is that resulting trim harmonizes perfectly with the rest of the garment.

Experiment with different color combinations, as well as with the number of working strands, to determine the desired thickness of the cord. This is best done prior to cutting the garment out, so you can pull the longest strands possible to create the necessary lengths of cord. To pull lengthwise threads, cut away the selvage, and remove thread lengths one at a time. When several threads have already been removed from the fabric, trim the tails of the warp or weft threads away, closer to the actual thread being pulled. This will facilitate easy removal of subsequent threads.

Multimedia trims

Beautiful trims can be made by combining a variety of different materials, including reembellished and recycled trims, knitting yarns, silk, rayon, metallic threads and cords, and narrow strips of bias-cut fabric. Experimentation is key to finding creative and exciting combinations!

Velvety trims

Velvet itself is somewhat difficult to use as a self-fabric trim. But gorgeous, velvety trims can be purchased or custom-made with cotton, rayon, and silk chenille yarns and can create a sumptuous look in a range of colors. Actual velvet trims are available commercially as well, most often as cord edges, inserts, or satin-backed ribbon.

the Spinster cord-making tool or bobbin winder positioned on the top of a sewing machine. Regardless of which method you use, the basic procedure remains the same. Here are the basic steps.

1   Cut two lengths of yarn, each approximately three times the desired finished length of the cord. The two lengths may each consist of more than one thread. The final cord will be four times as thick as one original length of thread. Prior to cutting actual lengths for your project, it is a good idea to work up a few samples that incorporate different numbers of threads so that you can ascertain how many threads it will take to produce the desired degree of thickness for your cord.

2   Join the two lengths at one end and put this end over a doorknob, stationary hook, or through the holes of a bobbin attached to the bobbin winder on your sewing machine.

3   Hold the threads taut and twist them in one direction to form a single length of plied thread. Continue in one direction until the twist in the thread is tight and springy, but stop before it starts to kink. To do this manually, tie the ends of the

yarn to a pencil and twist the pencil clockwise. If you are using the Spinster, simply spin the wheel forward until the yarn reaches the desired degree of twist. For the bobbin method, it is easiest to hold the foot control for the machine in one hand while holding the yarn taut in the other. If you are making a long length of cord that requires standing far away from the machine, it is frequently necessary to engage someone's help either to hold the cord or run the foot pedal for the machine.

4   Once the yarns are sufficiently twisted, fold the yarn back on itself to form two equal lengths that spiral in the opposite direction. It is important to keep both lengths taut while forming the fold. Here again, it is helpful to have an assistant.

5   Hold the loose ends tightly together, remove the folded end of the cord from its attachment, and let go of the cord. The two lengths will spiral together to form a single cord.

6   Monkscord can be attached to a finished edge by hand or by machine. For hand stitching, use a lightweight silk thread in a color that blends well with both the garment and the cord. Whipstitch the cord to the edge, matching the stitches to the twist of the cord. In this way, the stitches will remain virtually concealed.

7   To attach the monkscord to a finished edge by machine, use the edgestitch foot. Position the guide at the fabric's edge and the trim to the opposite side of the guide. Select a simple zigzag stitch or blind hem and adjust the stitch width so that the thread catches the monkscord when the needle swings to that side of the guide. The stitch width can be adjusted to remain virtually invisible or to enclose the cord, in which case the stitching becomes part of the design.

Three-strand braid

Like monkscord, this elementary braid works up rapidly and produces a pliable, versatile trim. Used primarily as an edge treatment for necklines, sleeves, unlined jackets, and hems, three-strand braid can be worked in a variety of materials, including turned fabric tubes, custom and commercial cords and flat trims, soutache, narrow ribbons, and novelty yarns (see the photo on the facing page).

To keep the strands of the braid in place and to allow for a steady, even tension on the braid as it's being worked (see the drawings on the facing page), secure the braid strands with a clamp or strong metal clip that is—in turn—tied to a doorknob or held with a Third Hand & Clamp. Another alternative is to tape the strands temporarily to the edge of a table or other flat surface while the braid is worked. This method tends to work best for simple braids that do not require a great deal of tension as the braid's being worked. To make a three-strand braid, follow these steps.

1   Measure three strands and secure them for working the braid.

2   Begin with two strands in your right hand, one in the left.

3   Pass the far right strand to the left, over the middle strand, to take the center position among the three strands of the braid.

4   Pass the far left strand to the right, over the middle strand. This strand will now be the center strand of the braid.

5   Alternate the sequence from left to right, always crossing the outer strand to the inside, where it will become the center strand in the braid.

6   The sequence is always over one to the left; over one to the right; with the strand moved from the right or left, to the center strand of the braid.

These custom-made three-strand braids were made from bias rouleau strips, reembellished soutache, and satin-wrapped cord obtained from pulling apart commercial gimps.

Four-strand braid

The four-strand braid is a round, firm braid that can be worked with thin and thick threads alike. Thin cords can be used for decorative couching, while thick cords make excellent edgings that are firmer, rounder, and more durable than monkscord. You can work the braid with strands of the same color or use a variety of colors to achieve a range of interesting effects. To make a four-strand braid, follow these steps.

1. Measure four strands and secure them to work the braid.

2. Hold two strands in each hand.

3. Pass the far right strand under two strands to the left, then back over one strand to the right. The working strand will now occupy the third position from left to right.

4. Pass the far-left strand under two strands to the right, then back over one strand to the left. This strand will now occupy the second position from left to right.

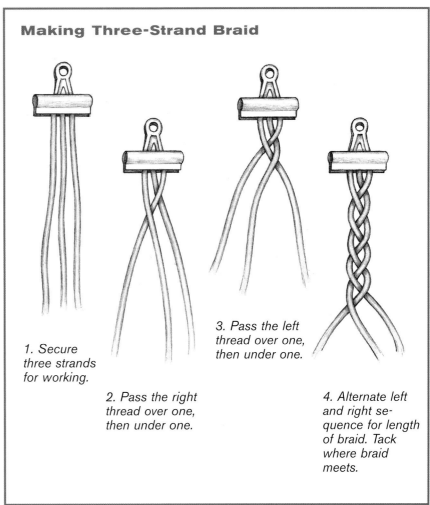

Making Three-Strand Braid

1. Secure three strands for working.

2. Pass the right thread over one, then under one.

3. Pass the left thread over one, then under one.

4. Alternate left and right sequence for length of braid. Tack where braid meets.

5   Alternate this sequence from right to left, always passing the outer strand over two strands, then back over one. The sequence is under two over one; under two over one; alternating the movement between the outermost strands to the left and right.

Five-strand braid

This flexible braid is firmer and stronger than its three-strand counterpart. Its appearance is similar, however, making it suitable for the same range of applications. Because five-strand braid is firmer than three-strand braid, it will lend a more substantial look to large braids, yet it can also be worked with finer threads that would look skimpy with three strands. Worked in fine threads such as silk buttonhole twist, the result is lovely narrow braid suitable for passementerie-style embellishments, as well as edgings.

Because the braid takes considerable time to make when worked in fine threads, keep the designs basic rather than elaborate to limit the trim yardage necessary to complete the design. Also, when making long lengths of a braided trim, it is helpful to reposition the trim in the clamp about every 12 in. to 18 in. so that you are never working far from the point where the braid is secured. The steps are as follows (see the drawings below).

1   Measure five strands and secure them for working the braid.

2   Begin with three strands in your right hand and two in your left.

3   Pass the far right strand over two strands to the center.

4   Pass the far left strand over two strands to the center.

5   To make the desired length of braid, alternate right over two, left over two.

Making Five-Strand Braid

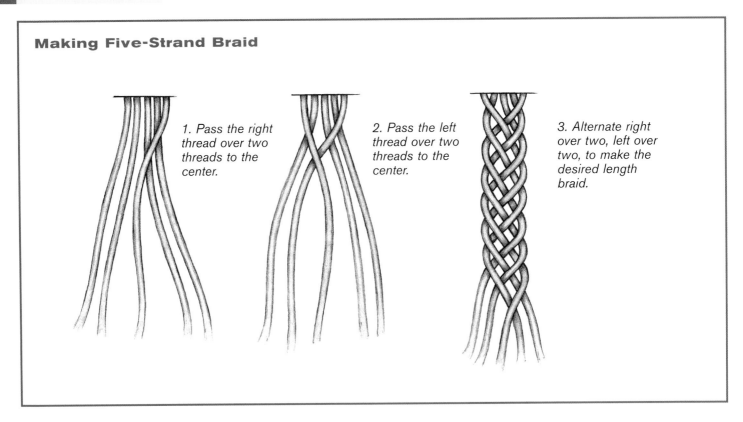

1. Pass the right thread over two threads to the center.

2. Pass the left thread over two threads to the center.

3. Alternate right over two, left over two, to make the desired length braid.

These custom five- and ten-strand braid variations were made from soutache and satin-wrapped cord.

Ten-strand braid

The two variations of the ten-strand braid are both wider than the others previously described (see the photo above). Variation I has an interesting structure, with flat edges to either side of a raised chevron that runs through the center (see the top drawings on p. 92). It is a very pretty braid, especially well suited as an edging for suits and coats and for outlining passementerie designs as well.

Variation II (see the bottom drawings on p. 92) is somewhat wider and flatter than variation I. Beautiful enough to stand on its own as an edging braid, variation II can also be stitched to a length of the raised chevron braid in variation I to produce a foldover binding for raw edges.

VARIATION I
In this variation, the working thread consists of two strands, rather than one.

1   Measure ten strands and secure them to work the braid.

2   Begin working with six strands in your left hand and four in your right. As you work the braid, alternate the six to four grouping from your left hand to your right and back again.

3   Pass the two far left strands over one strand and under three to the center of the braid. Grasp the strands with your right hand. There will now be six strands in your right hand and four in your left.

4   Pass the two far right strands over one strand and under three to the center of the braid. Grasp these strands with your left hand.

5   Continue this sequence, treating the two outermost threads as one working strand and passing it over one strand and under three, alternating left to right. As you work the braid, a raised chevron will form in the center.

VARIATION II
To work the braid, divide the strands into five groupings of two strands each, which are treated throughout as five working strands. For a narrow version of this same braid, simply use five individual—as opposed to double—strands. These are the steps.

1   Measure ten strands and secure them to work the braid.

2   Begin with six strands in your left hand and four in your right. Treat each group of two strands as a single unit for the entire length of the braid. As you work the braid, alternate the grouping of six strands in one hand and four in the other from your left hand to your right.

3   Pass the two far left strands to the right, over two, and under two toward the center of the braid. Grasp these strands with your right hand.

> To keep individual strands of the braid in place, sew or tape directly across the ends of the braid after working.
>
> **TIP**

Making Ten-Strand Braid

Variation I

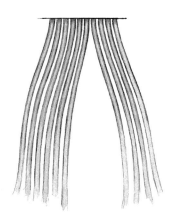 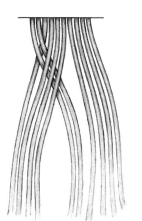 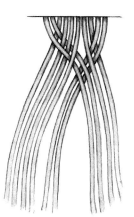 

1. Begin with six strands in your left hand and four in your right. Alternate the six to four grouping from your left hand to your right and back again.

2. Pass the two far left strands over one strand and under three to the center of the braid. There will now be six strands in your right hand and four in your left.

3. Pass the two far right strands over one strand and under three to the center of the braid. Grasp these strands with your left hand. Continue sequence, treating the two outermost threads as one working strand and passing it over one strand and under three, alternating left to right.

Variation II

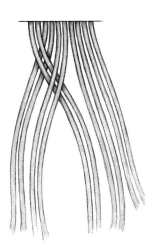 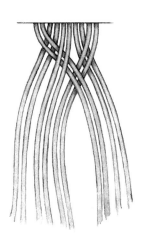 

1. Begin with six strands in your left hand and four in your right. As you work the braid, alternate the grouping of strands from one hand to the other.

2. Pass the two far left strands to the right, over two, and under two toward the center of the braid. Grasp these strands with your right hand.

3. Pass the two far right strands to the left, over two, and under two toward the center of the braid. Grasp these threads with your left hand. Continue sequence, alternating from left to right.

4 Pass the two far right strands to the left, over two, and under two toward the center of the braid. Grasp these threads with your left hand.

5 Continue the sequence, alternating from left to right.

Serger trims

A variety of custom-made trims can be made quite rapidly using decorative threads and a serger (see the photo at right). The resulting cords are beautiful and versatile and can be used for couching, edge treatments, and passementerie embellishments.

Serger trims can be made with or without a core, or filler. I generally prefer to use a filler because it adds body and helps the trim maintain a consistent round or flat shape. Suitable round fillers include gimp, pearl or crochet cotton, Pearl Crown Rayon, and purchased narrow cording. Suitable flat fillers include ribbon floss, narrow ribbons, and, my own favorite, soutache trim.

When selecting a filler, keep in mind that it is potentially a decorative element in the trim, since it will show through the spaces produced by the upper and lower looper threads. When making a trim for a specific garment, investigate thread combinations and play with tension settings on the upper and lower loopers of your machine. Experiment with normal settings first, then try various combinations of loosening the upper and tightening the lower looper until you acquire the unique look you're after. Keep notes on suitable settings for consistent results with particular combinations of thread, and tape a small sample to the side.

To make serger trims with a round core, it will be necessary to use a cording foot for your serger. The procedure will be basically the same as for a flat trim, except for that the cording foot will be used to help direct and feed the trim into the serger. To make a serger trim with a flat core, start with the following settings, and fine-tune adjustments as needed.

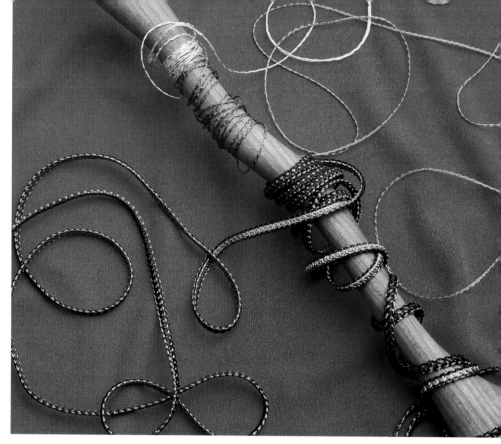

Flat and round trims in custom colors can be made in a flash using a serger.

1 Thread the upper and lower loopers with a heavy decorative thread, such as Pearl Crown Rayon or #8 pearl cotton, and a regular-weight decorative or polyester thread in the needle.

2 Raise the cutting knife, leave the tensions at normal settings, and set the stitch length to 2 in. to 2½ in.

3 Raise the presser foot of the serger and insert one end of the trim beneath the standard presser foot of the serger and to the right of the needle.

4 Lower the presser foot and begin stitching, holding onto the serger chain and pulling it through to the back side of the serger.

5 The trim should be fully enclosed by the upper and lower looper stitches, in which case it will continue to feed evenly through the machine.

6 Sew for a few inches, then check the results and make adjustments to tighten or loosen your upper or lower looper tension as required.

> **Braids are based on a repetitive sequence in which one or more strands are woven under and over other strands in the braid. The movement may be in one direction or may alternate from left to right. I find it helpful to say the sequence out loud when first learning the braid.**
>
> **TIP**

Reembellished trims allow you to create enriched color variation, in perfect accord with your garment.

7   When the settings produce satisfactory results and you hit upon a thread combination that will work for your garment, serge the entire length of trim needed for your garment.

Reembellished trims

The concept behind reembellished trims is simple: Start with a wonderful trim and make it even better. Reembellishing presents the opportunity to introduce colors that will marry the trim to the garment; establish interesting textures and color contrasts; and deepen the character and complexity of the trim overall (see the photo above).

My favorite ways to alter an existing trim include beading and bobbinwork. Beading is simple and usually consists of little more than adding a simple edging or a running-stitched row. For either purpose, I prefer to work with tiny seed beads.

Adding bobbinworked threads to common commercial trims is one of the fastest and most satisfying ways I know to transform a simple trim or to make a trim uniquely suited to a garment. A single row of bobbinworked straight stitch down the center of trim can be worked in a color to match or coordinate with the fashion fabric for a garment. The bobbin-work can be added after the trim is sewn to the garment, following the visible stitching line on the wrong side. Or, for braided trims, it can be added to the trim *before* the braid is worked. Simple stitching in the ditch to lay in decorative threads from the bobbin adds a beautiful touch to trims of all kinds. It can also be worked directly next to a trim, on the fashion fabric, to create a smooth segue between the garment and the trim.

Although I tend to use straight stitch most frequently, decorative stitches present infinite options for reembellished trims as well. Grosgrain and other stable ribbons stand up well to bobbinwork and decorative machine stitches and generally do not require an additional stabilizer. When a stabilizer is needed for softer ribbons, try a lightweight tear-away, such as Stitch & Ditch heirloom or water-soluble Solvy.

To reembellish trims, follow the usual procedure for bobbinwork and machine embroidery (see Chapter 2), but be sure to guide the trim smoothly beneath the presser foot. The edge of the trim must follow a consistent guide to keep the stitching spaced equidistant from both edges of the trim. In the case of soutache, consider feeding the soutache through a pintuck, braiding, or Sequins 'N Ribbon foot with an appropriate slot or groove to stabilize the trim as it's fed into the machine.

DESIGNING WITH TRIMS

Braid-Embellished Dress

Designing embellishments with trims entails selecting or making a trim that is appropriate in color and scale for the fabric you have selected for your garment. It also entails coming up with a design in keeping with the properties of the trim and using those properties to enhance the garment. Proper scale—including proportions relating to the trim, fabric, garment style, and embellishment design—are paramount, as are the methods used to apply the trim.

Also, with braids, design decisions should be guided by a sense of what will look good

When designing embellishments with braids, design decisions should be guided by a sense of what will look good on the garment's wearer rather than on the surface of the fabric. Ornamentation can be elaborate but not overbearing, ostentatious, or gaudy unless, of course, that's what you want.

Three Dresses with Simple Braid Embellishments

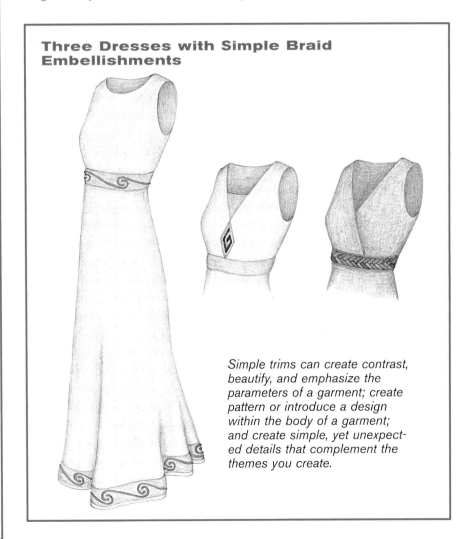

Simple trims can create contrast, beautify, and emphasize the parameters of a garment; create pattern or introduce a design within the body of a garment; and create simple, yet unexpected details that complement the themes you create.

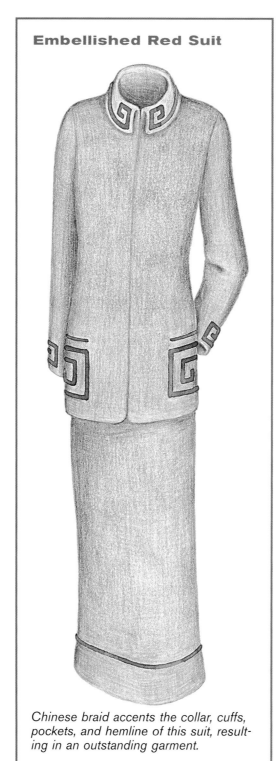

Embellished Red Suit

Chinese braid accents the collar, cuffs, pockets, and hemline of this suit, resulting in an outstanding garment.

For the most part, simple treatments produce favorable results. Use trims to create contrast, beautify, and emphasize the parameters of a garment; to create pattern or introduce a design within the body of a garment; and to create simple, yet unexpected details that complement the themes you create. Chinese knot buttons, bound buttonholes, inserts in seams, frog closures, a latticework passage for a belt, the belt itself, a woven inset or collar—these are the features that result in an outstanding garment.

Edge finishes

Using trim as an edge treatment is perhaps the most frequent use of it in garment design (see the photo on the facing page). Trims can be decorative in their own right or used to produce the look of binding or piping without the added bulk.

Any of the custom braids in the preceding section can be used as edgings, as can countless commercial trims. While some thought must be accorded to the order in which the trim is applied to a garment, as well as the method by which it will be sewn, edgings are fairly straightforward, both in terms of application and design. Nevertheless, experimentation will yield new and exciting variations on this basic theme. In addition to using monkscord and braided trims as edgings, consider the two following edge treatments, which are very easy to do.

NARROW EDGE WITH FLEXIBLE BRAID

Flexible braid is a wonderful, inexpensive trim suitable for simple to elaborate applications. This one is especially uncomplicated, and the results are wonderful, resembling baby piping, but far less time-consuming and without the added bulk.

The edging consists of a single strand of narrow (1/16 in. to 1/8 in.) flexible braid positioned directly at the garment's edge. An optional row of bobbinwork stitching further

on the wearer of the garment, rather than on the surface of the fabric. Ornamentation can be elaborate but should not be overbearing, ostentatious, or gaudy unless, of course, that is the intended effect.

augments the impact of the braid, which is sewn to the garment *before* hems are turned or facings are applied. To achieve perfect placement for the braid, follow these steps.

1   Baste in the hem and seamlines where the braid edging is to be applied, using a thread that contrasts with the fashion fabric.

2   Sew the flexible braid in place, matching one edge of the braid to the basting, which will serve as a placement guide. Use a cording foot to help position the braid accurately and attach it with a single row of stitching directly through the center.

3   If desired, sew in a row of straight-stitch bobbinwork directly next to the edge of the flexible braid. For accurate placement,

For the appearance of piping without added bulk, monkscord (made from strands of the same fabric used to make the garment) creates an elegant tone-on-tone edge treatment that's ideal for this wool crepe dress.

Pulling Gimps Apart and Using the Pieces

Commercial gimps are machine-made braids composed of one or more elements, many of which can be employed individually to embellish garments. In fact, taking a gimp apart and using the wrapped cords or knit tubes for trim is almost as fun as making custom braids and cords. Indeed, the elements that you take apart can be reconstructed or used in any manner you see fit.

One of the wonderful things about pulling apart commercial gimps is that it puts greater numbers of narrow round and flat trims at your creative disposal—many of which are otherwise difficult to come by. It also provides a wider range of color options, broadening the palette and increasing the likelihood of finding a perfect color match for your garment.

Rayon-wrapped (also referred to as satin) cords are a staple ingredi-ent of commercial Chinese braids and other decorative gimps. Wonderful to use decoratively in the bobbin or with a cording foot, rayon-wrapped cords are an excellent choice for passementerie-style embellishments and can be used with the wide trim in its original state, which serves as the perfect choice for outlining.

Knit tubes and flat, narrow ribbon elements can be used interchangeably with soutache or flexible braid; stuffed with a filler and used as round cord; or used as an embroidery ribbon in the manner that silk ribbon is employed. They also serve as a wonderful alternative to regular thread for whip-stitched or blanket-stitched edges.

In addition to the elements of composed gimps listed above, you're likely to come across useful staples such as chainette and bunka-style cords that can be put to creative use.

And keep in mind that the yardage of trim you acquire when you take a gimp or cord apart will be multiplied from the original yardage amount by however many strands were required to weave, ply, or braid the gimp or cord. In other words, 3 yd. of commercial braid composed of five strands of wrapped rayon cord will produce 15 yd. of individual cord for your use.

Some gimps are easy to undo; others are resistant or too tedious to bother with. Chevron braids and French braids come undone with ease. Also look for Chinese braids and other textured gimps with a chainstitch on the back of the braid. The chain can easily be unraveled when cut, making elements of the trim easy to pull apart.

use an edgestitch foot to mark the line first from the top side of the garment, using thread to match the garment on the right side, and contrast with it on the wrong side.

4 When the trim is placed and the bobbin-work is complete, turn up the hem or attach the facings so that the bottom edge of the trim precisely defines the edge of the garment.

RIBBON-THREADED EDGINGS

Ribbon-threaded edgings make for a great embellishment detail when care is taken to ensure that the path for the ribbon is evenly spaced and measures a consistent distance from the garment's edge (see the drawings at right). The threading path consists of a series of buttonholes spaced in a predetermined pattern, which creates a path for the ribbon to feed through. For best results, use a flat rather than a textured ribbon. This is a unique way to accent collars, cuffs, and pocket flaps or to thread a narrow belt. To create the threading path for this edging, follow these steps.

1 Determine the position of the finished embellishment in relation to the garment's edge.

2 Mark this line on the interfaced garment piece, prior to constructing the garment.

3 Determine and test the size buttonhole necessary to accommodate the trim. Decide as well how far apart to space the buttonholes, as this will determine how much of the trim shows through and at what intervals. When determining placement for a collar or any other portion of the garment that has a right angle, begin by marking the point of that angle first. Generally, a right angle is worked in two separate threading operations, which alleviates the need to actually turn the corner with a single length of braid.

4 Sew the buttonholes. If your machine offers a narrow buttonhole option, use it.

Ribbon-Threaded Edgings

Ribbon-threaded edgings are great for accenting collars, cuffs, and pocket flaps or to thread a narrow belt. Best results are obtained using flat rather than textured ribbon.

Cut them open and thread the trim through before attaching corresponding pieces of the garment. Secure the trim at both ends of the threading path by stitching it to the fashion fabric inside the seam allowance.

Border designs

Border designs represent yet another frequently used design option for trims (see the photo at right). They typically take more time to plan, prepare, and sew than do edgings, especially if the border incorporates a design or pattern that must be transferred to the fabric prior to sewing the trim. Simple approaches to creating borders with trims include the following.

- **Repeated lines** can be built up in crisscross formations or concentric bands to accent the perimeter of the garment. Worked in a color that complements the fashion fabric and with a trim of appropriate scale, even the simplest approach can create considerable impact and enrich the character of the garment.

- **Geometric designs** are simple to reproduce and transfer and tend to work up quite rapidly with the use of a braiding or pintuck foot. Numerous sources for Greek and Celtic key, and Chinese lattice patterns abound and provide rich inspiration for border designs that translate well to garment design. Alternatively, it is fun and easy to create original border patterns using the grid method described on pp. 116-118.

Designs within the body of the garment

While edgings and borders tend to dominate braid treatments for garments due to their simplicity in terms of placement, don't overlook the potential application of braided bands and allover designs within the body of the garment. These will be more time-consuming to plan, since final placement is best determined by working with a muslin of the garment to pinpoint the most effective presentation for the design.

Consider that designs placed in the main body of the garment can be the sole embellishment focus of the garment or can be a way to elaborate upon a striking edging or border design (see the photo below).

Also, though the conventional approach consists of using the line of the braid to create a pattern or image, which becomes apparent against the contrasting ground, consider that the braid can also be used to create negative space, in which the braid pattern recedes and the ground fabric dominates.

Regardless of which design approach you take, certain considerations will be universal and must be taken into account when planning any trim detail.

FABRIC AND TRIM COMPATIBILITY

Are the weight of the fabric and the weight of the trim compatible? Although it tends to be

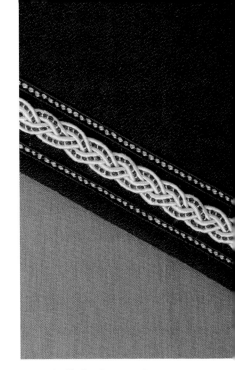

Reembellished soutache was used to create the three-strand braid that forms the foundation for this simple, yet effective edge treatment.

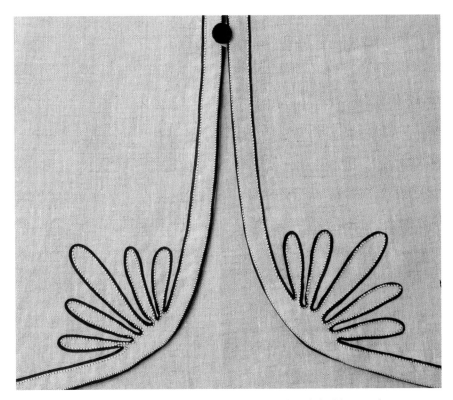

Narrow, black, flexible braid is further enhanced with bobbinwork to create the edging and motifs on this linen blouse. The design is repeated at the edge of the sleeves.

more problematic to have a trim that's too heavy for a particular fabric, it is also true that some trims will not be substantial enough. A melton can certainly handle just about any lace trim weightwise, for example, yet in most instances, the look of lace on melton is visually imbalanced and challenges our sense of an appropriate match for the delicacy of the lace as well as for the bulk and heft of the melton. While juxtaposition can sometimes be used intentionally, in most instances the basic properties of the trim and base fabric should roughly correlate. In other words, the more elaborate, dense, or ornate the trim, the heavier the base fabric; the more delicate the trim, the lighter the base fabric.

BALANCE, SCALE, AND PROPORTION

Is the scale of the design appropriate for the type of garment, and does the distribution of the pattern create an overall effect of balance and proportion that is flattering to the wearer? Both symmetrical and asymmetrical designs can work effectively or otherwise in this regard: It is simply a matter of approaching the garment as whole and balancing elements of the design in a manner that reflects consideration of the wearer. This holds true whether the design treatment is spartan or flamboyant.

GARMENT STYLE

Does the style and degree of embellishment suit the style of garment and highlight pattern details in an effective way? Does the amount of labor the design entails roughly correspond to the usefulness or longevity of the garment? Not everything we sew has to last more than a season; on the other hand, when the intent is to produce a perennial favorite, the quality and longevity of materials should correlate with the expenditure of time afforded them.

Trim placement

The correct placement of trim relies on two things: accurate measurement or transfer of the design lines in relation to the garment; and proper positioning of the trim along that line for sewing. For complex borders and designs, consult the Appendices (see p. 166) for transfer methods. For simple placement of trim on the body of a garment, it will be necessary to measure and mark in guidelines. This can be done with a ruler and water- or air-soluble ink or other appropriate fabric marking pens, or the guidelines can be basted in on the sewing machine using a seam-guide attachment and removed once the trim has been placed.

Once the proper position for the design has been established, it is necessary to decide how to place and sew the trim. Trim can be preplaced or sewn directly to the garment. Very narrow flat trims and round cords are best sewn directly with the aid of a suitable presser foot. One commercially available foot—the Sequins 'N Ribbons foot—allows for direct placement of ribbons up to $\frac{3}{8}$ in. wide.

Preplacing is an excellent way to ensure that the trim is placed correctly prior to sewing and helps stabilize the trim and keep it from shifting beneath the presser foot as it's being sewn. I almost always preplace wide trims, as well as elaborate designs for passementerie, in which case the preplacement results in a smoother line.

When preplacing the trim is necessary or desirable, there are a number of notions currently available to make the job easier. One is Wonder Tape. Another is a water-soluble fabric glue stick. Both wash out with water, do a good job of keeping the trim in place, and can be sewn through without gumming up the needle. While these are by no means the only feasible solutions, they are the ones I find most convenient and the least time-consuming.

SEWING TRIMS

Though there are times when sewing trims by hand is appropriate (see the sidebar below), sewing them by machine is by far the fastest, cleanest, and easiest method to sew flat trims and cords. It also produces favorable results with most textured braids, though it may take initial experimentation to determine a path and manner of stitching compatible with the braid.

The three basic ways to attach a trim by machine include edgestitching or topstitching the trim in place using the basic straight stitch; visible couching using decorative, zigzag, or utility stitches to encase or sew directly through the trim; and invisible couching, with the blind-hem or vari-overlock stitch, so the stitching remains discreet from the right side of the garment.

Each of these methods is made simpler and the results are more satisfying when you are able to take advantage of the wide variety of methods, notions, and materials that make the job easier. Among the options for proper presser foot, thread, needle, and stitch selection, there is likely to be a combination that will work with one of the methods listed previously to attach most trims artfully by machine. Be sure to preshrink and test the color fastness of your trims prior to sewing (see the sidebar on p. 104).

Narrow trims

Flat, narrow trims are generally sewn with visible straight stitching, either directly through the center of the trim or edgestitched on both sides. They can also be sewn in place using a

When to Sew Trims by Hand

In my book, sewing trim by hand is desirable only when machine stitching would somehow be detrimental to or detract from the finished appearance of the trim in relation to the garment. Among hand stitching's potential advantages are that it can be worked almost invisibly and that it does not add stiffness. It also affords a degree of control when sewing to certain types of fabrics.

Whether to stitch a trim by hand or by machine is generally something I decide on a case-by-case basis. There are, however, trims I would never elect to stitch by hand, as well as those that always fall into the hand-stitched category. I recommend attaching trims by hand in the following situations.

• When attaching highly irregular or textured trim that may be flattened, crushed, or hang up the presser foot if sewn by machine.

• For sewing any trim that may need to be removed for cleaning the garment; including metallic mesh trims, beaded trims, etc.

• To create decorative effects by attaching the trim using hand embroidery.

• To sew a trim invisibly, or when the look of hand stitches creates a more desirable decorative or discreet appearance than can be achieved with machine sewing.

• When machine sewing adds too much stiffness to the garment.

Beaded Skirt with Appliqué

This black velvet skirt is embellished with gold braid, metallic beads, and silk/metallic appliqué.

double needle (the width of the needle should be an increment less than the width of the trim) and with decorative machine stitches used to couch the braid. When using a double needle to attach trim, be sure to reduce the needle tension so that the trim lies flat.

Presser feet that are frequently use for sewing flat, narrow trims include braiding and cording feet, the open-toe embroidery foot (when a double needle is used), and the zipper and edgestitch feet.

Very narrow flat trims, such as $1/16$-in. flexible braid, are best sewn directly through the center using a small needle and fine thread in a color to match the trim. These trims are easiest to place with an appliqué, cording, or pintuck foot. Other trims that can be sewn with one row of stitching through the center of the braid include soutache, star braid, and narrow braids with a chevron formation that meets at the center. For braids that are too wide or too thick to fit through the holes, slots, or grooves of the already mentioned feet, the open-toe embroidery foot may work well, though in this instance some braids will benefit from the stability afforded by preplacement of the braid.

In the absence of a braid structure that creates a central "ditch" or line to sew through, flat trims $1/8$ in. and wider tend to look best edgestitched, using a zipper foot or edgestitch foot or couched invisibly on one or both sides of the trim.

As is true for any trim, choose a lightweight thread appropriate for the garment fabric and trim. Select the needle size according to the thread used, as well as the garment and the trim. I generally prefer to use machine-embroidery cotton or silk threads over polyester, which can cause puckering on light- to medium-weight natural fiber fabrics. Invisible nylon—available in smoke and clear—is another suitable choice. Generally, the strength of the thread is not as critical for sewing trims as it is for seams. The exception

Sewing Corners

Perfect the art of turning corners with any narrow, flat trim, and you'll be able to create beautiful geometric borders and designs. Unlike curves, which require a flexible trim (see pp. 105-109), corners can be manipulated with just about any flat trim, including those with an inflexible selvage (typical of most ribbons, for example).

For flat, narrow trims, there are two basic methods for turning corners. The trim can be pivoted to form a somewhat rounded corner, or it can be flipped to the other side, in which case the trim forms an angle at the point where the corner is turned. Which method to use will depend upon the trim. Ribbons and other trims with an inflexible selvage tend to look best when flipped, assuming they look the same on both sides. Flexible trims like soutache work well either way, so the decision hinges on aesthetic preference alone.

Either way, it will be helpful to use a tool to help position and hold the trim in place as the corner is turned. A tailor's awl, sewing stiletto, or even a seam ripper will suffice, but my favorite tool for this task is a pair of beading tweezers. In addition to the requisite pointed tip to hold the trim in place as it's pivoted, the bill of the tweezers can be used to lift and position the braid with ease.

Pivoting the trim

1. Sew the trim along the design line. Stop directly at the corner to be turned and sink the needle.

2. Raise the presser foot and pivot the garment and the trim on the machine needle, pulling the trim into formation and manipulating the outer corner with the point of the tweezers to form a smooth line at the inner and outer corners.

3. Hold the trim firmly in place along the new line.

4. Lower the presser foot and take one stitch directly across the corner of the braid.

5. Continue to hold the braid in place, and resume stitching along the new line.

Flipping the trim

1. Sew the trim along the design line. Stop one braid's width from the adjacent line and sink the needle.

2. Raise the presser foot and flip the trim over. The inside edge should be directly against the needle, and the outside edge positioned along the new angle of the design line.

3. Hold the corner of the trim in place with the point of the beading tweezers.

4. Lower the presser foot and take one or two additional stitches, as necessary, to cross the intersecting points of the trim until the needle reaches the center of the trim on the adjacent line. Sink the needle directly at this point.

5. Lift the presser foot. Pivot the fabric and trim on the needle to adjust for the angle of the new line and resume normal stitching.

here is sewing very thick or course braids, sewing to heavy or synthetic fabrics, or attaching trims to any form of outerwear, in which case using a strong, long-wearing thread is required to maintain the integrity of the stitching over time.

Wide trims

Wide trims generally benefit from preplacement using water-soluble fabric glue stick or Wonder Tape. The most common method of application is sewing a straight line of stitching down each edge of the trim. This can best be accomplished with an adjustable zipper foot, which allows the foot to snug up against the edge of the trim to produce an accurate line of stitching and to avoid the possibility of the foot hanging up on the trim.

As with narrow trims, some are flexible and others are not. Inflexible trims are suitable for straight lines and angles only, while braids that can be shaped or flexed can be used on curves. Gathering the braid along the inner portion of

TIP

To calculate the length of trim required for an edge or seam, measure that length and add 2 in. for leeway, attaching ends, or inserting ends in the seam. Trims are generally attached to individual components of the garment prior to sewing the seams, but this will depend on the trim and its placement in relation to the garment. Forethought is required to determine a logical sequence for attaching the trim to individual components of the garment, for matching the trim, and for sewing the seams. For example: Trim on a collar could be sewn to the right side of the collar before or after the collar was sewn but invariably before the collar was inserted into the neckline seam.

Preshrinking and Testing Colorfastness of Trims

It is a good idea to preshrink and test trims for colorfast properties prior to sewing. Check the label of the trim bolt to see if the trim has been preshrunk, is colorfast, or has any specific cleaning instructions. Not all companies include this information; most, however, do note the fiber content of the trim, which gives you something to go on.

Preshrink the trim in the same manner that you preshrink the fabric for your garment. If you intend to dry-clean, send it to the dry cleaners along with your fashion fabric and ask them to preshrink—not dry-clean—your materials.

To preshrink trim for garments that will be washed by hand or machine, secure the trim in a bundle and place it in a bowl of very warm water for 15 to 20 minutes, or until the water cools. Then dry the trim on a line, if that is how you intend to dry your garment, or place it in a lingerie bag and dry it by machine.

curves can be used to coax a somewhat flexible braid in place. Once the general shape is formed, steaming the braid will further help define its shape. Sharp angles are formed by mitering the braid.

Discreet joining and ending of wide trim is achieved when ends meet and are folded under or seamed together. When using gimp, I recommend a wide seam allowance because the ends have a tendency to fray. A seam sealant such as Fray Check will work on individual components, but the ends of the braid as a whole will stay together only when sewn or taped in place.

Round tubes and cords

Round tubes and cords must be couched in place with visible zigzag or decorative stitches or with invisible blind-hem stitches. The use of a suitable presser foot with a slot, hole, or groove that matches the tube or cord is essential, since preplacement of the cords is not an easy option.

To couch the tube or cord in place using zigzag or decorative stitches, adjust the stitch width according to the width and height of the trim. Suitable stitches will encase the tube or cord without the needle penetrating its surface.

To couch the tube or cord in place using the blind-hem stitch, set the stitch width to 1mm and the length from 1mm to 2mm. Adjust the needle position to the right of center. The exact position of the needle will be determined by the placement of the tube or cord when secured beneath the presser foot. Position the straight stitches along the right side of the trim. Swing the zigzag stitch to the left, catching just a narrow bite of the tube or cord but enough to secure it in place.

MAKING PASSEMENTERIE

The term *passementerie* refers to braid and bead trims, as well as to an ornate style of ornamentation with which these embellishments are applied (see the photo below). Characterized by loop, scroll, paisley, and floral motifs that pervaded the use of passementerie trims during the Victorian era and early 20th century, the technique remains an option for modern garment design, particularly when treated with at least a braid's width of restraint.

Selecting trims

Selecting appropriate trims and knowing how and when to use them are crucial to the success of passementerie embellishment. Narrow trims, such as flexible braid, soutache, and star braid, are generally appropriate in scale ($\frac{1}{16}$ in. to $\frac{3}{16}$ in.) and lie well when sewn. If you plan to use a braiding or cording foot to attach the trim, you will want to confirm in advance whether or not the braid feeds though the hole, slot, or groove on the foot prior to purchasing large amounts of trim.

To pare down choices for a specific project, test potential candidates for responsiveness to loop and scroll formation. Hold the trim in hand, keep it flat, and loop one end to form a small circle. A fluid trim that readily conforms, while retaining a smooth, round curve along the inner and outer edge is perfect for passementerie stitched flat to the garment through the center of the trim.

Trims with a great deal of body—such as soutache—may resist curves if you try to keep the braid flat. Try, of course, because there are exceptions; but as countless capes and collars of the Victorian era prove, soutache rolls much more readily when the braid is stood upon its edge, with the flat sides facing in, rather than upward. Use this property to advantage and attach the soutache along one side only using invisible machine- or hand-worked stitches. For tight curves and loops, this is a far more effective method of using soutache than sewing it flat, in which case it usually buckles and pulls, producing a strained look that is never quite right. Which is not to say that soutache cannot be sewn flat side down. It can, and it performs favorably in this vein for geometric designs, parallel rows, and gentle, sloping curves.

Passementerie **refers to braid and bead trims, as well as to a style of ornamentation characterized by swirling loop, scroll, paisley, and floral motifs.**

Passementerie Examples

The success of passementerie embellishments hinges upon choosing a suitable garment style and wedding that style to an appropriate passementerie design.

In addition to the narrow trims just described, wrapped, plied, serged, and braided gimp, and cords of all kinds can be worked to complement flat trims or as the mainstay of an entire passementerie design. Color selection is broad, and opportunities for creating custom cords further augment the possibilities.

Prior to buying large amounts of trim for passementerie, purchase a small length and test it to determine actual results. If you are pleased with its responsiveness and appearance, purchase additional trim in the amount required for your project. Use the string method described for bias appliqué (see p. 119) to predict actual yardage requirements for your project. But before you can estimate how much trim to buy, you must work up a suitable passementerie design in conjunction with a specific plan for an actual garment.

Designing embellishments

In addition to careful selection of fabric and trims, the success of passementerie embellishments hinges upon choosing a suitable garment style and wedding that style to an appropriate passementerie design. For garment styles, look at lined vests, suit jackets, coats, and capes made up in medium- to heavy-weight fabrics that will stand up to the degree of stitching required to attach the trim.

I tend to think that the more complicated the passementerie design, the smaller in scale the actual garment should be. A vest encrusted with braid embellishment may retain its appeal, while a coat requires a more selective approach if the result is to be anything less than overbearing. For a full-length coat, look for elements of the pattern that can be adapted to passementerie designs: rolled and shawl collars, sleeves, cuffs, insets, belts, and pocket flaps come to mind. If you love the basic lines of the garment and can envision a way to use passementerie to link individual

Sewing Passementerie to the Garment

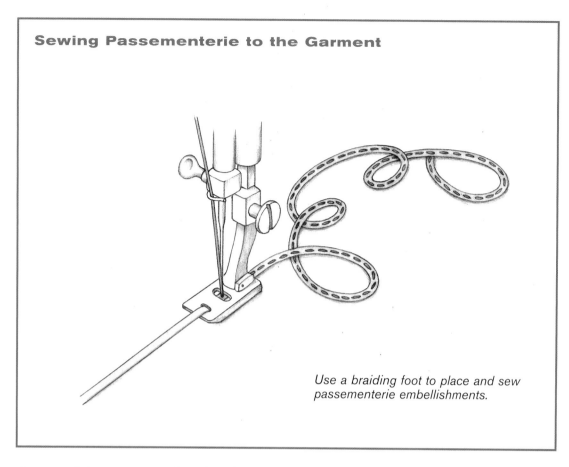

Use a braiding foot to place and sew passementerie embellishments.

elements of the pattern together, then the garment's worth a try.

As for the passementerie design itself, you can draw it freehand or adapt it from another source. Look for designs that spiral, wave, and scroll in a continuous line. Reproductions of old calligraphic, printing cartouche, and typeset manuals are often good sources for inspirational designs. To the extent possible, complete the entire design for one pattern piece in a single pass of the machine. This lends continuity to the design and facilitates sewing ease.

Preparing for passementerie

To prepare a garment for passementerie embellishment, first stabilize the fabric, then transfer the design.

Adequate stability is essential for working the ornate loops and scrolls of passementerie designs. Portions of the garment that are to be embellished should be interfaced, and to the extent necessary, additional water-soluble stabilizers should be applied. Use as many layers of a lightweight stabilizer as necessary to provide what your fabric and design demand. The added stability will pay off by way of a perfectly laid design.

Transferring the design to fabric can be done using direct or indirect methods. Which method to employ depends upon how you plan to sew the trim. Direct methods involve marking the actual garment fabric for placement of the trim. The advantage of this method is that it provides the option for preplacing the trim prior to sewing. For some designs and trims, such as braids, this may result in a smoother line.

Indirect methods feature a layer of water-soluble stabilizer (that functions as a design template) placed between the fabric and the trim, so preplacement of the trim is not an option. The design template is basted to the right side of the garment, and the trim is sewn to the design template, which is torn away when the design is complete. A braiding or cording foot is used to guide the placement of the braid (for more on transferring patterns, see the Appendices on p. 166).

Using a presser foot to guide and place the trim along the design line—as opposed to placing the braid prior to sewing—is the fastest and most direct way to attach braid for simple and straightforward designs. But complicated or elaborate designs may benefit from preplacement. If you already have access to a braiding foot, try it on a sample and see how guiding and sewing the trim with the presser foot works for your design. Then try preplacing the braid and compare both the end results of both placement methods, as well as the expenditure of time. Working up a sample will also give you the opportunity to test and adjust for the stability of the base fabric and its overall compatibility and scale in relation to your design.

In addition to balance, proportion, and scale, remember to ensure that designs mirror each other when mirroring is required, rather than tracing off two identically directed designs. To create a mirror image, simply flip the design template for the right and left sides, including the fronts of the garment, collar points, pocket flaps, and sleeves. For an asymmetrical design, double-check to see that the placement is correct and that the line moves from side to side according to your intent.

Applying passementerie

Each of the two methods that follow achieve the same goal. They differ in one respect only: In method I, the braid is placed as it's sewn, while in method II, the braid is preplaced prior to sewing along lines indicated for the passementerie design. Method I requires a braiding or cording foot to match the width of the passementerie trim, while method II can be sewn with a specialized foot or a standard presser foot.

METHOD I

This method relies on the use of an appropriate braiding or cording foot to guide the trim along the design line as the trim is stitched in place. It does not require placement of the braid prior to stitching. Using this method, the trim can be sewn directly to the marked fabric or to an intermediary stabilizer that includes a cartoon of the design. The trim can be straight stitched directly through the center of the braid; couched with decorative stitches; or sewn invisibly along one side by adjusting the needle positions and by selecting a narrow blind-hem stitch with a width of no more than 1mm, so the swing of the zigzag stitch just catches the edge of the trim.

1 Interface the garment piece to be embellished and transfer the passementerie design either directly to the right side of the garment or to a stabilizer basted to the right side of the garment.

2 Attach the braiding or cording foot to the machine. Use a size 65 to 80 universal needle in the machine, depending upon your trim, and invisible nylon or other suitable thread to match the trim. A small needle, lightweight thread, and short stitch length (2mm) will produce a less conspicuous stitching line. As the design is worked, it may be necessary to shorten the stitch to as little as 1mm to round tight curves. If you are able to reduce the sewing speed on your machine, do so, as it will be necessary to sew curves at a relatively slow speed.

3 Study the basic design and determine in advance where to start, which direction to work, and where to end the stitching line. If the design line is not continuous, determine what designs are continuous, and devise a logical sequence for working those designs.

4 If at all possible, begin and end the trim outside the seamlines. Where this is not feasible, start the design at the point where the trim will eventually cross over itself. This will hide the raw edge and maintain a clean, unobtrusive line. A seam sealant, such as Fray Check, will keep the ends of the trim from fraying. I recommend sealing at the start and finish of each section, whether or not the trim starts within the seamline.

5 Feed the trim through the presser foot according to manufacturer's instructions for that individual foot. For a standard braiding foot, the trim is usually fed in through a hole at the top of the foot. Other suitable feet may have different arrangements for securing and feeding the trim.

6 Secure the trim with a backstitch or two, then slowly sew it in place, keeping it in the center of the foot and stitching along the design line. To round tight corners and curves, shorten the stitch (you'll have to reposition the fabric frequently beneath the presser foot). If you have a needle down setting on your machine, use it; if not, always remember to sink the needle prior to raising the presser foot.

7 When the trim ends in a seamline, or where the ending will be covered by trim passing over the end, simply secure it in place with a backstitch. If the ending will be conspicuous and will not be covered by an additional layer of trim, you can unravel the ends of the trim and bring the resulting threads to the underside. To do this, it will be necessary to leave an adequate thread tail, which must be long enough to pull through and to knot off on the garment's wrong side.

METHOD II

This method varies from the first in that the trim is placed in its entirety prior to being sewn. In some instances, this allows for greater control in the placement of the trim. Although it takes time to glue baste (adhering the trim to a fabric using a water-soluble fabric glue stick) the trim, the sewing actually proceeds somewhat more quickly than in method I, since correct placement of the trim has already been achieved. The general directions regarding starting, ending, and joining new lengths of the trim are the same for both methods. The following directions include only those instructions that vary from the basic procedures outlined in method I, so in addition to the following, read through the general directions outlined there.

1 Interface the garment piece to be embellished and transfer the passementerie design directly to the right side of the fashion fabric.

2 Glue baste the trim in place. Work in lengths of 6 in. to 12 in. at a time, applying water-soluble fabric glue stick to the underside of the trim. Then place the trim directly to the garment, along the line indicated for the design.

3 Once the design is placed in its entirety, it is ready to be sewn. See step 2 in method I for instructions on threading the machine. In addition to the presser feet used in method I, it is possible to use a variety of other feet that provide a guide for stitching. The ¼-in. foot, standard embroidery foot, and standard zigzag foot are all possible choices.

Appliqué

Appliqué relies upon the effective use of fabrics to produce geographies of pattern and texture that consist of everything from unadorned bands and borders to graphically complex designs. Abstract or realistic, folkloric or refined, the effective use of appliqué expresses a passion for the properties of textiles and the power of design.

Worked in quality fabrics with an eye for detail and emphasis on technique, there are many unique ways to create embellishments that lend drama and sophistication to garments. High-contrast variations rely upon an eye for color and the ability to visualize effective patterning within the boundaries of a garment. Tone-on-tone applications utilize line, texture, and degree of sheen to the sewer's easy advantage by pairing wool with velvet, satin faille, or even self-fabric—embellished with embroidery, braid, or pintucks—or simply cut on the bias.

Never out of style, these expressive embellishments remain open to interpretation and versatile over time. As you'll see, the creative applications are limitless, and the techniques are simple.

MATERIALS AND EQUIPMENT

This lotus motif was embellished with fused and stitched appliqué and free-motion stitching with flat-filament metallic thread.

Several sewing-room staples and a few specialty notions are essential for the techniques featured in this chapter. As usual, having the right tools at your disposal at the onset of a project increases proficiency and rewards you with results worthy of your efforts.

- **Beautiful, well-selected fabrics** are at the heart of all good sewing, but never is this more the case than with appliqués and insets. More so than the technique, the workmanship, or the design, the fabrics you choose to work with will set the entire tone for your garment.

- **The Fasturn tube turner** is the essential tool for turning the bias rouleau tubes that are the foundations of faggotted rouleau and bias appliqué.

- **Celtic Bias Bars** are available in metal or plastic versions and in a variety of widths. These bars make it simple to press a perfect bias tube, stretch it to a uniform width, and keep the seam centered on the back side. They are invaluable for producing the bias tubes required for bias appliqué and faggotted rouleau.

- **Fusible web** is an essential ingredient for fused and stitched appliqué. When selecting a product, base your decision on its ease of use and handling, adhesive properties, and the degree of stiffness it imparts to the appliqué and base fabrics.

    Paper-backed Trans-Web, HeatnBond Lite Iron-On Adhesive, and Alene's Fusible Web are some of the lighter webs that achieve overall good results, but I recommend testing with the actual materials for your project, since results from one fabric type to another can vary. Among one of the newer products available, Sol-u-Web from Pellon is an unbacked web that can be used to hold an appliqué in place for stitching. Its primary advantage is that it washes away with water, leaving the resulting appliqué with a hand that is no stiffer than the equation of the base and appliqué fabric combined!

- **Tracing paper** will be required for drafting insets and altering patterns for rouleau. In the way of tracing paper marketed to sewers, I recommend two kinds (if possible, have both on hand). One is widely known as examination-table paper and is the width of the standard examination table in a doctor's office. You'll like this paper for cutting out slippery fabrics, as well, since the tooth of the paper diminishes the slip and slide of slippery cloth. For tracing off patterns, the advantage of this paper is that it comes with a lot of yards on a roll, and it's easy to reel off and use. Its limitation is size: It's not always wide enough for the pattern piece you need to trace.

    Burda pattern tracing paper is very wide (it's also the wonderfully durable paper that Burda patterns used to be printed on). Thankfully, the paper is still available in packaged form and comes in sheets large enough for any pattern tracing or altering venture you may care to undertake.

- **Clear gridded squares and rulers** are indispensable items in any sewing room and are a tremendous aid in making changes to patterns. Also essential is some kind of fashion ruler, or a long French curve, for producing smooth curved lines. Flexible curves, while not imperative, are wonderful to have, particularly those with rulers.

- **Thread** for working the faggotting stitches for faggotted rouleau should be colorfast, strong, durable, resist kinking and knotting, and be compatible with the fabric used to make the rouleau. Threads that meet these criteria, include silk buttonhole twist, linen embroidery threads, such as Londonderry linen 50/3, and crochet cotton, including DMC's Cebelia and Coats Opera. Weights 10, 20, and 30 are the most suitable.

- **A water-soluble fabric glue stick** has many wonderful uses, and it's invaluable in placing bias appliqué.

- **Paper-backed, double-sided ⅛-in. basting tape** comes packaged in rolls and offers an alternative to hand basting, which is especially welcome for placement of designs for faggotted rouleau.

- **The presser feet** required for each technique are listed in the materials list or directions. (For more information on presser feet, see Chapters 2 and 3.)

- **Stabilizers** may be called for when working with particular fabrics, as well as for appliqués that incorporate a lot of machine stitching in the design. Lightweight tear-away stabilizers that can be worked in layers, including Stitch & Ditch and Totally Stable, are useful in this case, and 100% cotton flannel used as an underlining is often a good solution as well. In addition to acting as a stabilizer, it adds body and warmth.

TIP

The base fabric for fused and stitched appliqué must be suitably stable, but you don't want the finished garment to feel like a coat of armor when worn. Test a variety of fusible interfacings on your fashion fabric and use them in the course of working up samples related to your design. Then select the interfacing according to basic performance and the overall hand that you like best.

APPLIQUÉS

Fused and stitched and bias appliqué methods share in common the technique of layering one fabric upon another as a means of ornamentation. Yet they differ significantly in use, treatment, and effect, and entail various methods of application. None of these embellishments is very difficult to master, though it does take initial time to latch on to new techniques, let alone envision how to incorporate them in your next garment. Allow yourself the luxury of taking time, and seek pleasure in the process. The garments you give yourself permission to create will surely be worth this allowance.

Inspirations for appliqué embellishments are rich and varied—as are the materials used to create them. Floral sprays, meandering vines, Celtic knotwork, and all manner of ornamental flourishes head the list of possible designs. Worked in cotton, silk, leather, or lame, appliqué can be the focal point of a garment or the foundation for further embellishment.

Fused and stitched appliqué

If your main association with fused and stitched appliqué still conjures up images of Holly Hobbie sweatshirts, it's time to take another look at what's going on in the realm of garment-related appliqué. Here you'll find a profusion of color, pattern, and texture; the bold use of prints, solids, and sheers; and rich encrustations of threadwork, as the commonplace satin stitch teams up with free-motion embroidery, a host of decorative stitches, and lush applications of cord.

DESIGNING WITH FUSED AND STITCHED APPLIQUÉ

Designing with fused and stitched appliqué is like making a collage. There are an endless array of colors, textures, and images at your disposal. The challenge and fun of it are creating a coherent pattern from these fragments—a little world of your own making.

Translating your ideas for appliqué to garment form requires selecting a suitable garment style, working effectively within the perimeter of that design, and taking into account the way the garment will lay upon the body. One of the characteristics of fused and stitched appliqué is that the process of bonding the appliqués to the fabric backing adds a degree of crispness that is commensurate with both the overall area of the applied embellishment and the degree of layering that takes place. The type of fusible web used and how that specific brand interacts with your selected fabrics is also a variable that affects the end results.

What all this means in light of picking out a pattern is that fused and stitched appliqué works best when worked on a base of medium- to heavy-weight fabrics and is most compatible with garment styles that require a fabric with body, as opposed to drape. Look for lined vests and jackets worn close to the body; not necessarily tailored (though tailored is fine) but by no means oversized.

In addition to the fun of creating and stitching the appliqué, one of the things that is undeniably lovable about this technique is its versatility. I have used it on everything from pinwoven vests to tailored silk dupioni jackets, for off-the-cuff and over-the-shoulder treatments to allover embellishments, painstakingly designed.

The image range includes any and everything you can imagine. For my own garments, themes vary with my mood, and I draw inspiration from the fabrics, textures, and colors I happen to be working with at the time. From single lotus flowers to branching floral sprays and lush borders, the nascent images are fashioned through layers of free-motion stitching, decorative machine stitches, and perhaps cording, bobbinwork, or beading, until they not only transform the garment but also take on a life of their own.

FUSING APPLIQUÉ

Fusing is the first part of creating an appliqué. The garment piece is backed with fusible interfacing, then the appliqué is fused to the top of the fabric.

1 Cut out the garment from fashion fabric and fuse a suitably stable interfacing to all portions of the garment that are to be embellished with appliqué. For vests and jacket fronts, fuse the entire section of the garment and its corresponding piece (right and left front, for example). If desired, add a 100% cotton flannel underlining to create additional stability and substance. Stitch around the entire garment section just inside the seam allowance.

2 Following the manufacturer's instructions, apply fusible web to the wrong side of fabrics that will be used for the appliqué. Fuse to uncut yardage as opposed to individual designs. Use a nonstick (Teflon or polylon) press sheet to help keep your iron and pressing surface clean. The appliqué pressing sheet also makes it possible to assemble separate pieces of the appliqué directly on the sheet, then peel away the assembled appliqué, and fuse it to your garment in one piece.

3 Draw or trace outlines for designs or shapes that are to be used in the appliqué directly to the paper backing on the wrong side of the appliqué fabric(s), as shown in the drawings above. (If you are

Border Grids for Appliqué

Grid drawn in for border design

Alternate grid using basic pattern from previous design

working with prints, eliminate this step, since you can use the designs that are printed on the right side of the fabric.)

4 Cut out all designs from the appliqué fabrics using small, sharp scissors.

5 Peel away the paper backing from the appliqué designs.

6 Play with the arrangement of the appliqué pieces (fusible web side down) on the right side of the fused pattern pieces for the garment. When you settle upon an arrangement you like, fuse the appliqué in place, following the fusible web manufacturer's instructions for bonding to fabric.

7 When all motifs are fused in place, follow up with any of the following techniques for stitching the design.

STITCHING APPLIQUÉ

Appliques can be secured to fabrics with narrow zigzag stitches, decorative machine-embroidery stitches, or free-motion embroidery stitches.

115

Narrow zigzag stitches

Narrow zigzag stitches are the simplest way to secure the appliqué and, depending upon the desired effect, can be worked for minimal impact or treated decoratively. The width and length of the stitches will determine how much thread is sewn into them, but the type of thread used will also impact the results. Try setting up with a stitch width and length of 1½mm, and make adjustments as necessary.

For the least impact, use invisible nylon or select a color that matches the appliqué in the needle. Contrasting decorative threads, includ-ing metallics, will draw attention to the stitch-ing, which can be desirable or not, depending upon the design.

To sew around the appliqué's edge, select a presser foot with a guide in the center of the foot. Align the guide with the edge of the fab-ric and zigzag around all edges, checking to see that the width of the stitch actually bites the appliqué fabric.

Cording around the edges of the appliqué is also accomplished with narrow zigzag stitches. It is necessary to use a presser foot that will feed the cording under the foot as you sew. The standard embroidery, appliqué, cording, and pintuck feet are possible choices, though the first two allow for greater visibility and are typically shorter feet, which make them more apt for curves.

An alternate way to produce a corded effect is to add heavy threads from the bobbin. To do this, it will be necessary to have a guide that you can readily see on the wrong side of the cloth. To produce the guide for stitching, use a contrasting thread in the bobbin and work narrow zigzag stitches around the cir-cumference of the design. Then, turn the gar-ment wrong-side up. The previous line of stitching should be readily visible on the underside. Now reload the bobbin with a heavy decorative thread and sew along the guidelines, with the wrong side facing up (see p. 76 for instructions on sewing heavy threads in the bobbin).

Decorative machine-embroidery stitches

Decorative machine-embroidery stitches can be an excellent way to secure appliqués (see the drawings below). They provide good cov-erage and can be adjusted for width and length to produce a range of effects. I rarely use these stitches as the sole treatment for an appliqué, but they are an essential part of the way I like to construct borders (see the sidebar on the facing page). Worked in rich, decora-tive threads, they add character, depth, and complexity, especially when they serve as the foundation for other techniques.

Free-motion embroidery stitches

Free-motion embroidery stitches are yet another way to treat a fused and stitched appliqué. This method is very fun to try and produces marvelous, high-impact results. I liken it to Jackson Pollock's scribble method of painting, because the motion is loose, repeti-tive, and unconfined. A variety of decorative threads can be used, but I especially like the metallic hit of the flat-filament threads like Sulky Sliver.

To work free-motion stitches over the sur-face of your design, use a darning foot, drop the feed dogs, and sew! Since the feed dogs are disengaged, it's up to you to move the fab-ric, and you can do so in any direction: for-ward, back, down, to the side, in circles, or

Appliqué Designs

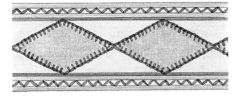

Border design with appliqués, machine stitching, cording, and bobbinwork

Machine- and hand-embroidered accents and beads

Simple Methods for Beautiful, Lush Borders

Borders are bands of color and pattern used to outline and define particular parts of a garment or accessory. Characterized by symmetry and repetition, they rely on the repetitive use of motifs, in combination with straight or fluid lines; bands of color and pattern; and possibly some kind of decorative ground.

The center band (or bands) of the border contain the central, or dominant design. The center band may be constructed off a grid that allows for easy and accurate placement of the designs. Designs can be worked into the center band and may be used intermittently on the garment, as well. Frequently, designs are placed at regular intervals above the border. Bands of color and design are used in combination or alone to outline and accentuate the central design, as well as to add color, variety, and interest to the border. They are also used to separate and define larger bands.

To construct a lush border using fused and stitched appliqué, follow these steps.

1. Interface the fashion fabric and stabilize it with additional layers of Totally Stable tear-away stabilizer.
2. Sew in the band and grid lines for the border. These are the lines that will indicate where bands of color and motifs are to be placed. They must be straight stitched from the top side of the fabric. The top thread should provide just enough contrast to remain visible while sewing. The bobbin thread must contrast sharply with the stabilizer on the back.
3. There are two ways to sew in an accurate grid. One is to premark with chalk, using a clear ruler to produce accurate measurements. Then sew the stitching along the premarked guidelines. A faster method is to use a seam guide with a ruler. To use this method, adjust the seam guide to create the desired distance from the needle to the foot of the guide.
4. To mark or sew the grid, begin by stitching in the ⅝-in. seam allowance. Then determine the desired placement of the center band for the border and sew the first line in, parallel to the edge of the garment. Sew the second line parallel to the first to create the desired width of the center band for the border.
5. Next, use the seam guide to divide the band into squares or rectangles and, if desired, diagonal lines (all sewn in). The point is to create a simple grid that serves as the base for your appliqué and threadwork design.
6. Based on the grid structure, decide on basic shapes and placement for the fused appliqué.
7. Experiment with a range of decorative stitches that can be used to outline the areas that are to be appliquéd, and enrich the ground (the background patterning will remain visible against the base fabric). Play with the settings on your machine—stitch, length, width, tension, stitch elongation, and memory—to come up with patterns you like.
8. Play as well with a variety of machine-embroidery threads until you find combinations you like.
9. Sew in the ground stitches for your design, using an open-toe embroidery foot.
10. Cut and fuse the appliqués in place at regular intervals along the border.
11. Stitch in place using decorative machine stitches, working in a logical sequence along the entire border.
12. Cord the appliqués along the edge, either by machine couching or by sewing in heavy threads from the bobbin. (Refer to Chapter 2 for complete instructions on bobbinwork.) Continue to build up the designs until you're satisfied with the results.
13. Finish off the edges of the band with satin-stitch cording and inlaid bobbin threads. Expand the border and bands as desired.

following basic shape and lines of your design. For best results, move the fabric smoothly and slowly and keep the machine running at a fairly good speed.

Bias appliqué

The fluid properties of bias—defined as the line that cuts diagonally across the grain of the fabric—can be used to create appliqué embellishments of exceptional beauty. At the heart of bias appliqué borders, medallions, and designs of all kinds is a simple trim called bias rouleau. Made from individual fabric strips that are cut on the true bias, then sewn, turned and pressed, bias rouleau adapts to curves like fish to water, which makes bias appliqué pure pleasure to create, sew, and wear.

DESIGNING BIAS APPLIQUÉ

My own inspirations for working with bias appliqué stem from the precise, graceful lines of Celtic ornamentation. To translate the intricacy of these designs garments, I turned to bias appliqué as the method and supple silk as the medium for realizing my design. Not wanting to spend hours sewing by hand, I developed a relatively fast, simple method of appliquéing bias fabric tubes by machine (see the drawings below) that sacrifices neither subtlety nor precision and produces a finished garment that looks like it took a great deal of time. In reality, the process is simple, as the entire embellishment is sewn with the blind-hem stitch on a machine. Applying these methods requires planning and care, but once you prepare the fabric and practice the techniques, the work progresses quickly.

Anchor Bias Appliqué by Machine

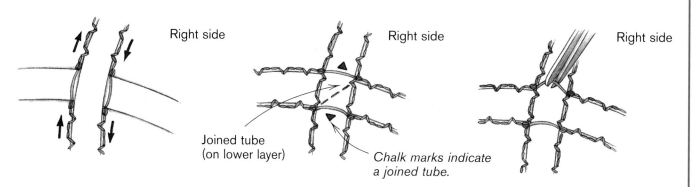

Right side

Right side

Right side

Joined tube
(on lower layer)

Chalk marks indicate
a joined tube.

Stitching tubes, jumping intersections

You can stitch tubes in a braided design and sew a regular intersection.

1. Blind-hem stitch along the appliqué edge, taking a tiny bite.
2. At the corner of the intersection, drop the feed dogs and sew several stitches.
3. Lifting foot and needle, carry the thread over the intersection (you'll trim it later).
4. Anchor corner on the other side.
5. Raise the feed dogs and blind-hem stitch to the next intersection.

Stitching joined intersections

Where abutting bias tubes are glued, stitching across the intersection on the top layer adds stability.

1. Stitch the underpass tube like any other intersection, jumping it.
2. Sew the overpass tube with a blind-hem stitch through the intersection, without dropping the feed dogs.

Trimming extra threads on the right side

Lines of stitching become invisible when you trim excess threads.

1. Clip where the threads cross the intersection.
2. Cut the loose threads as close to the fabric as possible, without nicking the fabric.

Of course Celtic inspirations are just one design option for this technique. Look to battenberg lace patterns for equally elaborate blueprints with similar flair. Or pare the ornamentation down and try your hand at creating simple braids, spirals, scrolls, and spontaneous, gentle curves to enhance the lines of your garment (see the photo on p. 120). Once you decide upon a design, fine-tune its placement and scale. Use a photocopier, if necessary, to reduce the design or to enlarge it to size.

FINDING SUITABLE FABRICS

Many fabrics are well suited to bias appliqué. Look for light- to medium-weight natural fiber fabrics with an even, supple stretch on the bias. I've seen beautiful results with silks of all kinds, from three-ply crepe, to noil, and to dupioni. Other elegant choices include wool and rayon crepe and handkerchief linen. Avoid twills, knits, and heavy-textured fabrics, as well as those with a pile or nap.

Prior to placing and sewing the appliqué, the base fabric must be suitably stable. For fabrics like wool crepe, silk dupioni and noil, backing the base with a tricot knit fusible interfacing may be sufficient.

Fluid, drapey fabrics like silk crepe, on the other hand, may require a different approach. To temporarily transform even the lightest, slipperiest silk to the consistency of heavy paper, consider a water-soluble liquid stabilizer, such as Perfect Sew. In addition to making it possible to stitch the appliqué to the base fabric with minimal distortion, a water-soluble liquid stabilizer dissolves completely when washed. Also, the fabric returns to its original, supple state.

Once the base fabric has been stabilized, transfer the appliqué design. For interlacing designs and borders, I prefer to create and use a plastic template. You can make a template by tracing the design directly to the plastic, then cutting out the design with a mat knife. For single motifs and medallions, it is necessary to trace the entire design. For borders, you'll only need to trace 8 in. to 12 in. of it, beginning

How Much Bias Do You Need?

To determine the quantity of bias strips needed for a design of bias appliqué, first photocopy the design. Place a length of string on the outermost edge and follow the design in a clockwise fashion. Mark the spot where you begin and, when you return to that point, cut the string and measure it.

To calculate the amount of bias needed for a braided border, for instance, use the string to measure a single 1-ft. strand of the border. Multiply this amount (in inches) by the number of strands that make up the braid and divide the results by 12. This is the number of feet of bias needed for the border design.

Now measure your pattern pieces to determine the total length of all borders for your garment. Divide this amount (in inches) by 12. This is the number of finished border feet needed.

To find the amount of bias needed for a border appliqué, multiply the first number by the second. To convert this amount to yards, divide by three. Use this measurement to calculate how much bias to cut and sew. A 1¼-yd. piece of 45-in.-wide fabric yields more than 80 ft. of 1½-in.-wide bias strips for ⅜-in. tubes.

and ending in the middle of a repeat, so you can realign the template for a perfect match.

PREPARING BIAS ROULEAU

Fluid bias rouleau forms the design lines for your appliqué. To produce this even bias tubing, you need to cut the bias strips, then fold, turn, and press them. Whether you cut with scissors or with a rotary cutter, strips

Bias-rouleau strips were used to create a three-strand braid that adorns the shoulder and neckline of this dress.

must be cut on the *true bias*, without seams. (For more information on cutting bias strips, see p. 148.) In other words, methods for making continuous bias are not recommended for bias appliqué.

To get the longest unseamed strips possible, start with a true square of 36-in.- to 60-in.-wide fabric (1¼ yd. of 45 in.; 1⅔ yd. of 60 in.). Mark the square in half along the diagonal, then working from the center line out, cut the fabric in strips—1¼ in. to 1½ in.—for resulting ¼-in. to ⅜-in. rouleau tubes. For accuracy, cut one layer at a time.

Working with a rotary cutter, ruler, and cutting mat is the quickest way to cut strips. If you use scissors, premark the fabric with chalk along the cutting lines. I prefer a disappearing chalk, such as Clo-chalk.

To sew the tubes, fold the bias strips in half, right sides together. You can use a ¼-in. foot to sew a perfect ¼ in. from the folded edge. If your tubes are ⅜ in., use a zigzag presser foot and alter the needle position, or use a marker on the machine bed as a guide.

A quick way to sew uniform tubing is with a Fastube foot, which guides the folded strip to the needle. It eliminates the stress of guiding length after length accurately and saves time. The companion product for this foot is called Fasturn and makes turning the finished bias tubes a breeze! You can even open the seam as you turn the tube, which helps distribute the bulk of the seam to either side.

Finally, the tubes need to be pressed with the aid of a Celtic Bias Bar, which helps to center the seam and stretch the rouleau to a uniform width. To use the bias bar effectively, follow these steps.

1   Insert the bias bar into the tube.

2   Roll the seam to the center so that it will be hidden when the appliqué is sewn.

3   Press, using steam and a lightweight press cloth.

4   Reposition the bar, moving it through the entire length of each tube. Press after each adjustment.

5   After the bar is removed, press the entire length once more using the press cloth. The bias rouleau is now ready to be applied to the base cloth.

6   To position the appliqué for sewing, use a fabric glue stick.

7   Apply the glue stick to the wrong side of the bias rouleau, coating just a few inches at a time, then place the rouleau along the design line.

STITCHING THE APPLIQUÉ BY MACHINE

With careful attention, this method will allow you to attach the appliqué almost invisibly (see the photo at right).

1   Thread the needle and load the bobbin with 60-wt. machine-embroidery thread in a color to match your fabric. If you can't find a good color match, use a fine invisible nylon as the top thread and fine cotton in the bobbin. Lightweight silk thread is also an option.

2   Select the blind-hem stitch and adjust both stitch width and length to 1mm. You want the sideways stitch to take the tiniest bite possible while still catching the appliqué fabric. Test this on a sample swatch prior to sewing on your actual garment and adjust the width to a slightly wider setting if the needle doesn't catch the fabric. Or adjust to a slightly narrower setting, if the bite is so wide that the needle thread shows. To some extent, the visibility of the stitch will vary with the fabric. Fabrics with more loft will tend to conceal the stitch, while flatter fabrics will conceal it less.

3   Adjust the needle position to the right and use an open-toe embroidery foot so that you can see clearly.

4   If you have a half speed setting on your machine, engage it (or sew slowly). Likewise, if it's an option, select needle down.

5   Align the edge of the appliqué with the inside of the right presser-foot toe, which will serve as a guide. Stitch along the edge of the appliqué.

6   If you are appliquéing a design where the lines cross over and intersect, it will be necessary to "jump" the intersections, meaning you move the presser foot over the intersecting bias tube without taking any stitches through that intersection. To do this, drop the feed dogs when you reach the corner of an intersection.

7   Sink the needle so that it barely catches the appliqué and stitch up and down two or three times to secure, forming a knot on the back.

8   Raise the presser foot and needle and gently push the work forward until the unbroken thread crosses the intersection (don't worry, you'll trim the threads later). Lower the foot and secure the intersection's next corner by stitching up and down two or three times.

9   Now raise the feed dogs and continue stitching to the next intersection, along the edge of the appliqué.

10 Lower the feed dogs at all intersections, except those that contain a join in the bias, and push the work across the intersection to begin sewing again.

11 At the intersection with a bias join on the underlap, keep the feed dogs raised, and continue to sew directly through the intersection.

12 After you complete an entire edge of the appliqué, turn the work around and sew the other edge. Repeat with each strand of the design until the entire appliqué is secured.

13 When all appliqué sewing is complete, trim away any threads that are visible across the intersections. Cut loose thread as close to the fabric as possible, without nicking the fabric. I use a Gingher tool called a Berling nipper for this purpose, which is more comfortable to use than scissors, and its tweezerlike blades can cut close to the cloth without nicking. Hold the nipper perpendicular to the fabric and cut the excess thread close to the cloth.

Machine-stitched bias appliqué works up quickly, maintains the hand of the cloth, and looks as though it were made by hand.

Although you can cut bias strips clear to the corner of your yardage, there's a point at which the strips become too short to use conveniently. Rather than cutting up strips that can't be put to use, start cutting the bias strips far enough away from the corner so that all of your strips will be useful. The leftover yardage in the corner will be useful, too.

TIP

INSETS

Embellished Silk Crepe Dress

Insets produce contrasts in color, texture, and line. They set the tone for the rest of the garment and are frequently reinforced with the use of bands, bindings, or covered buttons worked in the same fabric as the insets. This dress features sheer chiffon insets and woven ribbon.

Insets are shapes or bands seamed into the structure of the garment to produce contrasts in color, texture, and line. Used effectively, insets set the tone for the rest of the garment and are frequently reinforced with the use of bands, bindings, or covered buttons worked in the same fabric as the insets.

Insets can be used anywhere on the body of the garment. You can cut them from a con-

trasting color, work tone on tone, pair sheer with opaque, embellish them, or leave them plain. Creating and sewing an inset is easy. In the way of extra work, it requires just a few simple alterations to the pattern, and staying the inset seams.

Selecting a suitable garment pattern

Simplicity is the password when it comes to a garment pattern amenable to insets. Look for well-cut renditions of basic styles, with few pattern pieces and clean lines. Of course, you can always seek out a pattern that supplies the inset for you and work from there to put your own spin on an already fabulous design.

Designing an inset

To create your own inset, start with the line drawing that comes with your basic pattern. Enlarge this image, using a copier, and run off several copies, so that you can tinker with more than one idea as you perfect the design.

Once you hit upon an idea you like, try it out full scale. There are a couple of ways to do this. One is to draw the basic shape of the inset, cut it out, pinfit the pattern, locate and mark the placement for the inset, and perfect the shape of the inset from there.

Another approach is to cut an actual muslin and pin it to the dress form or the actual wearer by marking corresponding dots. Designate the shape and location of the inset directly on the muslin. Remove the muslin from the dress form and lay it flat. To perfect the line, connect the dots, using rulers and French curves. Proof the results on the dress form or the actual wearer. When you like the basic look, it's time to prepare the pattern pieces for the inset (to get some ideas for effective inset designs, see the sidebar below).

Preparing the pattern

In the following steps, you will redraw the pattern piece to make room for the inset and establish reference points to make the assembly easy and accurate.

1   Trace the pattern piece onto pattern tracing paper. Indicate the grainline, and carry it through the entire pattern.

2   To draft the actual design, use the muslin as a guide. You can trace off reference points directly from the muslin, but for the actual pattern, draw in the straight lines with a straightedge and curved lines with a fashion ruler or French curve. Where insets run parallel to the edge of the garment, measure to ensure that the space between them remains consistent.

3   When the accuracy of the lines has been checked, and the pattern pinfitted once more to proof the effect, draw in the actual seamlines with a fine-point pen.

4   Draw in the grainline on each pattern piece. Measure accurately so that the grain indicated for all pattern pieces runs absolutely parallel. Finally, draw in notches on both sides of each seamline to

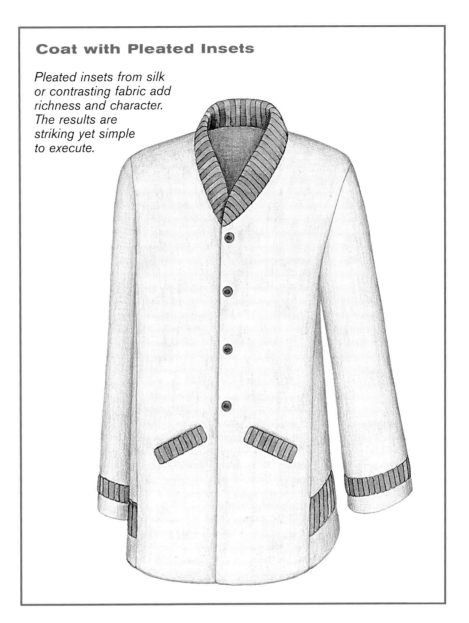

Coat with Pleated Insets

Pleated insets from silk or contrasting fabric add richness and character. The results are striking yet simple to execute.

Ideas for Creating Effective Insets

Use this list to jump-start your own ides for insets. Experiment with unique fabric pairings, color, and line to make a statement or as the foundation for further embellishment.

Fabric pairings
Velvet and wool; velvet and faille; wool crepe with silk crepe; self-fabric bias inset (for plaids and textured wools); reverse side of fabric; linen and lace; silk charmeuse and silk chiffon; wool crepe and wool batiste.

Line
Asymmetrical, curved, geometric, concentric.

Texture
Smocked, pleated, quilted, channelstitched and corded, pintucked, faggotted rouleau.

Applied embellishments
Appliquéd, beaded, embroidered, passementerie.

Details
Topstitched, piped, bias bound.

help match the pattern pieces when they're sewn.

5 Cut the pattern apart along the lines for the inset (see the drawing below).

6 On a new piece of pattern tracing paper, retrace each portion of the pattern, including the grainlines and the notch. Add seam allowances to all newly cut edges. This includes the inset and all adjoining edges of the garment that were cut away. (The original seam allowances provided in the pattern are not to be altered in any way. Do not add seam allowances any-where else, unless your original pattern did not provide seam allowances.) The seam allowance can be the same as the rest of the garment seams or smaller.

7 Label all pattern pieces clearly (upper front inset, lower front inset, etc.). Indicate how many pieces will need to be cut from fashion fabric and label right and left sides of the garment if they are treated differently.

8 Throw away the first set of cut-up pattern pieces so they do not accidentally get cut out instead of the pieces with the seam allowances added. Then cut out individual pattern pieces from appropriate fabrics.

Dividing a Pattern for Insets

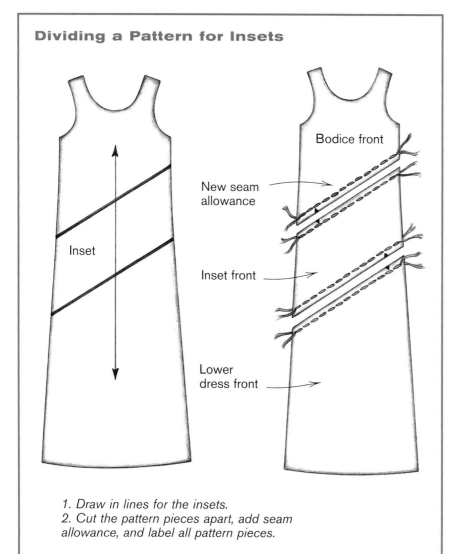

Inset

New seam allowance

Bodice front

Inset front

Lower dress front

1. Draw in lines for the insets.
2. Cut the pattern pieces apart, add seam allowance, and label all pattern pieces.

Sewing the inset

The addition of an inset creates at least two additional seams that will be unaccounted for in the commercial pattern instructions for your garment (for garments that did not have an inset to begin with). These seams should be sewn at the onset of garment construction (see the top left drawing on the facing page), since doing so will re-create the original pattern block that is referred to in the instructions. From there on, the commercial pattern instructions will apply to all phases of construction.

Careful, precise seaming of the inset is a must. Because the inset is a design detail, it will draw attention to that portion of the garment, including the seams. If the workmanship is consummate, these seams will only add to the beauty of the garment. But seams that stretch and curl, curves that bulge when they should lie flat, and points that pucker instead of point are hardly attractive and are potential pitfalls when it comes to sewing an inset.

Sewing Pattern Pieces

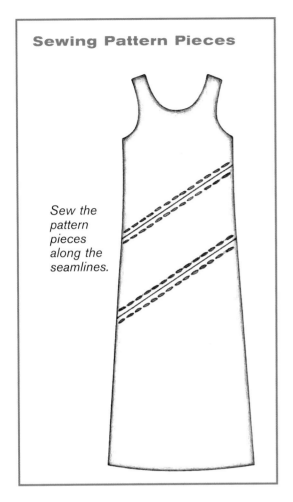

Sew the pattern pieces along the seamlines.

Curved Seams for Insets

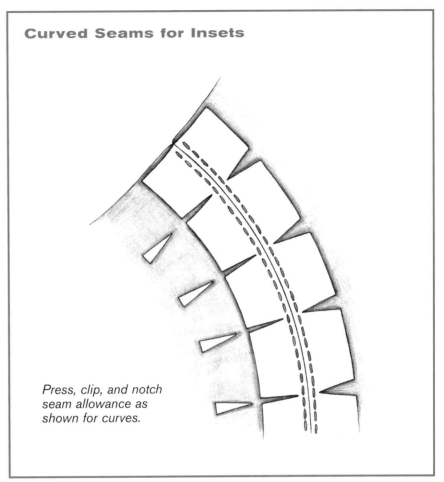

Press, clip, and notch seam allowance as shown for curves.

Though there is sometimes no cure for a seam ill-sewn, there are practical ways to ensure first-rate results. They include staying seams that fall on the bias (to prevent wavy seams); clipping, notching, and pressing curved seams so that curves lie flat (see the right drawing above); and preparing corner seams by sewing reinforcement stitches (see the drawing at right), then clipping to the corner prior to seaming (for perfect points, not puckers). Once the inset is sewn, simply proceed with instructions for sewing the rest of the garment.

Sewing and Pressing Points for Insets

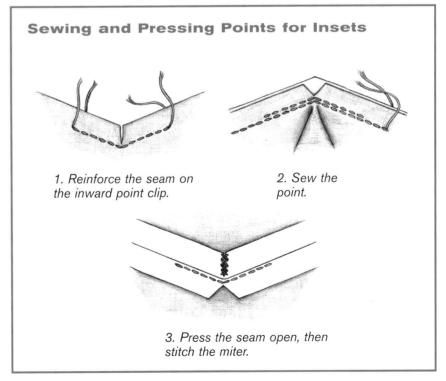

1. Reinforce the seam on the inward point clip.

2. Sew the point.

3. Press the seam open, then stitch the miter.

125

FAGGOTTED ROULEAU

MATERIALS LIST

FAGGOTTED ROULEAU

Bias rouleau: light- to medium-weight silk, wool crepe, cotton, and linen

Cotton or silk organdy

Stabilizer: iron on (optional)

Fusible interfacing (optional)

Permanent-ink pen (with a fine point)

Pencil

Pattern tracing paper

Press cloth

Measuring and drafting tools: clear grid ruler, flexible curve, French curve, and compass (optional)

⅛-in. basting tape or lightweight silk basting thread

Thread: silk buttonhole twist, crochet cotton, or pearl cotton

Hand-embroidery needles: size according to thread used

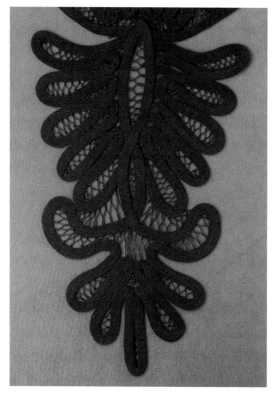

Contrary to its delicate, lacelike appearance, hand-faggotted rouleau creates a sturdy cloth and can be used to create entire garments. This sample was made from three-ply silk, faggotted with silk buttonhole twist.

The term rouleau refers to tape, ribbon, braid, or fabric trim that is pliable enough to shape in the form of tight curves for purposes of creating decorative laces, insets, appliqués, and garment closures. The following methods for faggotted rouleau rely upon the same type of turned fabric tubes used to make decorative braid and bias appliqué (see pp. 119-120).

For this embellishment, fabric tubes are coaxed into elaborate, passementerie-like designs and applied to a temporary fabric or paper base for stability. Faggotting—a type of stitchery that connects two pieces of cloth separated by an open area—is worked by

hand, between the rouleau strips, across all open areas of the design.

The purpose of the faggotting is structural and decorative. Worked in heavyweight thread, such as crochet cotton or silk buttonhole twist, it connects the rouleau strips and maintains the shape of the design. When the stitchery is complete, the finished rouleau is separated from its base, and the lacelike beauty of the faggotting is revealed.

Contrary to appearance, this distinctive, elegant, and utterly feminine embellishment works up more quickly than one might first imagine and is suitable for inserts, edgings, or entire garments. Even so, if the treatment is to be extensive, it is unrealistic to expect overnight results. Like most embellishments, the biggest expenditure of time is in the planning and preparation (see the sidebar on the facing page).

Once the design is worked out and the rouleau strips are sewn, turned, pressed, and applied to a base, however, this project can leave the sewing room! Like knitting or hand embroidery, it's portable. So come up with a fabulous design and work on it here and there for relaxation, while conversing with family and friends, whenever time allows. Before you know it, you'll have a garment that you'll cherish for years to come.

The following instructions are for faggotting by hand only (see the photo above). Though it is possible to use machine methods typically associated with Battenburg lace for this technique, the use of a hoop poses size limitations. In any case, my preference leans toward the clean look of handwork, which in reality is equally simple and no more time-consuming than comparable machine methods—particularly if you use my method of using basting tape to place the design.

Plotting the Order of Construction for Faggotted Rouleau

Once you've figured out how to alter the pattern to accommodate your rouleau design, it's a good time to consider how the rouleau embellishment will impact the sequence in which the garment must be sewn. The order of construction should never be an afterthought, since faggotted rouleau edgings, appliqués, and insets are sewn in a logical sequence governed by the design of the embellishment in relation to the garment style. To plot the order of construction for a garment, keep the following considerations in mind.

• Read through the commercial pattern instructions so that you are familiar with the general order of construction recommended for your garment. As you read through, add instructions that pertain to alterations you've made to the pattern and cross out all instructions that no longer apply. (If you're adding faggotted rouleau to a collar, for example, added instructions would include appropriate sequence for sewing the main collar piece and adding the faggotted rouleau to that collar piece; if you eliminated a facing, instructions for sewing that facing no longer apply.)

• Construct cut-away rouleau appliqués directly on the garment. The outer edge of the appliqué always consists of rouleau outline, which is sewn directly to the fashion fabric using a blind-hem stitch. When the faggotting is complete on the inner portion of the appliqué, cut away the garment fabric, leaving a margin of cloth that is pressed back and sewn in place. Sew appliqués that fall within the seamlines of the pattern piece before sewing that piece to another. Place and stitch appliqués that cross a seamline after sewing the seam that they cross.

• Shape and attach edgings and insets to a separate base fabric. Complete faggotting worked on the interior portions of the insets while attached to the base and baste the base fabric to the main garment so that the rouleau is spaced a precalculated distance from the edge of the main garment section(s). Then attach the edging or insert to the garment section with faggotting stitches. Remove all basting from the main garment, rouleau, and base fabric. Remove the base altogether.

• Apply insets and edgings that cross a seamline to the garment after sewing that seam. For example, for a rouleau yoke that extends from back to front, sew the shoulder seams of the bodice and bind (or turn under) the bodice edge prior to basting the base fabric to that edge and faggotting the yoke to the bodice along the connecting line. Likewise, edgings at the hem of a skirt would be added once the side seams were sewn.

• For entire garments made from faggotted rouleau, construction is slightly more complicated. It is possible to treat the back and fronts as one (attached at either the shoulders or the sides), or each portion of the pattern can be placed and faggotted individually, then joined by a straight strip of rouleau at what would be the seams. Bands that travel around the neckline, center front, and bottom hem, all the way around the back, pose a construction dilemma that can be resolved by treating the band as a separate piece; treating the fronts and back as one piece; or simply calculating the location of the bias joins so that they end up in an inconspicuous place.

To prepare for this technique, create or adapt an appropriate design, make a template, determine the amount of fabric needed, alter the pattern to accommodate the application of the design, and transfer the design to a fabric base. Then apply bias rouleau strips that have been sewn, turned, and pressed to this base following the lines of the design. The application of rouleau in this manner leaves open areas, which are, in turn, worked with faggotting stitches that permanently join the strips together.

Finding design inspiration

Simple interpretations of this technique involve little more than following the basic lines of the affected components of the pattern. Replace a conventional collar with one that features one or more rouleau strips faggotted to the edge, and you've added an extraordinary detail without a lot of fuss. On the other hand, if you're looking for an epic project, fuss all you will: This technique invites elaborate interpretation limited only by your willingness to comply with its demands.

You can easily locate design sources for Celtic spirals and knotwork, Battenberg lace, and Chinese latticework, which inspire countless design options that can be adapted to this technique. Or work up your own visual theme based on hieroglyphs, ferns, suns and stars, or leaves. Play with fragments of designs; combine them. Make copies of those you like, toying with enlarging designs, fracturing them, and recombining. Then take your copies home; trace off and pin-fit your pattern; and play with design placement, honing in on the one you like best and locating the perfect placement. But before getting hooked on a specific pattern or idea, sample the basic technique. Get a feel for the amount of work involved and make an informed decision regarding the scope of your project.

Selecting the perfect pattern

Faggotted rouleau embellishments are suited to a variety of garment styles. Edgings can be used to accent virtually any collar, cuff, neckline, or hem. Insets and appliqués can be used to produce bands or motifs to enliven the front of a blouse, back of an unlined jacket, hem of a skirt, or bottom of a sleeve.

Look for pattern details that will complement your work: convertible and shawl collars; and one-piece fronts, back, and sleeves. A nice pattern feature for a blouse is a hidden front placket, which allows for a rouleau inset down the center without sacrificing the ease of a button-down front. For insets or edgings on skirts and dresses, check the bottom width of the finished garment. Generally, narrow widths show the work to best advantage and involve less work and time.

If you like the idea of creating an entire garment from rouleau, consider vest or jacket patterns with simple shaping and straightforward lines. Round, V-neck, and mandarin-collar necklines are suitable, and it's especially nice if you can find a pattern where the front edges meet in the center, since this treatment maintains the openwork effect of the design. If you have an otherwise appropriate pattern, however, don't hunt high and low for this detail, as just about any pattern can be suitably altered by removing the front overlap and redrawing the line (see the sidebar on the facing page).

When you review pattern choices, think as well about closures and how you might treat them relative to the designs. Buttonholes are out of the question, unless you create an under placket and go with the overlapping front. A better solution for standard buttons are loops attached to the garment's edge. Yet another alternative are frog closures that join at the center and are tacked in place on either side.

Making a design template

Once you have settled on a design, enlarged it to scale, and fussed over and finalized its placement on the pattern, you can make a paper design template that corresponds to the portion of the garment to be embellished. The template will be used to trace the entire rouleau design to the base fabric.

All designs must be drawn to scale and placed directly where you want them in the final garment. As you will see when you actually do this, making the design template will force you to begin thinking about what adjustments will be necessary to make to the pattern. To make a template, follow these steps.

1   Use pattern tracing paper to trace around the outline of all pattern pieces to be embellished. Label all pattern pieces clearly and trace off the grainline.

2   Pencil in the actual seamlines to ensure accuracy in placement of the designs.

3   Draw directly, trace, or glue a copy of the design in place exactly where you wish to have it positioned on the finished garment.

Determining the amount of fabric

In addition to being the blueprint for tracing the rouleau design to the base fabric, the design template is used to determine how many yards of rouleau are required for a design. The string method described for bias appliqué (see the sidebar on p. 119) provides an accurate estimate of how much rouleau you will need to produce. In turn, this will answer the question of how much fabric to buy.

Simple applications can sometimes be based on the yardage called for in the pattern, depending upon the margin of the layout. If all you need are a few rouleau strips to edge a collar, see if there's a way to arrange the pattern pieces to include the bias strips necessary to make the rouleau.

To calculate how much additional fabric to purchase for long, uncomplicated insets, motifs, and border designs, measure the longest continuous line in your pattern. Use a tape measure to duplicate that length on the bias of your fabric, positioning the tape so that the beginning and end of the tape measure align with the lengthwise selvages. Use a pin to mark the farthest point from the crosswise edge, where the end of the tape intersects

Guidelines for Altering a Pattern for Insets or Faggotted Rouleau

• Never alter the original pattern. Trace off the original directly to pattern tracing paper. All subsequent alterations should also be traced as well.

• Fine-tuning the alterations may take a series of adjustments to the pattern. Most alterations require at least two tracings: one to divide the pattern along the new seamlines; the other to create individual pattern pieces that include the new seam allowance.

• All information relevant to cutting and sewing the pattern should be noted on the individual pattern pieces. Relevant information includes the name of the pattern pieces (front, back, left front, inset, etc.), grainline, notches to match pattern pieces for sewing, seam allowance, and an indication of how many pieces to cut from the pattern piece.

• In addition to the above notations, pattern pieces for faggotted rouleau may include notations that indicate where an edge is to be bound, where faggotting will be sewn, and where the rouleau is to be placed.

with the selvage. Measure the length from this point, back to the crosswise edge, along the lengthwise grain. In most instances, this measurement will provide ample extra yardage.

Extensive, or complex edgings, insets, or appliqué, as well as the use of rouleau to create an entire garment, present a different scenario in terms of how much yardage to buy. Exact yardage amounts are difficult to gauge precisely, so allow some latitude in this regard.

Keep in mind that facings, hems, and seam allowances will be eliminated, and that much of the garment's surface will consist of openwork stitches rather than fabric. All edges and seamlines will be outlined with rouleau, so be sure to measure around the entire edge of the garment, including the neckline, front openings, and hemlines—including sleeves.

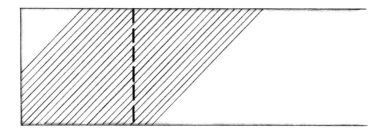

Because the percentage of usable bias yardage increases with the length of fabric, shift the initial cutting line farther from the corner edge. This will result in cutting longer lengths of fabric and leaving a larger portion of the corner uncut.

In addition to these measurements, calculate the length of all seams. For an unstructured cardigan, this would include two side, two shoulder, and two armscye seams. A jacket with a mandarin collar would include an additional seam for the collar band. If you plan to make your own frog or knot buttons from rouleau, be sure to include the yardage for that as well.

To calculate how many yards of rouleau are required for completion, use your design template and the string method described for bias appliqué. When you arrive at a figure, compare it with the number of usable bias strips you can cut from a perfect square of fabric.

For a rough approximation of how much rouleau yardage this square of fabric will put at your disposal, divide the length of usable yardage by 1½ in. or the width of the strips. This tells you how many strips the square will yield. Then multiply the number of strips available by the length (in inches) of the mid-length strip—not the longest or the shortest strip. Now divide this amount by 36 in. to convert this calculation to yards. This yardage figure indicates approximately how many yards of rouleau a perfect square (1⅓ yd. of 45 in.; 1⅔ yd. of 60 in.) of fashion fabric yields. Finally, divide the rouleau yardage required for your project by the number of yards of rouleau a perfect square yields. Multiply the result by the length of your yardage square (1.333 for 45 in. of fabric; 1.666 for 60 in. of fabric). This final figure indicates how much actual fabric to purchase.

If your estimated yardage amount exceeds the length of the square measurement you used for estimation, you will actually end up with more available bias than you calculated for, because you'll be cutting from a rectangle, not from a square. In other words, the percentage of usable bias yardage will increase with the length of fabric. My recommendation, in this instance, is that you shift the initial cutting line farther away from the corner edge (see the drawing at left). This will result in cutting longer lengths of fabric (this is good!) and leaving a larger portion of the corner uncut (also good!).

If it turns out that you need to cut this up for bias, after all, you can at a later point. If not, you'll end up with more usable leftover fabric than you otherwise would. I do not recommend buying less than the calculated amount, however, since it's better to have a little leeway built in to a project like this, as opposed to coming up short in the end.

Preparing the pattern

Embellishments with faggotted rouleau require adjustments to the pattern. The adjustments for making edgings, appliqués, insets, and entire garments from rouleau vary, as explained. In each case, alterations to the pattern must be complete before the garment is cut out. In some instances, it may be necessary to combine techniques based on your vision for the completed garment.

Regardless of how extensive the treatment, properly thinking through the alterations that need to be made is essential to success. Likewise, think in advance about how the addition of rouleau will affect the order in which the garment is constructed.

To avoid irreversible mistakes, double-check all of the alterations you make before you cut into your fashion fabric. In particular, reexamine all edges and seam allowances to ensure they will fit together as intended. You can remove a seam allowance, if necessary, but you sure can't put one back!

Finally, use proper tools to trace off the pattern and make all subsequent changes. A permanent-ink pen with a fine point, clear grid ruler, compass, French curve, and flexible curve are useful for this purpose.

ALTERING THE PATTERN FOR A FAGGOTTED ROULEAU EDGING

Edgings are the simplest treatment to make with faggotted rouleau. To use rouleau edgings to transform collars, cuffs, and hemlines, begin by making the following alterations to the pattern.

1 Trace off the entire pattern piece to be embellished. Trace all seamlines, and mark in hems. Generally, a measurement for the hem is marked on the original pattern. Mark in grainline.

2 Trim away the seam or hem allowance on all edges to be embellished. Do not trim away the seam allowance that will be used to construct the garment. On a collar, for example, trim away the outer seam allowance, but leave the neckline seam allowance intact. This paper pattern piece will be your working template. It will be used to create the new pattern pieces for the unembellished portion of the original pattern piece, as well as the template for the embellished edging on your garment.

3 Determine how wide you want the rouleau edging to be. The narrowest width would consist of one rouleau strip, plus the desired width of the faggotting (generally ¼ in. to ⅜ in.). The width and complexity of the edging should remain proportionate to the pattern piece that is being embellished and to the rest of the garment. A large shawl collar on a robe, for example, will stand up to an ornate

border or looped edging, while a convertible collar for a blouse calls for a simpler approach.

4 Align the clear grid ruler with the edge to be embellished and make a series of dots to indicate the width of the edging, progressing around the circumference of the working template. Connect these dots with a solid line, maintaining an even distance from the edge. A flexible curve is an excellent way to produce a smooth line around curves and collars.

5 Alternatively, if you already have a design template for your garment, lay the working template over it and trace the outline of the edging design directly to your working template.

6 Label the main portion (i.e., collar) and the edging (i.e., collar edging) of the working template. Check to see that the grainline is indicated on the main pattern portion. Cut out the edging along the indicated line.

7 The remainder of the template is your main pattern piece. The outer edge of this piece can be left without a seam allowance, in which case this portion of the garment must be bound with bias trim. Alternatively, the new pattern piece can be retraced, and a seam allowance can be added. Either way, be sure to label the pattern piece and indicate whether or not there is a seam allowance along the edge, and if so, how much.

ALTERING THE PATTERN FOR CUT-AWAY ROULEAU APPLIQUÉ

When rouleau is used to create a cut-away appliqué, the resulting effect is similar to an inset, but both the techniques and possibilities for each method differ (see the drawings on p. 132). One major difference is that the edge of the appliqué always consists of a rouleau strip, which allows for more intricate shaping along the margins of the design.

No alterations to the pattern are necessary with the appliqué method, because the designs

If the seams aren't marked on the pattern, the easiest way to remove a seam allowance is to use a rotary cutter with a guide attachment.

TIP

131

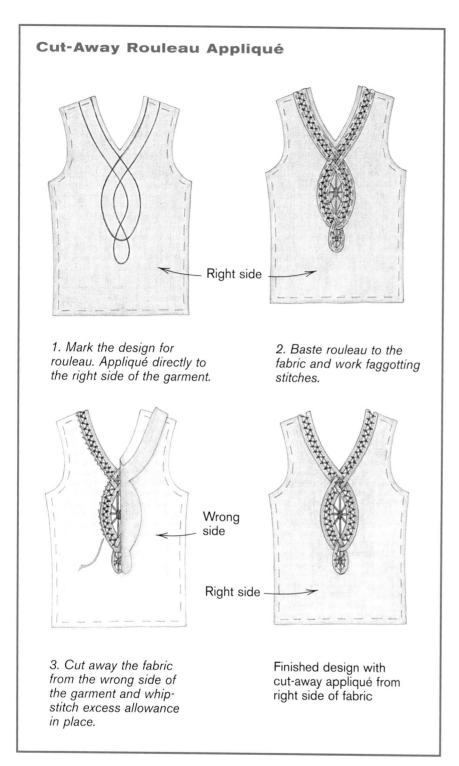

Cut-Away Rouleau Appliqué

1. Mark the design for rouleau. Appliqué directly to the right side of the garment.

Right side

2. Baste rouleau to the fabric and work faggotting stitches.

Right side

3. Cut away the fabric from the wrong side of the garment and whip-stitch excess allowance in place.

Wrong side

Right side

Finished design with cut-away appliqué from right side of fabric

template for the appliqué design. The template in this case would be traced off the pattern, with the front and back pattern pieces pinned together, matching the shoulder seamlines. The outer edge of the design template will correspond to the neckline, minus the seam allowance.

ALTERING THE PATTERN FOR A FAGGOTTED ROULEAU INSET

Rouleau insets vary from edgings in that at least two edges are connected to the main body of the garment. They vary from appliqués in that they are less versatile in terms of shaping and that no fabric from the inset actually comes into contact with the main portion of the garment. Use rouleau insets to set in beautiful bands on the front of a blouse, a wide border on a vest or cardigan, or an entire faggotted rouleau panel on a dress or coat. Pattern alterations for rouleau insets should be made in tandem with or based on a design template, which in this instance doubles as the working template. The methods are as follows.

1   Trace the entire pattern piece onto pattern tracing paper. This will be your working template.

2   Determine the embellishment design, size, scale, and its exact location on the pattern. Draw, trace, or apply the full-scale design to the working template.

3   Using a straightedge, pencil in a line that runs flush with the outermost edge and parallel to the design. Repeat for all edges of the inset design.

4   Pencil in a second line parallel to the first and spaced approximately ¼ in. to ⅜ in. apart. The distance between these two lines allows for the faggotting stitches that will hold the design in place. Assess the line for consistency and effective placement on the pattern. When you're satisfied, redraw the outer lines in ink.

are applied directly to the surface of the garment rather than to a separate base fabric. However, where an appliqué design crosses seamlines—for example, a yoke that includes both the front and back necklines—it will be necessary to work with the pattern to create a

5 Label the inset, as well as the parts of the pattern to either side. Mark grainline on pattern pieces that surround the inset.

6 Cut apart the working/design template along the inked-in line. The portions of the template to either side of the inset are now your new pattern pieces for the un-embellished portion of the original pattern piece. Add seam allowances to the cut edge if you prefer to turn the edges under rather than bind them.

7 The inset portion of the template represents the area to be embellished and will be used to trace the rouleau design to your base fabric.

ALTERING THE PATTERN FOR ROULEAU CONSTRUCTION

When rouleau is used to make an entire garment, all seam allowances, facings, and hems are eliminated from the garment. However, since the entire edge of the garment will consist of a band of rouleau, a more accurate template is produced by including the seam allowance and by indicating the seamline. When the design is transferred to a base fabric, the inclusion of the seamline will visually aid in accurate placement of the rouleau.

For purposes of making a design template, the only other alteration may be creating a complete pattern piece for a back or sleeve that may normally have been cut on a fold.

TRANSFERRING THE DESIGN TO A BASE

Once the necessary alterations to your pattern have been made to accommodate your rouleau design, you are ready to transfer the outline of the design from the design template to a base fabric. If a working template was used and resulted in a separate pattern piece for an edging or inset, superimpose this pattern on the design template directly over the design for rouleau. Pin matching edges and seam allowances where they coincide. Trace around the pattern piece directly to the template.

When the rouleau design is traced off the template to the base, trace the new pattern line rather than the entire template. For insets, appliqués, and edgings, draw a ¾-in. to 1-in. margin around the entire design.

To trace directly to the fabric base, use a fine-point permanent-ink pen. The base fabric should have a crisp hand and be sheer enough that you can easily see the lines of your design template when it's placed beneath the cloth. Cotton organdy is ideal for this and is relatively inexpensive. Silk organza or cotton muslin are also fine (see the left drawing on the facing page).

Pattern tracing paper offers desired stability for small pieces but becomes cumbersome for a larger design and is subject to tearing. Also, it is difficult to reposition the rouleau without tearing the paper, while the cloth base is quite amenable to repositioning and to last-minute adjustments to the design.

Paper's advantage, however, is stability. Unlike fabric, it does not stretch and is not subject to distortion. If you are working on an elaborate design and are concerned about this factor, use interfacing or an iron-on stabilizer to back the base fabric. If you elect to do this, the stabilizer should be added after the design is drawn.

If you plan to use the tape method to apply rouleau to the design, place the rouleau right side up and work the faggotting stitches from the right side of the design (see the right drawing on p. 134). In this instance, the finished design will appear exactly as it does when attached to the fabric base.

If you plan to use the hand-basting method, however, this is not the case. The aesthetic advantage of hand basting is that the rouleau can be placed facedown on the fabric base so that the faggotting is worked from what will be the wrong side of the garment. Faggotting done from the wrong side of the garment produces a cleaner look. The point at which the needle enters the fabric remains discreet, and the rouleau strips appear to frame the stitched designs. Also, it is possible to fold and miter

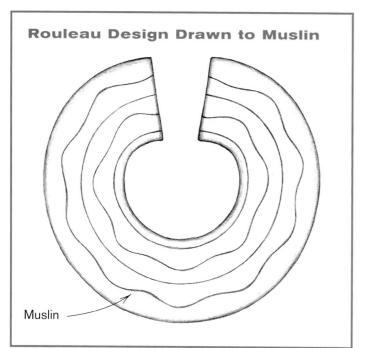

Rouleau Design Drawn to Muslin

Muslin

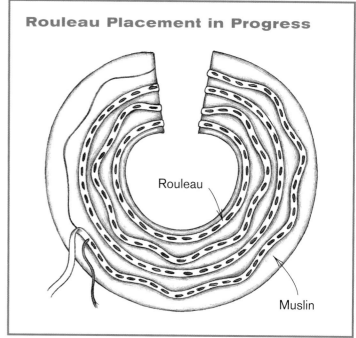

Rouleau Placement in Progress

Rouleau

Muslin

corners on the back side of the garment to produce what will be a point on the front and to accomplish the finishing stitches, such as tacking the rouleau at intersections and adding new strips to complete the design.

Unless you reverse the design prior to application, however, placing the design face-down will mirror, or reverse the direction, of the design. A simple way to correct this is to work from the design line that bleeds through to the wrong side of the base fabric. If you wish to do this, simply be sure that the ink from the marker bleeds through and is readily visible on the opposite side of the cloth when you trace the design. That way, you can simply flip the base fabric and work directly from this side.

Perhaps it has already occurred to you that if you have two front sections or sleeves that are essentially mirror images, it is not necessary to trace each side to a separate base. Assuming that you use the bleed-through method, so that the rouleau design is visible from both sides, one base will suffice. The rouleau will be applied to one side of the base to complete the right side of the garment and removed prior to working the opposite side of the garment, on the other side of the base. It

is a good idea in this case to label the base cloth clearly in advance so that you don't inadvertently end up with two right sides!

Placing rouleau strips to a base

The success of faggotted rouleau depends upon placing the rouleau so that it lies smooth and adheres firmly to the fabric base. This way, the shaped fabric strips remain stable while various stitches are used to secure them, preserving the integrity of the design.

The following methods include both traditional and time-saving techniques for applying rouleau strips to a fabric base. Likewise, methods for permanently joining the rouleau with lacelike stitchery allow for levels of treatment that range from simple to complex. Prior to placement, all rouleau strips must be sewn, turned, and pressed flat.

Hand basting the strips to the base with silk thread is the traditional placement method for faggotted rouleau. It provides ample adhesion, yet allows for some further shaping and redistribution of the fabric once the rouleau is attached to the base. It can also be pressed, which helps to "set" the shape of the trim. Its primary advantage, however, is that the basting in no way mars or alters the fabric. The rouleau can be applied facedown and worked to advantage from the back side of the embellishment. Once the faggotting is done, the basting is withdrawn, the stitching looks beautiful from the right side of the garment, and no trace of the method remains. Needless to say, if you are working a complex design or perhaps an entire garment, hand basting can be cumbersome and time-consuming—particularly in light of the handwork yet to be done when the basting is complete. Nevertheless, its advantages should not be overlooked.

An alternate method that is much quicker and, for most applications, satisfactory is to use ⅛-in. basting tape to tack the rouleau to the base temporarily. The tape is narrow enough that it allows for the flex of the curves, yet it holds the trim securely in place. It also has the advantage of being repositionable, so if the rouleau doesn't lie well around a particular corner, for example, it is feasible to take it up and rework its placement without any fuss.

It is preferable to adhere the tape to the wrong side of the rouleau and place it on the base fabric right side facing up. Using the tape in this manner avoids the possibility of the tape forming a slight residue on the right side of the garment. Since it requires working the faggotting from the right side of the garment, designs worked in this style should avoid loops and points, which tend to work best when there is full access to the back side of the design.

Although it is preferable to use the tape primarily for applications where the rouleau is placed right side up, it is possible to use the tape selectively on the right side of the rouleau. If you choose to use it in this manner, be sure to pretest the tape on your fabric and work up the design as quickly as possible once

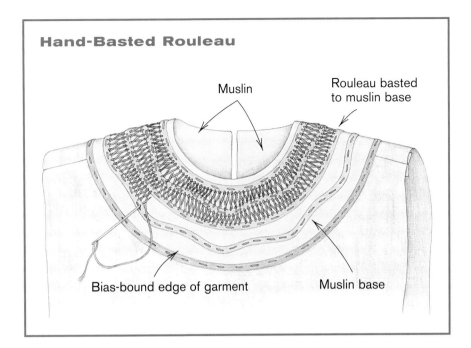

Hand-Basted Rouleau

Muslin

Rouleau basted to muslin base

Bias-bound edge of garment

Muslin base

the rouleau is attached to the base. Likewise, remove the fabric from the base and the tape from the surface of the rouleau immediately upon completion of the faggotting.

Regardless of how you elect to position the tape, under no condition should the rouleau be pressed while the tape is adhered to its surface.

HAND BASTING

Silk thread leaves no impression when pressed, so make the effort to use it for hand basting rouleau.

1 Select a lightweight silk basting thread that contrasts sharply with the rouleau and base fabric.

2 Place the bias rouleau facedown and baste it to the base fabric along the design line, stretching and molding it to the curves as you go. The rouleau will conform readily to most curves, but for especially intricate ones, it is possible to preshape the rouleau by working it into the desired loop or curve, then lightly pressing it before basting it to the design (see the drawing above).

3 The surface of the rouleau should remain flat, smooth, and retain the flow of the design. Bear in mind that, as long as it's not twisting or turned in upon itself, it will relax in the final pressing and will most likely appear to conform more precisely to the design.

4 Work a longer running stitch for straight or slightly curved lines and shorten the stitch as you shape the bias around curves. Aim to keep the width of the rouleau consistent.

5 To the extent possible, attempt to complete long passages with a single length of rouleau. When it is necessary to join two strips to complete a pass, do so at an inconspicuous point. Take small tacking stitches as necessary and whipstitch the ends in place, making sure that all raw edges will be hidden from view on the right side of the garment.

6 Where one strip of rouleau crosses another, simply baste the top strip directly to the one below. In addition to faggotting, tacking stitches are used to secure the rouleau at intersections, add on new lengths as the design requires, and ensure that fabric joins remain invisible from the right side of the garment.

7 To form points, as called for in the design, pinch the rouleau so that the tip of the point coincides with the design. A miter will form on the working side. Baste directly through the base of the miter, then continue basting along the design line. When all basting is complete, individual points can be worked with permanent stitches through the base of the miter, as well as one or two whipstitches to keep the point to one side.

8 After the entire design is basted to the base fabric, proof the lines. Although you can't make significant alterations without breaking the basting, it is possible to redistribute the rouleau to round out the edges, to smooth more fabric into narrow spots, and to firm up the basic line. If there are spots where the rouleau is really twisted or otherwise contorted in a way that will interfere with the design, break the basting and remove as many stitches as necessary to release the tension at this point. Smooth the rouleau back into proper position and rebaste, stitching beyond the break in the original basting.

9 After you've made corrections and are satisfied with the results, press the entire basted design. Press from the wrong side first, then flip the base over, and press the right side of the rouleau through the fabric base.

USING BASTING TAPE

Basting tape is quicker than hand basting, but it's harder to manipulate accurately.

1 Apply ⅛-in. basting tape to the wrong side of the rouleau strip.

2 Peel away the paper backing, approximately 12 in. to 15 in. at a time, and apply the rouleau to the base fabric following the design line.

3 Shape the rouleau as it's applied and keep it as uniform, smooth, and flat as possible.

4 Reposition the rouleau as necessary.

5 Where lines intersect, the tape will be caught between layers. It will need to be removed before tacking, which can be done after basting is complete or after the faggotting is complete.

6 Do *not* press the rouleau while the tape is adhered to fabric.

Stitching faggotted rouleau

Numerous faggotting and insertion stitches can be used to join the rouleau, but by no means is it necessary to entertain the possibility of using them all. The basic faggotting stitch alone is sufficient for an entire garment and works up quite rapidly once you've hit your stride. On the other hand, if simple rhythms are not your cup of tea, perhaps you'll enjoy exploring a few additional stitches here and there, introducing a sprinkling or profusion of beads, incorporating silk buttonhole rings into your design, and for the final indulgence, making your own frog closures or Chinese knot buttons from rouleau.

The drawings below illustrate a few of the basic stitches that you can incorporate into rouleau designs. To begin faggotting at any point in the design, bring the needle through the cloth on the back side of an intersection. Take a small backstitch to attach the intersecting layers of rouleau, bring the needle to the corner of the nearest open area, and begin to work the faggotting stitch across the open portion of the design.

Be sure to use a thread that is sufficiently strong and that resists shredding, knotting, and kinking when you sew. Linen, silk buttonhole twist, and crochet cotton are excellent choices. Select a color to match or contrast subtly with your fabric.

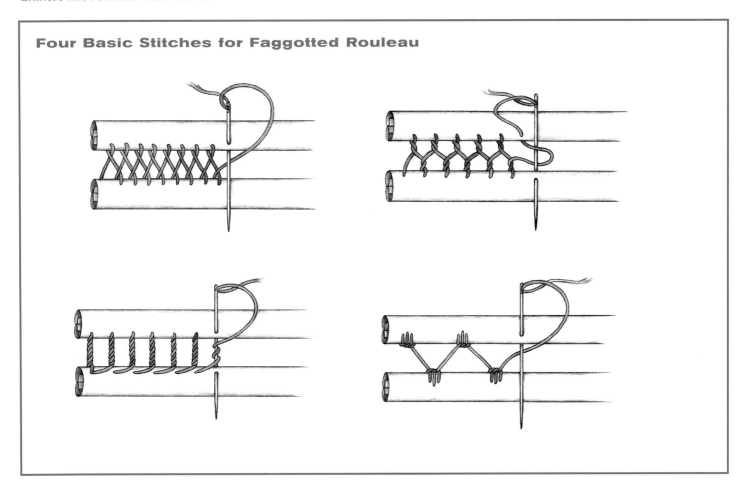

Four Basic Stitches for Faggotted Rouleau

Bindings and Pipings

For effects that range from delicate to dramatic, bindings and pipings are both practical and beautiful. Knowing when, why, and how to apply them will put new methods at your fingertips for making garments uniquely your own. Try a silk charmeuse binding on the collar and cuffs of a blouse; triple piping on a shawl-collared robe; the slim allure of a narrow French binding on silk chiffon. Details such as these take time but reward you with garments whose beauty and longevity often exceed your efforts.

Although you may tend to think of bindings and pipings first in terms of the visual impact they provide, learning to use them functionally is also rewarding and frees your creativity as well. The methods presented in this chapter unravel the mystery of achieving professional binding and piping results across a range of applications.

MATERIALS AND EQUIPMENT

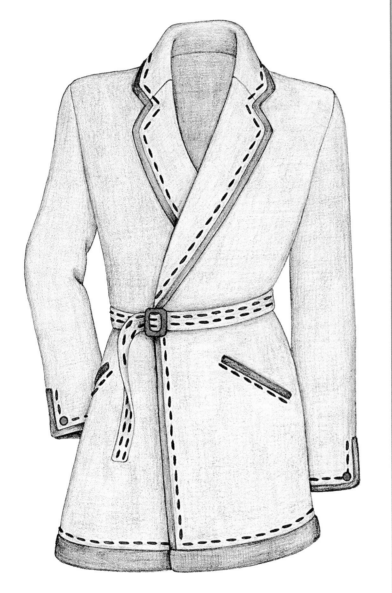

Jacket Embellished with Bindings

Bindings can provide effects that range from delicate to dramatic. The lines of this jacket are highlighted with bias bindings and topstitching details.

Exquisite bindings and pipings require just a few simple notions and basic sewing supplies. The emphasis in materials selection lies in creating elegant and eclectic fabric combinations to achieve the effect you desire.

Fabrics and alternatives

Not all fabrics are equal when it comes to suitability for bindings and pipings. The choice will be dictated by numerous considerations that include aesthetic as well as practical decisions. In addition to selecting a material according to its compatibility and effect relative to the fashion fabric and garment style, it is necessary to consider how that material will perform in terms of ease of use, added bulk, and in some cases, durability.

For bindings and pipings alike, the fabrics that tend to perform best are natural fiber fabrics with a smooth or lightly textured surface and an even, supple stretch on the bias. Crisp fabrics with body, such as linen, cotton, and silk dupioni, are generally easier to control, while slippery silks and rayons require greater time and care in handling. Fabrics with a twill weave structure, such as denim and wool gabardine, make durable bindings but have a tendency to twist out of shape more readily if care is not taken to straighten the grain initially and to cut the fabric strips on the true bias (see the sidebar on p. 148).

Knits are quite suitable for bindings and pose an economical advantage, since the strips are cut on the crosswise grain. Wool double knit, wool jersey, stretch velvets, and stretch Lycra of all kinds make suitable bindings for a variety of applications.

For lush or eclectic effects, look to silk charmeuse, velvet, silk metallics, silk chiffon, and cotton or silk tulle. Look as well to incorporate unusual plaids, stripes, and the wrong sides of double-faced self-fabric for eye-catching effects that are never overbearing.

Base your selection on aesthetic intuition, bearing in mind that bindings and pipings are often an open door for the creative use of bold colors and highly ornamental fabrics you may never elect to use for an entire garment.

Though fabric tends to dominate, it's by no means the only choice for bindings and pipings. In the way of bindings, custom and commercial foldover braids, ribbons, lace, twill tape, and petersham (or grosgrain) pose intriguing possibilities. Likewise, there's more than one way to pipe a seam, so if corded piping doesn't make you turn cartwheels, maybe commercial or custom cord-edge will.

Stabilizers

Fabrics that are especially prone to stretching, as well as lightweight fabrics and sheers, can be difficult to cut and sew on the bias and may benefit from starching. Regular spray starch will tame most fabrics considerably, but for extremely slippery silks and rayons, you may want to try a water-soluble stabilizer like Perfect Sew prior to cutting the bias and throughout its application. Perfect Sew can be applied directly to the fabric from which the binding is cut, as well as to the portion of the garment where the binding is to be applied, and removes completely upon washing. (Always test on a sample prior to using any water-soluble stabilizer. These stabilizers are not compatible with all fabrics; however, I have had excellent results with most silks.)

Cords for piping

Most sewers who use piping frequently develop strong preferences for particular types of filler cord. Plied or braided, suitable filler cords vary in density, flexibility, and resilience, all of which effect the character of the piping

---

Designing with Bindings and Pipings

Bindings and pipings are among the easiest embellishments to use effectively. My theory is that it's because their application is limited to the edge of the garment, with an emphasis on the seams. Not about motifs or endless decorative options, bindings and pipings are straightforward embellishments. Their success hinges upon workmanship, color selection, and placement of line.

Though bindings and pipings can be a focal point, they are frequently employed to highlight yet another embellishment or simply to emphasize the structure of the garment by drawing attention to or away from particular lines. Use them as well to create continuity, either by using a fabric for the binding or piping that appears elsewhere in the garment, or by introducing a color next to which disparate elements can abide.

---

when used as its core. Since a number of options are available, it's initially worthwhile to experiment with all of them so that you experience the properties and performance of each firsthand. From there, you can make an informed decision. If you couldn't be bothered, simply choose the type of cord that is most accessible and convenient, as all of the options that follow are perfectly suitable.

- Polyester cable cord is a soft, plied cord that comes in a complete range of sizes for pipings $\frac{1}{8}$ in. to $\frac{5}{8}$ in. wide. It is inexpensive, guaranteed shrink proof, and can be purchased at most fabric stores.

- An easy-to-find cord is 100% cotton Siene twine, available from hardware stores. This cord is basically household string. It has a firm twist and comes in sizes suitable for piping to $\frac{1}{8}$ in.

- Also favored for "baby" piping are #5 and #3 pearl cotton, crochet cotton, and cotton gimp, available from specialty needlework sewing-supply stores.

Commercial foldover braids, trims, and cord-edges are easy to use and expand the options available for bindings and pipings.

- Sash cord is a round sinnet cord or braid, so it is very firm and produces clean, well-defined piping. It can be purchased from most hardware stores and wherever drapery supplies are sold. Look for the preshrunk 100% cotton variety, which comes in several sizes suited to standard piping applications.

- Another firm cord favored by many sewers is rattail cord, which is a satin cord made from rayon. More expensive than most fillers, it comes in $\frac{1}{16}$-in. and $\frac{1}{8}$-in. widths and a wide range of colors. Rattail can be purchased at most fabric and craft stores.

Presser feet

The most versatile presser foot for piping is an adjustable zipper foot, which slides to the right or left of the needle and allows you to stitch as close to the piping as possible. A nonadjustable zipper foot, which relies on the needle positions of the machine for placement, can be used but is not as accurate for all applications. A generic version of the adjustable zipper foot is available and, along with a shank adapter, can be used on most machines.

Other presser feet that are useful for piping are those with a round groove on the bottom of the foot. These feet rely on the foot groove to hold the cord firmly in place and utilize the needle positions on the machine to fine-tune the distance of the stitch from the piping cord. The size of the piping cord must be comparable to the groove on the foot base, which limits the size of piping each of these feet can produce. Nevertheless, when you find a perfect match for a piping size that you use frequently, it makes both the production and application of piping a breeze! Feet that fall into this category include the corded appliqué foot, all of the pintuck feet, Bernina's bulky overlock foot, and the generic Pearls 'N Piping foot.

Presser feet and machine attachments that are useful for machine application of bias bindings include the $\frac{1}{4}$-in. foot, the edgestitch foot, the zipper foot, and bias binder attachments.

Some binder attachments are designed for prefold bias trims, while others perform a one-step binding from a flat-bias strip. Also, some binders accommodate multiple binding widths, while others are limited to one size—or size range as the case may be.

Bias-tape maker and rotary cutting guide

A bias-tape maker allows you to create your own prefold bias bindings from virtually any light- to medium-weight woven fabric. The flat bias is inserted into the tape maker, and the emerging end comes out folded. The folds are pressed in place as the tape maker is pulled in the opposite direction to expose new lengths of the folded trim. Tape makers are available for making $\frac{1}{4}$-in., $\frac{1}{2}$-in., $\frac{3}{4}$-in., 1-in., and 2-in. finished binding widths.

A bias-tape rotary cutting guide is a clear grid ruler that corresponds directly to the individual bias-tape makers listed above.

Markings on the guide indicate precise widths for cutting strips for the desired prefold binding.

Marking and cutting tools

For most applications, a rotary cutter and mat provide the quickest, cleanest cut for bias strips. If you use a mat and rotary cutter, however, the mat should be as wide as the length of bias being cut so that you don't have to readjust the position of the mat beneath the cloth.

A rotary cutter will often work fine, but if you're working with slippery fabrics, it is sometimes difficult to maintain the position of the cutting edge, and, as well, the fabric may slip, slide, or bunch with the pressure of the blade. In this instance, you may get better results by premarking the bias strips to be cut with Clo-chalk disappearing fabric chalk or a Chalkoner wheel, then cutting them with scissors. A pair with a microserrated edge will keep even the most slippery fabrics in place during cutting.

Duckbill appliqué scissors are extremely sharp and are the perfect solution for grading seams. Both the bent, raised handle and the scissors blades are parallel with the fabric's surface when in use. This feature maximizes comfort and control when cutting close to the surface of the cloth or when attempting to get beneath one layer of fabric and cuts without nicking the layer below. For grading, trimming, and clipping seams, use 5-in. tailor's points—also known as Craft Shears.

Whether you cut your bias strips with a rotary cutter or scissors, a long, clear grid ruler is a necessity. The longer the ruler, the better for cutting out long lengths of bias. I have one that is about 40 in. for cutting long lengths, and a 24-in. ruler for short lengths.

Altering a Pattern for a Binding

When a bound edge is used in place of a facing or hem, the seam allowance must be eliminated from the pattern. Rather than cutting the seam allowance away from the original pattern piece, I recommend tracing the original onto pattern tracing paper and eliminating the seam allowance on the copy. That way, if you care to make the pattern again, the original is still intact.

When you eliminate the seam allowance from a portion of the pattern, always make a notation of that change directly on the new pattern piece. I note the alteration in the pattern instructions as well, while my thought process is clearly locked into thinking through the ramifications of the planned embellishment. That way, I don't have to rethink the process when I sit down to sew.

Clockwise from upper left: long, clear grid ruler; Chalkoner, rotary cutter and mat; duckbill appliqué scissors; tailor's points; scissors; and bias tape makers in a variety of sizes.

BINDINGS

BINDINGS

MATERIALS LIST

Presser feet: Consult specific binding methods for proper presser-foot selection

Fabric for bias bindings or single or double-fold bias tape

Bias-tape maker (optional)

Rotary cutting guide (handy for use with bias-tape makers)

Long, clear grid ruler

Rotary cutter and mat or microserrated edge scissors

Clo-chalk or Chalk-oner wheel

Stabilizers: spray starch or water soluble (optional)

There's more beauty to bindings than meets the eye. By making these fully functional embellishments and learning how best to employ them, you'll see that even ordinary garments become special. Use bindings with confidence to eliminate show-through facings and maintain the transparency of sheer garments; to alleviate the problem of bulk when working with heavy fabrics; to bind the edge of double cloth so that both sides will show. Also use bindings to join a single layer collar to a neckline; to hold pleats in place; to accent a pocket or seam; to cord a narrow hem or to bind a scalloped one.

Basic bindings

Bindings are classified by both the number of layers that bind the edge of the cloth and the method by which the bindings are applied. A single binding consists of one layer of cloth, cut at least four times the finished width of the binding. A double binding—also referred to as a French binding—consists of two layers of cloth folded from a single fabric strip that is at least six times the finished width of the binding.

If the garment or the binding fabric are especially heavy, cutting widths for these bindings may need to be increased from this basic formula to provide the allowance necessary to wrap easily around the edge. It is possible to measure the thickness of the finished binding with calipers, which will give you a fairly accurate notion of how much extra to cut. In any case, the seam allowance for attaching the binding is always the same as the finished width.

Single and double bindings alike can be hand felled or machine sewn. A hand-felled binding is most often applied to the right side of the garment by machine and turned to the wrong side and whipstitched in place by hand. This produces a lovely finish in which no stitching is visible on the right side of the binding.

Bottom: Commercial foldover braid on wool coating. Top: silk satin binding from unfolded bias on silk jacquard, applied with binder attachment.

Tulle binding on silk chiffon and narrow French binding on silk satin.

HAND-FELLED SINGLE BINDING

A hand-felled single binding is suitable for all weights of fabric (see the top drawing below). The machine stitching is done from the right side of the garment, and the hand felling from the wrong side. If the material being bound is on the heavy side, accommodate the thickness of the fabric by cutting the strips that much wider. If the binding itself is thick, that may also impact the width of the strip, since the binding is folded back on itself. If you're in doubt about the width, pretest with a short length of binding prior to cutting out the entire length required. Here are the basic steps.

1   Measure and cut a bias strip the length of the seam plus 2 in. and four times the desired finished width of the binding.

2   Pin one edge of the binding to the garment, right sides together. Pin across rather than with the seamline.

3   Hand baste the binding, just inside the seamline (see the bottom drawing below). Although you don't have to do this, hand basting offers added control for placement of bias bindings and pipings prior to the actual stitching. Basting may seem cumbersome at first, but it tends to produce better bindings, particularly when the edge to be bound is shaped; when the material being worked frays easily; and when the binding or piping is a different weight and texture than the garment fabric.

4   Sew the seam by machine, binding face-up. The seam allowance is equal to the finished width of the binding.

5   Wrap the binding firmly around the raw edge. Turn it to the wrong side of the garment and match the seam allowance of the unfinished binding to the seamline as you baste it in place, stitching in the ditch from the right side of the garment. Or, pin the binding in place along the seamline.

6   Lightly press the binding from the right side of the garment and let set before handling.

7   Remove the basting and turn the raw edge of the binding under to create a fold even with the seamline. Pin in place.

8   Slipstitch the folded edge in place along the seamline.

HAND-FELLED DOUBLE BINDING

A hand-felled double binding is commonly used for reversible garments and is the mainstay for sheers. Like the hand-felled single binding, no stitches are visible on the finished binding on either side of the cloth. As a rule, double bindings are cut six times the desired finished width of the binding, but be just a

TIP

Never hurry a binding! It will show and may actually take more time in the long run. Instead, take time initially to ensure that the bias is cut correctly and that all subsequent steps are worked with care and precision. That way, your binding will be perfect the first time around.

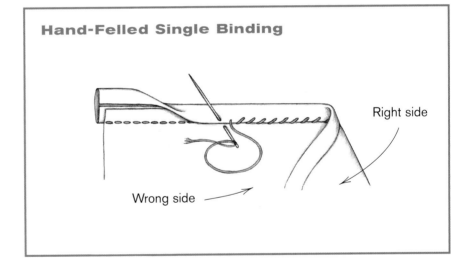

Hand-Felled Single Binding

Right side

Wrong side

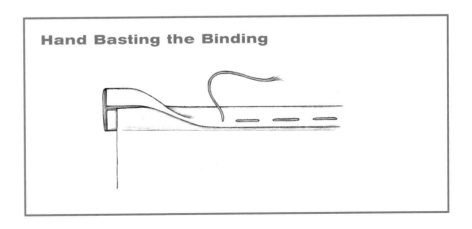

Hand Basting the Binding

little more generous if you're working with heavy cloth. Here are the steps.

1   Measure and cut a bias strip the length of the seam plus 2 in. and six times the desired finished width of the binding.

2   Fold the binding strip in half, wrong sides together, taking care not to stretch it. Lightly steam along the fold.

3   Pin the raw edge of the binding to the garment's edge, right sides together.

4   Hand baste inside the seamline, if desired.

5   Machine stitch along the seamline, binding faceup.

6   Bring the binding up and over the edge of the garment to the wrong side.

7   Pin in place, matching the folded edge of the binding with the seamline.

8   Steam and finger press along the seamline on the right side of the garment.

9   On the wrong side of the garment, slipstitch the binding in place.

NARROW FRENCH BINDING

Reserve the narrow French binding for necklines of silk chiffon, crepe-de-chine, georgette, and other lightweight, silky sheers. Practice making the binding as narrow and as smooth as possible. To make a narrow French binding, follow these steps.

1   Measure and cut a bias strip 1 in. wide and the length of the seam plus 2 in.

2   Fold the binding in half, wrong sides together, and press, taking care not to stretch the binding.

3   Pin the raw edges of the binding to the garment's edge, right sides together and across the seamline.

4   Hand baste the binding just inside the seamline.

5   Use the ¼-in. presser foot on the sewing machine. Sew the binding, stitching ¼ in. from the raw edge.

6   Trim the seam to a scant ⅛ in.

7   Wrap the folded edge of the binding firmly around the raw edge and baste or pin it in place.

8   Steam the binding from the right side of the garment and finger press near the seamlines.

9   On the wrong side of the garment, slipstitch the folded edge to the seamline.

IMITATION FRENCH BINDING

Like the traditional French binding, the imitation French binding is sewn in two steps but is finished by machine rather than by hand felling (see the drawings on the facing page). Also known as the stitch-in-the-ditch binding, the back side is longer than the front, which creates a fabric allowance that is caught when stitched from the right side of the garment. No stitching is visible on the binding itself because the stitching is done directly in the ditch of the seam—between the binding and the garment—which makes this the least conspicuous of the machine-stitched bindings.

The front and back of the binding must be unequal widths, so the back allowance extends no more than a scant ⅛ in. beyond the seamline and is caught when the binding is stitched.

This method can be used for single as well as double bindings. Either way, add on ⅛ in. to ¼ in. to the standard width measurement to allow for the extra width needed on the back side of the binding. For the least-conspicuous results on light- to medium-weight fabrics, use 60/2 cotton machine embroidery thread, and a 65/9 or 70/10 denim or Microtex sharp needle to stitch in the ditch on the front of the garment. Here are the steps.

1   If applying a double binding, fold the bias strip in half and press along the fold, taking care not to stretch the bias.

2   Match the raw edge of the binding to the edge to be bound, right sides together, and pin them in place.

3   Hand baste inside the seamline, if desired.

4   Machine stitch along the seamline, with the binding faceup and the seam allowance equal to the finished width of the binding.

5   Turn the binding up and wrap firmly around the raw edge. Turn it to the wrong side of the garment and baste in place so that the edge of the binding extends beyond the seamline. The double binding is now ready to be machine stitched from the right side of the garment (see step 9).

6   If applying a single binding, lightly press the binding from the right side of the garment and let set before handling.

7   Remove the basting and turn the raw edge of the binding under (on the wrong side of the garment) to create a fold that extends just beyond the seamline.

8   Baste the binding in place, working wrong side up. Double-check to see that the edge of the binding exceeds the seamline along the entire length to be bound.

9   Attach an edgestitch foot or adjustable zipper foot to the machine and sew on the right side of the garment, directly in the groove or ditch of the seam.

NARROW CORDED EDGE

The simple narrow corded edge is actually a facing that is corded along one edge and stitched under on the other. When sewn and turned, the covered cord extends from the edge of the garment to produce a piped effect (see the photo on p. 149). As a rule, the cord used is no larger than ⅛ in., which produces a delicate, yet distinct appearance. This

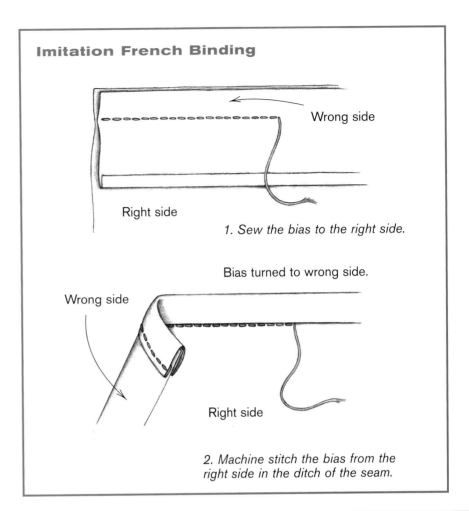

Imitation French Binding

Wrong side

Right side

1. Sew the bias to the right side.

Bias turned to wrong side.

Wrong side

Right side

2. Machine stitch the bias from the right side in the ditch of the seam.

finish is especially well suited to round or wide bateau necklines and is charming as well on a hem.

For an added touch, try whipstitching around the cord. Work one row from the front of the garment, stitching left to right; then flip the garment and work another left to right row from the back side, placing the stitches between those in the first row. The stitches will cross one another and, if worked closely together, will form a netlike effect over the cord. Experiment with other wrapping stitches as well. To make and apply this edge, follow these steps (see the drawings on p. 149).

1   Reduce the seam allowance on the garment to ¼ in. Do not cut it away!

Staystitching the garment edge prior to applying a binding strengthens the edge and makes it more resistant to stretching. Any edge can be staystitched in advance, though it is especially recommended for curves and diagonal lines.

TIP

Cutting Bias

If you wish to incorporate beautiful bindings and pipings in your sewing, make them yourself. The key to making pipings that neither twist nor turn and bindings that are smooth and flat lies in how you prepare the fabric before cutting.

Being sure that the fabric is properly straightened and "on grain" will help you make perfect bias bindings and pipings. (Fabric preparation is just as essential for making garments that fit, drape well, and maintain their appearance over time.) Prior to cutting bias strips from fabric, preshrink the fabric, then straighten the end, and check the grain alignment.

Straightening fabric along the crosswise grain is necessary to check the alignment of the grain. To straighten it, either clip the selvage and tear quickly and firmly, or pull a crosswise thread through the fabric and cut along the resulting line. Which method you use will depend upon the fabric: Fabrics with an even weave can generally be torn; fabrics where either the warp or weft is distinctly heavier should always be pulled and cut. Test by tearing a narrow strip off the crosswise end if there is any doubt about which method to use.

Realigning the grain is required if the length of fabric is off grain, or skewed. Though all fabrics are woven straight, it is not uncommon for the grain to be skewed in the manufacturing process when it is printed, finished, or rolled onto boards. To determine whether a fabric is on or off grain, fold the fabric lengthwise so that the sel-

Cutting on the true bias

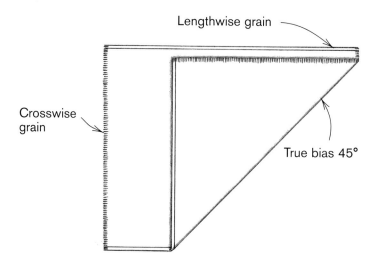

vages meet. The crosswise edges should align along the end, and the fabric should lie smooth along the lengthwise fold. If the edges don't match, or if the corners curve or fail to form a right angle (90°), the fabric grain must be realigned prior to cutting.

To realign the grain, dampen the fabric until the fibers are sufficiently relaxed, then stretch the fabric on the bias to pull the lengthwise and crosswise fibers back into right-angle formation. It may be helpful to do this with another person. Pull firmly and smoothly until the yardage is squared and the fabric folds into perfect right angles. When this is accomplished, allow the fabric to dry on a flat surface, then press prior to cutting. (In the case of fabrics that water spot, omit dampening the yardage.)

Once you've determined that the fabric is on grain, it is possible to cut a true bias (see the drawing

above). By definition, true bias is any diagonal line at a 45° angle to the lengthwise and crosswise grain. If you have a long, clear ruler with markings that include a 45° angle, it is possible to find the true bias by aligning the 45° line along the crosswise edge of the fabric and marking in the line or cutting directly with the rotary cutter.

Another method is to fold one corner of the cloth over so that the crosswise edge lies on top of the lengthwise selvage and that the lengthwise threads from the opposite selvage run parallel to the crosswise grain. Lightly press along the folded edge, then open the cloth, and, with chalk and a ruler, retrace along this line. All subsequent measurements will proceed from this point, using the clear ruler to measure the widths of the bias strips with ease.

2 Cut a bias strip 1½ in. wide and the length of the edge to be bound, plus 2 in.

3 Finish one edge with a serger or turn in a slim ⅛ in. (toward the wrong side of the fabric) and stitch along the edge.

4 To cord the opposite edge, wrap the bias around the cord at the top of the strip so that the distance between the raw edge and the cord is approximately ¼ in. Secure it with pins or use a glue stick.

5 With the raw edge faceup, insert the cord beneath the groove of a three- or five groove pintuck foot. Adjust the needle position to sew close to the cord and sew the length of the strip, maintaining an even distance from the folded edge to the raw edge.

6 To attach the corded facing to the garment, place the finished side of the strip faceup with the cord facing the garment. The raw edge that extends beyond the cord (on the underside of the strip) will face the raw edge of the garment. Align this edge and pin it in place.

7 Use a zipper or cording foot to sew the facing in place, stitching just outside the previous line of stitching, with the needle snug against the cord.

8 Press the facing allowance toward the back. The cord will extend beyond the seam.

TOPSTITCHED BINDING

The fastest way to bind an edge is to attach it to the garment in a single sewing operation. It is possible to do so, using single- or double-fold bias tape topstitched directly to the front of the garment, with or without the use of a binder attachment. The binder attachment simplifies and speeds up the process because it eliminates the need for pinning or basting and can be used with single- or double-fold bias tape (see the drawing on p. 150). Some binder attachments eliminate the need for prefolding

the bias strip, as well. This type of attachment folds and secures the binding as the flat-bias strip is fed through the binder.

Depending on the model, a binder may be limited to use with one width of prefold or flat binding only or have multiple slots that accommodate a wide range of widths and will sew both prefolded and flat bias. For specific details regarding its use, consult the instructions that accompany the binder attachment.

To bind an edge using double-fold bias tape without a binder attachment, follow these steps.

1 Cut and prepare the double-fold binding. This will be simplified with the aid of a bias-tape maker, which will create the first fold required for the double-fold tape. The proper widths to cut the flat bias for folding are indicated in the in-

In the center is a narrow corded edge from silk satin shown prior to application. The finished edge treatment was applied on paisley rayon jacquard.

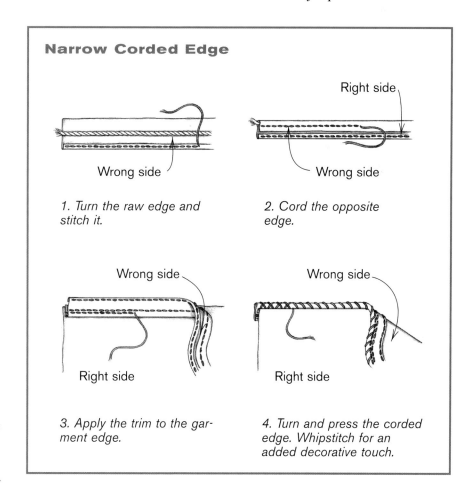

Narrow Corded Edge

1. Turn the raw edge and stitch it.

2. Cord the opposite edge.

3. Apply the trim to the garment edge.

4. Turn and press the corded edge. Whipstitch for an added decorative touch.

Machine-Sewn Binding with Binder Attachment

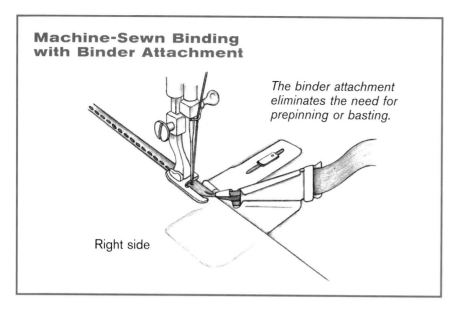

The binder attachment eliminates the need for prepinning or basting.

Right side

TIP

Bindings can be used to eliminate a gaping armhole or neckline by drawing the garment in so that it lies closer to the body. Use this to advantage when making V-neck cardigans and bias-bound vests of all kinds. Simply stretch the binding slightly when applying it to the edge and sew with the base fabric positioned beneath the binding, which allows you to use the motion of the feed dogs to ease the garment fabric in.

Using Continuous Bias

Continuous bias refers to a method of making long lengths of bias binding from a small amount of yardage. It is an economical way to produce bias because it yields a lot of length for the amount of cloth used.

The problem with continuous bias from an embellishment standpoint is that it produces a lot of seams. When the binding is applied, there is no way to control its placement. For that reason, I do not recommend continuous bias for bindings or piping on outer edges or seams. Use it only for binding seam allowances and hems of the inside edges of a garment and for bindings that are turned to the inside of the garment.

structions that come with the tool (or you can use the bias-tape rotary cutting guide).

2 A second fold is required to make the resulting single-fold tape suitable for a one-step binding: Fold the single-fold tape, wrong sides together, so that the width on the bottom exceeds the width on the top by a margin of a millimeter or so. (Increase the margin when binding to a heavy cloth, or to multiple layers.)

3 Press and lightly stretch the binding to eliminate any slack.

4 Preshape the double-fold binding directly to the garment edge to which it will be applied. If the binding is applied to an inward curve, such as a neckline, it will be necessary to ease the folded edge in and gently stretch the turned edges to the wider portion of the curve. If binding a collar, or scalloped edge, it will be the fold that is stretched, and the turned edges that need to be eased in.

5 Apply the double-fold bias tape to the garment, encasing the edge to be bound. The fold of the tape should be snug against the edge, and the wide portion of the tape must be on the wrong side of the garment.

6 Baste or pin through all layers to secure the tape.

7 Topstitch the binding in place using an edgestitch or zipper foot.

Joining bias strips

Bias strips must be joined when long lengths of binding are required for a garment and when they are used as a finishing technique on an enclosed edge, such as a neckline without a placket, a plain sleeve, or a hem.

As a rule, bias strips are joined on the straight grain of the fabric (which forms a diagonal line edge to edge on the bias). The easiest way to do this prior to application of the binding is to cut the ends of the two strips to be joined squarely across the bias. Place them right sides together at a right angle and mark the straight grain at a 45° angle. The line will cut diagonally across the corner. To the extent possible, patterns should be matched so that the joining seam remains as unobtrusive as possible. If you extend the top strip just a little beyond the bottom layer, it provides a little extra leverage when taking the first few stitches and sewing the strips together. Sew along the indicated stitching line using a short stitch length so that no back stitch is required. After the seam is sewn, press it open, then trim to a generous ⅛ in. If the binding is to be applied with a binder attachment, press the seam to one side, and each consecutive seam in the same direction, as this will keep the seam allowance from catching as it's fed through the binder.

On garments where the appearance of a seamless binding is desired, the length of the binding strips can be calculated in advance so that seams in the binding perfectly match the garment seams, in which case the adjoining strips are seamed together directly across the binding. For the most accurate results, it is best not to join the strips in advance but to join them when you near the seamline.

Joining the bias ends for hand-felled bindings can be done a number of ways (see the drawings below). One method is to measure the total circumference of the edge and to join the binding prior to attaching it to the seam.

A second method—which I prefer—is to calculate an additional inch for each end of the binding, which is initially left free when the binding is stitched to the garment. When the line of stitching reaches the point where it must join the other end, fold up one side of the garment out of the way. Then join the binding ends and stitch them at a right angle to one another on the straight grain of the fabric. Press the seam open, then align the edge of the binding—and stitch it—to the remainder of the garment's edge.
Yet another way to join a hand-felled binding is to lap it, with the ends of the binding

Joining Bias for Hand-Felled Bindings

Joining a two-step binding to match the seamline

Right side — Hand-felled neckline

Match seam.

Wrong side

A two-step binding can be joined across bias to match the seamline (suitable method for hand-felled and imitation French bindings).

Joining a two-step binding in continuous seam

Wrong side

45° angle

Right side

Excess binding

1. Join the binding ends on grain.

2. Stitch through the join.

Wrong side

Right side

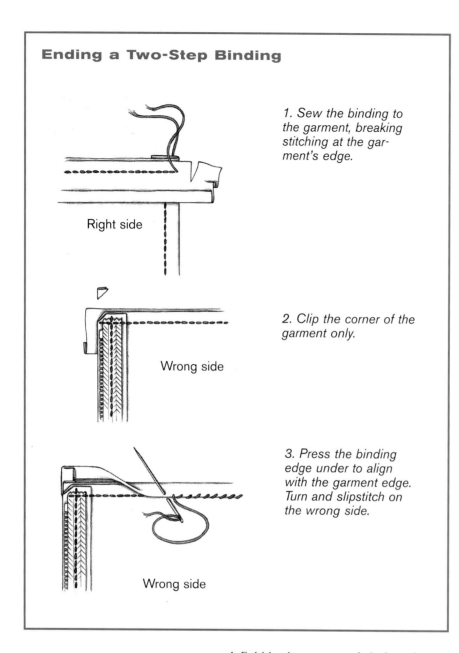

Ending a Two-Step Binding

Right side

1. Sew the binding to the garment, breaking stitching at the garment's edge.

Wrong side

2. Clip the corner of the garment only.

Wrong side

3. Press the binding edge under to align with the garment edge. Turn and slipstitch on the wrong side.

Topstitch the binding to the edge of the garment and turn under the end of the binding so that its edge coincides with the seamline and overlaps the beginning of the binding.

Ending bindings

To end a binding at a finished edge, including slit, placket, or zipper openings, the end of the binding must be turned under for a neat finish. Bindings are always applied after zippers are installed or facings are complete. On a two-step binding (sewn in two steps), turn the edge under after the binding has been stitched to the garment but before it is turned to the wrong side (see the drawings at left). Sew the binding clear to the edge of the garment, with a margin extending beyond the garment edge. Then trim the margin and fold it under to align with the edge. For a one-step binding (made with prefold tape or a binder attachment), simply fold the edges under prior to attaching the binding.

Binding corners

Binding a corner neatly requires mitering the corners on the front and back side of the binding. Mastering miters (45° cuts) on inward and outward corners is useful for binding square necklines, cuffs, and collar points.

This method is suitable for binding an outward corner with single and double bindings (other methods that relate to corners are included in the drawings on the facing page). Here are the basic steps.

1. On the wrong side of the garment, mark the point where the seams intersect.

2. For single and double bindings alike, press the flat binding strip in half, wrong sides together.

3. For the single binding, open the binding. Fold and press one edge of the binding to the center fold, wrong sides together.

squared. Fold back a margin of cloth at the beginning of the binding and align it with the seam allowance of the garment. Stitch on the binding and lap the end of the strip beyond the original starting point to meet the edge of the turned-back fold. If desired, the lap that occurs in the right side of the garment can then be slipstitched in place across the width of the bias.

A machine-stitched binding on an enclosed seam is joined with an overlap as well, but the procedure is different. If the joining is to coincide with a seam, the beginning of the binding overlaps the seam by approximately ½ in.

4   For double and single bindings, align the raw edge of the bias to the raw edge of the garment, right sides together and pin.

5   Find the point where the seam intersects on the back side of the garment and poke a pin directly through to the top side. Mark this point on the binding strip pinned to the front of the garment.

6   Stitch the binding to this point and stop. Secure it with a backstitch and remove the garment.

7   Fold the binding back on itself to create a 45° diagonal fold and align the raw edge of the binding along the unstitched side of the garment. The binding will form a straight fold along the adjacent edge and will match the 90° angle of the corner. Pin the binding in place.

8   Stitch along the pinned edge, beginning precisely at the upper edge.

9   Fold the binding to form a miter at the corner.

10   Slipstitch the binding in place on the wrong side of the garment, forming an opposing miter on the back side when you reach the corner.

11   When the felling is complete, stitch the miters invisibly in place.

Binding curves

In general, shallow curves—including shallow scallops—pose no more difficulty than straight edges and can be bound with ease using any of the hand- or machine-felled methods. When using topstitch methods, use shorter stitches to round the curves and, if necessary, alter the needle position farther to the right to keep it directly on the bias edge.

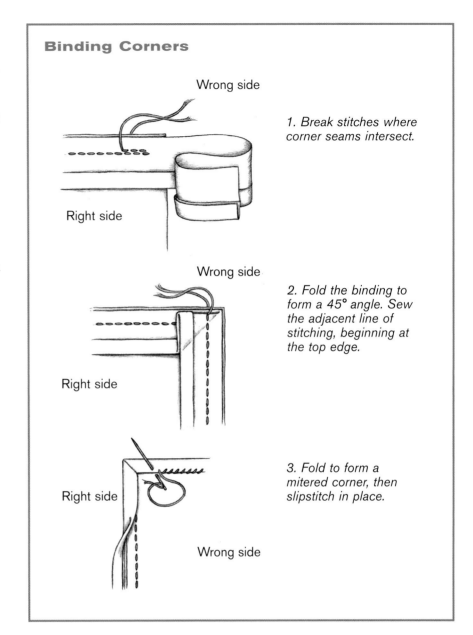

Binding Corners

Wrong side

Right side

1. Break stitches where corner seams intersect.

Wrong side

Right side

2. Fold the binding to form a 45° angle. Sew the adjacent line of stitching, beginning at the top edge.

Right side

Wrong side

3. Fold to form a mitered corner, then slipstitch in place.

The deeper the curve, the more the bias will need to be stretched along the fold and eased in along the open edge. For very deep curves, a closely worked running stitch along the edge can ease the fullness in. Staystitching the curved edge just inside the seamline prior to attaching the binding will help keep curved edges from stretching. If additional stability is required, use a lightweight tear-away stabilizer or interfacing as well.

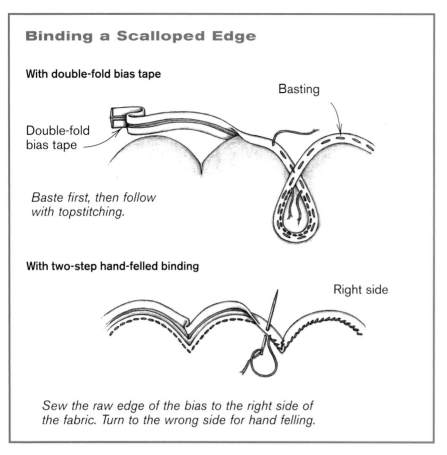

Binding a Scalloped Edge

With double-fold bias tape

Double-fold bias tape

Basting

Baste first, then follow with topstitching.

With two-step hand-felled binding

Right side

Sew the raw edge of the bias to the right side of the fabric. Turn to the wrong side for hand felling.

Binding scalloped edges

Deep, bound scallops can be beautiful hem accents, but they must be calculated for the exact bottom width of the garment. That way, the scallops will be identical in size and shape and meet neatly at the seamlines.

Once you have determined how deep and wide the scallops for your garment will be, make a full-scale plastic or cardboard template that consists of two or more scallops. Using the template as a guide, draw the outline of the scallops directly to the right side of the garment. The scallops can be bound using a two-step, hand-felled binding or with double-fold bias tape, which is hand basted, then top-stitched in place.

TWO-STEP HAND-FELLED BINDING

This method is done entirely by hand (see the bottom drawing at left).

1 Stitch the flat-bias tape directly to the line indicated for the scallops on the right side of the garment. Then cut the excess fabric away, following the stitching line. Alternately, the line drawn for the scallops can be staystitched and the scallops cut directly next to the stitching line. In this case, stitch the binding to the edge of the right side of the garment following the scalloped line.

2 Regardless of the order in which the binding is applied to the right side of the garment, it is felled on the wrong side. Turn the binding to the wrong side of the garment and turn the raw edge under. Hand baste or pin it in place and press the binding.

3 Slipstitch the turned edge of the wrong side of the garment. At the point of each scallop, there may be excess fabric, which should be caught with the needle and worked into a tiny pleat.

DOUBLE-FOLD BIAS TAPE

This is first basted by hand, then topstitched by machine (see the top drawing at left).

1 Slash between each scallop to the depth of the binding.

2 Baste the double-fold bias to the edge of the hem, drawing it up into the slashed portion of the scallop. Loop the binding under itself and encase the edge of the next scallop at the point of the slash. If necessary, an additional row of running stitches can be used to facilitate the turn of the loop.

3 Press in place, then topstitch along the edge of the binding.

Other Fabrics for Bindings

Once you understand and have mastered the basic techniques for bindings, try some or all of these unique variations in materials: velvet, petersham, lace/tulle, and leather or suede.

Velvet

Velvet bindings require special care and handling every step of the way. They are not exceptionally difficult but require patience and a bit more time than a regular single binding since they are best sewn entirely by hand. Use only silk thread for sewing, as it will not mar the velvet. For good results, cut out the bias for a single binding and modify the basic application as follows.

1. Sew the velvet binding by hand. Use a lightweight silk thread to match the garment for sewing and a small running stitch, with a short, intermittent backstitch to attach the flat bias to the garment.
2. Roll the allowance to the back side and loosely double baste the binding in place with a contrasting silk thread.
3. Pickstitch the binding from the wrong side of the garment. Catch the layer below but do not stitch through to the right side of the garment. Take tiny stitches that sink into the pile of the velvet. Because of velvet's pile, it is difficult to see the edge of the fabric. Move the stitching line in by a slim margin so that the stitches secure, rather than miss the binding.
4. Remove the double basting.

Petersham

Petersham is a type of grosgrain ribbon that is woven without a selvage. Widely used as a millinery ribbon, it's more flexible than standard grosgrain and richer in appearance as well. Petersham responds extremely well to curves when pre-shaped and steamed. It can be used as a foldover binding, but I prefer the effect of seaming and turning it to enclose the edge, in which case it is finished as a stitch-in-the-ditch-style binding.

Petersham is especially beautiful paired with tweedy wool and linens and is a nice binding for sturdy tapestry prints as well. Try it on pocket flaps and collars, vests, and suits. It's not as soft as some bindings, so use it where structure presides over drapability.

Lace/tulle

Fine silk or cotton tulle makes a lovely binding for sheer voiles, chiffon, and georgette. Try it alone or lightly baste a silk ribbon to the right side before turning the binding, and then encase the ribbon at the garment's edge.

Leather or suede

Leather and suede bindings can be sensational for elegant coats and sportswear and pair exceptionally well with wool, canvas, and velveteen. Cut these trims on the crosswise grain, as you would for knits, and sew them as a foldover or stitch-in-the-ditch binding. For best results, equip your machine with a Teflon foot to prevent the foot from sticking to the leather as you sew. Use a leather needle and a long staple polyester thread for sewing.

PIPINGS

Pipings add visual interest and definition, strengthen seams, and act as a stay prior to attaching the facing to a garment. They also lend polish to points and corners and smooth the transition between light- and heavy-weight fabrics.

Like bindings, pipings are decorative edge and seam treatments (see the photo above). But while a binding encloses an edge or seam, piping is inserted between seams or, in some cases, beneath one seam turned under. Used primarily to add visual interest and definition, piping also strengthens seams and acts as a stay prior to attaching the facing to a garment. It also lends polish to points and corners and smooths the transition between light- and heavy-weight fabrics—hence its popular presence in the application of linings.

From the delicate charm of baby piping on a collar, to the regal effect of double piping on a kimono band or cuff, mastering the basics of piping will put yet another embellishment mainstay at your creative disposal.

Piping can be flat or corded. Flat piping is softer and more flexible, while corded piping adds body and—in the case of thicker pipings—a degree of stiffness just outside the seam. Although flat and corded pipings can be used interchangeably, they are generally treated somewhat differently. Flat piping tends to be used as a transitional element between seams while thick, corded piping is most commonly used as an edge treatment. This makes sense, since it takes into account not only the visual effect of the embellishment but also the way it functionally alters the seam.

In addition to choosing between flat and corded pipings, practical considerations must attend to the added bulk of the piping. As a rule, the material used for the piping should be no heavier than the cloth used to make the garment. Light- to medium-weight garment fabric generally works well with piping of the same weight. Heavier fabrics often call for lighter piping materials, however, to reduce the bulk of the piped seam.

Preparing fabric for piping

The fabric strips for piping can be cut on the straight or bias grain, but piping made on the straight grain can be used only on straight seams. Fabric strips for flat and corded bias piping are cut in the same manner as for bindings, with attention accorded to the proper alignment of the grain so that the piping lies smooth and rounds curves and corners gracefully. Pipings made from knits are cut on the crosswise grain.

Flat piping is formed by simply folding the bias strip in half, wrong sides together, and basting just inside the seamline or attaching it directly to the seam to which it's being sewn. Preparations for corded piping include sewing the cord between the folded layers of the fabric so that the piping is fully assembled prior to sewing it to the seam.

CALCULATING THE STRIP WIDTH FOR FLAT AND CORDED PIPING

Flat piping is cut two times the width of the seam allowance, plus two times the desired width of the piping. For a narrow ⅛-in. piping, the strip width would be 1½ in. Its folded width would be ¾ in., and sewing the piping strip with a ⅝-in. seam would leave ⅛ in. of exposed piping.

To determine how wide to cut the strips for corded piping, you must first select the piping fabric and filler cord. The width to cut the strip will be equal to two times the seam allowance plus the width of fabric it takes to cover the cord. To find this distance, fold over the corner of the straightened fabric, just enough to cover a small length of the cord. The fold should be at a 45° angle to the selvage. Wrap and pin the fabric firmly around the cord; then measure and mark the fabric ⅝ in. away from the cord. Cut through both layers of fabric along this line. The width of the cut-away triangle is the width to cut the strips for the cord.

A less conventional approach that results in a perfect seam allowance of any desired width is to measure the required width, as directed above, then add ½ in. to ¾ in. to the cutting measurement for the covering strips. After the cording has been covered, cut a cardboard template 12 in. long and as wide as the seam allowance. To trim the excess seam allowance away from the corded piping, match one long edge of the template to the inside edge of covered cord, just outside the line of stitching. The fabric that extends beyond the opposite edge of the template is the excess: Trim directly with a rotary cutter along the edge of the template or mark in the line with a Chalkoner wheel and cut the excess away with scissors.

COVERING THE CORD

Covered cord for piping can be hand basted or stitched quite rapidly by machine. Some sewers like hand basting because it isn't as stiff and can be easily removed once the piping has been attached to the seam (see the drawings at left). But for most applications, I prefer covering the cord by machine. Machine-covered cord can be made using a zipper or cording foot. An adjustable zipper foot can be used to sew just about any size piping while cording feet are limited by the size of the groove on the underside of the foot.

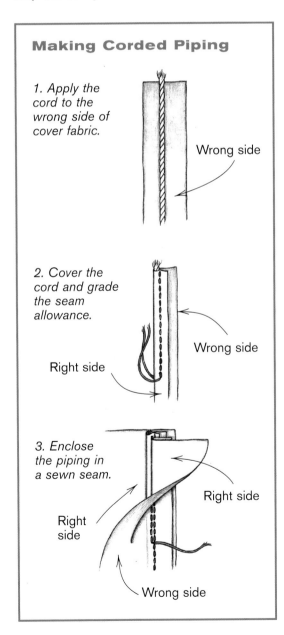

Making Corded Piping

1. Apply the cord to the wrong side of cover fabric.

Wrong side

2. Cover the cord and grade the seam allowance.

Right side

Wrong side

3. Enclose the piping in a sewn seam.

Right side

Right side

Wrong side

Covering the cord with a zipper foot

1   Wrap the bias strip around the cord, wrong sides together. Pin the edges together at a right angle to the length of the cord, matching the edges of the fabric strip.

2   Lengthen the straight-stitch setting to 3.5mm to 4 mm, depending on the thickness of the binding material. (Use a longer stitch for heavier fabrics.)

3   With the cord placed to the right of the needle and the zipper foot riding on top of the seam allowance, stitch next to the cord. Although the cord should be secure, this first row of stitching should not snug up tightly against the cord.

Covering the cord with a cording foot

1   Wrap the bias around the cord, wrong sides together, matching the raw edges. With the folded (corded) edge positioned to the right, pin the left facing seam allowance together.

2   Place the covered cord beneath the presser foot so that the groove of the foot rides on top of the covered cord. (The size of the groove on the underside of the foot and the size of the filler cord used for the piping must correlate. The cord should basically fill and lie securely in the groove but must not exceed it in diameter.) The fold may need to be placed to the left or the right, depending on the foot.

3   Try various needle positions to determine which ones will stitch the desired distance from the cord. The needle position will vary with the cord size, as well as with the placement of the groove beneath the foot. The more needle positions you have at your disposal, the better, as they will allow for consecutive stitchings that allow you to get closer to the cord when you stitch the final seam.

Sewing the piping

Regardless of the size of the piping, the basic method of application remains the same. To ensure that the stitching used to attach the piping remains discreet, keep in mind that each consecutive row of stitching must be worked closer to the cording. This can be done by adjusting the position of the zipper foot (on an adjustable zipper foot), or by changing needle positions on a stationary zipper foot or cording foot. If you use a contrasting thread in the needle and bobbin when you attach the piping to the garment, it will make it easier on the next pass to see—and stay within—that line. Prior to sewing the actual seam, however, switch back to a thread that matches your garment.

To enclose piping in a seam, follow these steps.

1   Align the raw edge of piping to the raw edge of the garment. Hand baste or pin it in place.

2   With the needle to the left side of the zipper foot, stitch the piping in place along the seamline so that the row of stitching lies to the left of the previous row used to cord the piping.

3   Baste or pin the facing to the main garment piece, right sides together, with the garment piece positioned on top. That way, the row of stitching used to attach the piping will be visible.

4   Using the visible stitching as a guide, sew through all layers. Snug the needle up to the piping, keeping the stitching to the left of the visible row so that no stitching will show when the seam is turned.

5   Press and grade the seam.

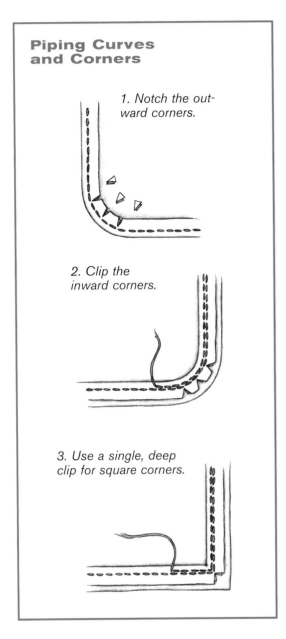

Piping Curves and Corners

1. Notch the outward corners.

2. Clip the inward corners.

3. Use a single, deep clip for square corners.

REMOVING BULK

To reduce bulk at the point where the corded portion of the piping is inserted back into a seam, remove the filler cord at the point where it intersects the seamline. To remove the cord, pull the cord out and away from the fabric cover using tweezers. Cut the cord away and smooth the fabric back into place, then enclose the end of the piping in the seam.

Baby piping adds delicate charm. The baby piping here is on silk jacquard and has a contrasting band cut from the opposite side of the fashion fabric.

PIPING CURVES AND CORNERS

To apply piping to curves and corners, clip the fabric so that the seam allowance can turn the corner (see the drawings above). For a curve, clip about ¼ in. to ⅜ in. along the entire portion of the curve. For a corner, make one clip directly where the piping turns the corner, cutting almost to the stitching line of the cording.

In addition to clipping, it will be helpful to shorten the stitch length while rounding corners and curves alike.

Piping variations

The following piping variations are applied like any standard piping. They vary in effect, in materials used, and in the way they are constructed.

BABY PIPING

This miniature piping is generally about ¹⁄₁₆ in. to just under ⅛ in. wide. Delicate piping like this is most frequently used to highlight seams or accent edges (see the photo above). It is also used as a transitional element between fabrics of different weights, colors, and textures. Baby piping can be made corded or flat. Sew the flat piping with a standard presser foot. To make the baby piping, try the pintuck or corded appliqué foot.

DOUBLE AND TRIPLE PIPING

Double and triple piping are truly elegant embellishments. Reserve these techniques for styles and fabrics that can carry them off and deserve that little bit of extra effort. As you'll see, multiple rows of piping are not difficult to make or use, but it does take at least twice as long as single piping to prepare.

Keep in mind that two and maybe three layers of piping will produce added bulk and body in and at the edge of the seam. To reduce the stiffness, use the softer cable cord for the filler, and to the extent possible, close-grade the seams. I recommend making a sample that includes all the materials you plan to sew with so that you can determine the appropriateness of the materials chosen and fine-tune your piping technique.

In terms of basic preparations of cutting the fabric and covering the cord, the only deviation from the norm is that it may be necessary to cut the covering cord different widths, depending upon the size of cord you use, and whether you make double or triple piping. The potential problem with using the standard $5/8$-in. seam allowance for all three rows is that—at the outermost piped edge—the seam allowance may not be sufficiently wide to make it into the seamline. This is more likely to happen with triple than with double piping, but the size fill cord used will also impact results.

To compensate for the additional rows of piping, add an allowance to the initial row of piping and to the second as well, if needed. How much wider to cut the strips will depend on the size fill cord used, but for triple piping using $3/16$-in. fill cord, I usually add at least another $5/8$ in., since with the standard allowance, the raw edge of the outermost piping just barely reaches the seam. Apart from that, the piping is covered in the usual manner (see p. 157). Each row of piping is covered separately, then the piping is assembled and stitched to the garment as one trim.

For double piping, snug one row of finished piping up against the other (see the drawing on the facing page). Stitch the layers together, with the needle positioned closer to the cord than the previous row of stitching (visible on the inner row of piping). Add a third row of piping, if desired, and stitch it to the second, again keeping the needle as close to the cord as possible.

How Much Binding or Piping Do You Need?

To calculate the amount of finished binding or piping for your project, use a flexible tape measure. Write down the length of each edge and seam that you plan to bind or pipe. Add 2½ in. to each measurement for seam allowances and to give yourself some leeway. The resulting figures indicate how many pieces you will need to cut and what their lengths should be.

I prefer to use individual strips rather than continuous bias, so my calculations generally end here. I buy enough extra yardage to produce the longest bias strip I will need. For some applications, it may be necessary to piece the longest strip, as would be required for a shawl collar jacket, for example. In that case, I would measure the entire distance around the edge, beginning at the side seam, measuring up the center front and around the collar; down the opposite front, around the side seam and back; returning to the point of origin. I would construct the bias for this edge in three pieces, joined at the side-seam hem of the garment and at the center back collar. Bias strips should always be joined on the lengthwise, crosswise, or diagonal grain of the fabric. For a pieced binding seam to align with other garment seams, it must be joined across the width of the bias on the diagonal grain.

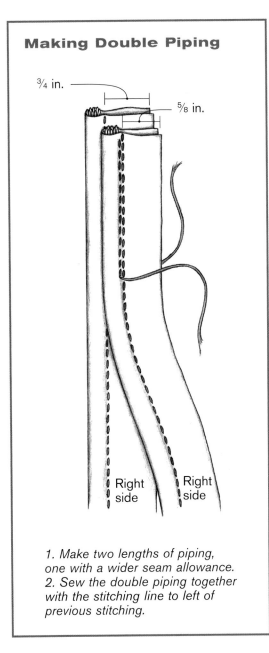

Making Double Piping

¾ in.

⅝ in.

Right side

Right side

1. Make two lengths of piping, one with a wider seam allowance.
2. Sew the double piping together with the stitching line to left of previous stitching.

CHUNKY PIPING

It takes the right garment style and fabric to pull this one off, but chunky piping can be sensational. Use it for fluid unlined jacket styles made from crinkled wools and rayons, and boucles, which will benefit from the piping's additional texture, body, and weight. If you use it in a more structured garment or pair it with a heavy fabric, consider using a light-weight covering fabric to keep the piping

itself soft and fluid, rather than stiff. I recommend ½-in. to ¾-in. cable cord for the fill. Be sure to remove the excess bulk of the cord prior to tucking it into the seam allowance.

CUSTOM CORD-EDGE

Cord-edge is a cord or braid attached to a tape for inserting into a seam. A variety of commercial cord-edges are available, and they can be used interchangeably with piping. You can make your own custom cord-edge, as well, by attaching commercial cords—or those you've made yourself—to a strip of flat or folded bias trim.

Attach the round trim to the fabric with a blind-hem or vari-overlock stitch. Use invisible nylon in the needle. Any of the large-grooved presser feet used for piping are suitable (the braiding foot is also a good choice). If the bias strip is folded in half, the edgestitch foot can also be used.

Adjust the stitch width to 1mm so that the stitch remains small and inconspicuous, and the bite of the zigzag just catches the cord. Adjust the stitch width and length as necessary if the zigzag foot doesn't catch the cord. Use the foot to guide the trim and adjust the needle position so the straight stitches are right alongside the cord. When the stitching is complete, you can roll the braid directly on top of the stitching line to conceal the stitching.

EMBELLISHED PIPING

Piping can be embellished before or after it is applied to the garment. Whipstitching around the covered cord of the piping is fast and simple and adds a welcome decorative touch. Work up a few samples using this method and see what you think. Flat braids and narrow ribbons work especially well, including flexible braid, Kreinik ¹⁄₁₆-in. and ⅛-in. metallic ribbons, and silk ribbon.

DECORATIVE THREADS

Thread	Characteristics/Applications	Brand Names
Machine Embroidery 100% Rayon	Delicate thread imparts rich color and glossy sheen. Subject to fading and wear over time. Fiber is weakened with exposure to water; sensitive to hot iron temperatures. Use in the needle for decorative applications, including machine embroidery, decorative stitches, decorative bobbinwork, satin stitch cording, topstitching, and channel-stitching. Threads can be doubled up in the needle for additional impact. Available in wide range of solid and variegated colors.	Sulky 30, 40 wt. Madiera 40 wt. Coats & Clark Mez Alcazar & Color Twist Finishing Touch 30 wt. Natesh 50 wt.
Machine Embroidery 100% Cotton	Imparts rich color and matte sheen for distinct embroidery designs. Stronger than rayon thread; greater resistance to wear due to abrasion, repeated washing, and heat. Available in a variety of weights and a broad selection of colors. Use for same range of applications as rayon embroidery thread.	Mettler 30, 60 wt. Madiera Cotona 30, 50, 80 wt. DMC Broder Machine Tanne 30, 50, 80 wt. Cotty Tanne 12 to 20 wt.

Machine Embroidery 100% Silk	Stronger and more elastic than cotton or rayon, it produces a rich, lustrous sheen that retains its strength and beauty over time. More expensive than cotton or rayon. Use for machine and hand basting, buttonholes, and same range of applications as rayon and cotton machine-embroidery threads.	Tire Silk 100 wt., 2 ply
		Tire Machine Twist 50 wt.
		YLI 1000 denier silk
		   sewing thread
		YLI Kanagawa Silk
		   Sewing Thread 50 wt.

Machine Embroidery 100% Acrylic	High-sheen acrylic thread resembles rayon embroidery thread. It is stronger and more durable but not as lustrous sewn out. Use for projects where color and high gloss are desired, and durability is a prime consideration.	Janome YLI Ultra Sheen

Metallic	Shiny, light-reflective thread. Use for machine embroidery, rolled hem edges, and decorative stitches. Lightweight metallics are not recommended for topstitching, since it appears insubstantial. Frays, breaks, and balls up more readily than most threads, so use special embroidery or metallic needle. Heavy metallics are not for use in the needle but can be couched or used in the bobbin.	Sulky Metallic
		   Kanagawa
		   Madiera Supertwist
		   Madiera Metallic #40,
		   #50
		   DMC Metallic
		   Mettler Metallic
		   YLI Fine Metallic

Tinsel/Mylar	Flat, metallized polyester thread adds brilliant, highly reflective sheen that glimmers and sparkles when sewn in. Flat filament reduces fraying and breakage associated with metallic threads.	Sulky Sliver Stream Lame Tinsel Prizm Hologram (Madiera Jewel)
Decorative Serger	Thicker and more textured than machine-embroidery threads in 100% rayon and metallic blends. Use for straight and decorative stitches in the bobbin.	YLI Candlelight Madiera Glamour Madiera Decor 6 Ribbon Floss

162

For Decorative Use in Needle	For Decorative Use in Bobbin	For Handwork	Compatible Needle Choices (correspond to thread used in needle)
YES Fine cotton or synthetic thread in bobbin	NO	NO	Embroidery 40-wt. thread 75/11; 30-wt. thread 90/14 Topstitch (N) 80/12 to 90/14 Twin embroidery 2.0/75 to 3.0/75 3.0 Drilling/triple
YES Fine cotton thread in bobbin	NO YES Embroidery thread in needle	NO YES	Embroidery 75/11 to 90/14 Topstitch 80/12 to 90/14 Twin embroidery 2.0/75 to 3.0/75 3.0 Drilling/triple Topstitch 90/14 Denim or universal 100/16 to 110/18
YES Fine cotton, silk, or synthetic thread in bobbin	NO	Pickstitch Running stitch with threads doubled	Embroidery 75/11 to 90/14 Topstitch 80/12 to 90/14 Denim 70/10 to 90/14 Twin embroidery 2.0/75 to 3.0/75 3.0 Drilling/triple
YES Polyester or fine synthetic thread in bobbin	NO	NO	Embroidery 75/11 to 9014 Topstitch 90/14 Twin embroidery 2.0/75 to 3.0/75
YES Fine synthetic thread in bobbin	NO	NO	Metafil 80/12 Metallica 80/12 Metallica twin
YES Fine synthetic thread in bobbin	NO	NO	Embroidery 75/11 to 90/14 Metafil 80/12 Metallica 80/12 Universal 80/12 Metallica twin
NO	YES Invisible, metallic or machine-embroidery thread in needle	Experiment	Select needle according to application and thread used in needle.

Thread	Characteristics/Applications	Brand Names
Specialty Needlepoint/Knitting Yarns	Produce rich color and textural effects when used for decorative bobbinwork or hand stitches. Kreinik braid and ribbon is available in a wide assortment of lush metallic colors. Other needlework threads in rayon, silk, cotton, wool, and blends are also suitable. Keep an open mind and experiment. Any thread/yarn is a candidate!	Kreinik #8, #16 Braid 1/16-in. ribbon Rainbow Gallery: Patina, Gold Rush, Pebbly Pearl Broider Wul DMC Medeci, Flower Thread, and Pearl Cotton Caron Collection Threads Edmar Rayon Threads Madiera Metallics #3, #5, #6, #8, #10 Sashiko Thread 20/4, 14/6
Polyester Topstitch/Buttonhole Twist	Use for high-impact topstitching on casual wear. Extremely strong, durable. Can be difficult to sew. Combine with regular weight polyester in bobbin.	Cordonnet 30 wt. (Mettler) Gutterman Coats & Clark YLI Jeanstitch
100% Silk Topstitch/Buttonhole Twist	The thread of choice for decorative machine topstitching and handworked stitches. Has high twist and elegant sheen. User-friendly for hand sewing; reduce needle tension for machine sewing. Fewer yards are on a spool—be sure to estimate yardage for project and buy accordingly, as dye lots can change.	Tire Line Twist 30 wt., 3 ply Gutermann Silk Topstitch Tire Buttonhole Silk 8 wt., 3 ply YLI Kanagawa Silk Stitch Trebizond Zwicky
Pearl Cotton/Rayon	High-luster plied thread. Rayon is springy; cotton is soft. Lightweight cotton can be used in the needle. Reserve heavier-weight cotton and rayon thread for the bobbin.	DMC Anchor YLI Pearl Crown Rayon
Lightweight Bobbin Threads	Substantially lighter than standard sewing thread, these threads are used in the bobbin to promote quality stitch formation when a decorative thread is used in the needle. Promote proper stitch formation and prevent thread buildup and needle jams. Cotton is available in many colors; others are limited to white and black. Prewound bobbin spools are available but aren't compatible with all machines.	Madiera Bobbinfil 60-wt. cotton Sulky Bobbin Thread YLI Lingerie & Bobbin Thread Sew Bob (Convenient prewound bobbins also available from some manufacturers)
Invisible Nylon Threads	Available in smoke and clear, these soft, transparent threads are for use wherever invisible stitching is desired.	Sulky Premier Invisible YLI Invisible Wonder Thread Coats Monofilament

Notes

1. Brand names listed indicate quality products that have been used successfully by the author for the techniques featured in this book. Most are available from mail-order sources listed on p. 168. This list is not conclusive. Comparable products with different brand names may also produce satisfactory results.

2. Needle choices listed indicate a range of possible selections for good results. Testing is always recommended, since results will vary with different combinations of thread, fabric, and interfacing. For best results, test with the exact combination of materials you intend to use.

For Decorative Use in Needle	For Decorative Use in Bobbin	For Handwork	Compatible Needle Choices (choices correspond to thread used in needle)
NO	YES Machine-embroidery, invisible nylon, or metallic thread in needle	YES	Select needle according to application and thread used in needle.
YES Polyester thread in bobbin	YES Polyester thread in needle	NO	Topstitch 90/14 to 110/18 Denim 100/16 to 110/18 Universal 100/16 to 120/19 Microtex sharp 100/16
YES 50- or 30-wt. silk 60- to 50-wt. cotton thread in bobbin	NO YES Metallic, invisible, or embroidery thread in bobbin	YES	Embroidery 90/14 Microtex sharp 90/14 to 100/16 Topstitch 90/14 to 110/18 Twin denim or universal 4.0/100 Denim 100/16 to 110/18 Universal 100/16 -120/19
YES #16, #12, #8 cotton 60-wt. cotton thread in bobbin	YES Machine-embroidery thread in needle	YES	Topstitch 90/14 to 110/18 Denim 100/16 to 110/18 Embroidery 90/14
NO	NO	NO	Select needle according to application and thread used in needle.
YES	YES	NO	Universal 70/10 to 80/12

APPENDICES

Appendix A

Transferring Designs to Fabric

Various methods are used to transfer designs to fabric. Each has its strengths and limitations. Which method to use will depend on a number of considerations, including the compatibility of care requirements for the fabric with removal methods for the transfer medium; the color, texture, and hand of the fabric; the type of embellishment to be applied; and the extent of the design.

Designs can be transferred directly to the right side of the fashion fabric or to an intermediary stabilizer basted in place. Some transfer mediums produce a permanent mark, and others are temporary. These are the fundamental divisions among methods and materials.

DRAWING ON THE RIGHT SIDE OF THE FABRIC

Designs can be traced or drawn freehand directly to the surface of the garment, using permanent-ink pens, dressmakers chalk pencils, or water- or air-soluble fabric markers. As with any of the direct methods, it is also possible to transfer the design to the wrong side of the garment, and thread trace along the design line, so the design is visible from the front, if removal of the transfer line is at all questionable.

Tracing an image directly through fabric is easier if the paper with the image is pinned or basted to the fabric with double-sided tape. A light table or some other light source behind the image and the fabric will make the design easier to read and transfer. The light table is also useful for reversing directional or asymmetrical designs that need to be mirror-imaged on the garment.

USING IRON-ON TRANSFER PENS

Iron-on transfer pens produce a permanent design transfer. Trace the design to paper using the transfer pen. Then iron it facedown to the right side of the fabric. The heat of the iron results in a direct transfer of the design. If the image is directional, trace it in reverse so that it will appear the way you intend for your design. Once ironed, you cannot alter the position of the transfer. For this reason, placement of the design must be absolutely accurate and precise. The advantage of this method is that the lines of the transfer are easy to read and remain distinct throughout the process of working the design. Because the transfer ink cannot be removed from the fabric, however, the embellishment must completely cover the design line.

USING TRANSFER FABRIC

This method is fast, easy, and accurate. Pin the design beneath the transfer fabric (silk organdy, crinoline, or net) and trace directly using an air-soluble,

water-soluble, or permanent-ink fabric marker. Then place the transfer fabric on the garment fabric and retrace to transfer the design through the cloth.

I favor the smooth, strong line that can be acquired using silk organdy, which I use to trace and transfer routinely. By tracing and transferring the design with an air- or water-soluble marker that removes from the cloth with ease, my transfer cloth can be used again and again. Another advantage is that the design is clearly visible on both sides of the cloth, which negates the need to make another copy of the image in reverse, to create a mirror-image design. The design can simply be flipped over and traced from the opposite side. This method can also be used with permanent-ink pens, in which case the design cannot be removed from the fabric. Silk-organdy transfers tend to work best with ink markers, as opposed to chalk pencils. Chalk pencils do work quite well using the same transfer principle but are best used with crinoline or net rather than with silk organdy.

To use crinoline or net, the basic principle is the same: Simply trace, place, and transfer the design. In this case the chalk or ink will not penetrate the fabric but will be transferred through the open areas of the crinoline or net.

Regardless of which material you use, baste or tape the transfer fabric to the garment fabric prior to transferring the design. For best results, work on a hard surface and, if desired, use pattern weights or use Sewer's Fix-It Tape to secure the garment piece to the table. This will help stabilize the fabric while transferring the design.

USING PLASTIC TEMPLATES

Templates are a practical way to transfer knotwork, braid, key, and other simple designs with repeat patterns. Once the templates are traced and cut, the transfer to fabric is very quick, and the template can be stored for future use.

To make a template, trace the embellishment design directly to a clear template plastic. For borders, it is necessary to cut a complete pattern repeat, beginning and ending at a halfway point, so it is easy to match the design. Use a utility knife or hot knife template cutting tool to cut the template plastic. Position the template as desired on the fabric and hold it in place with double-sided basting tape on the back of the template. Draw around the template with chalk dressmaker's pencils or with air- or water-soluble fabric markers.

USING DRESSMAKER'S TRACING PAPER AND TRACING WHEEL

This method is simple, direct, and well known, as most sewers use it to transfer darts and other pattern markings to fabric. In terms of embellishment transfers, it works best on light- to medium-weight woven materials, with an even texture and weave.

Place the transferable side of the paper facedown on the right side of the fabric, sandwiched between the fabric and a paper copy of the design. Then trace the design onto the fabric using a tracing wheel or inkless ballpoint pen to exert pressure while tracing the lines. Dressmaker's tracing paper is available in a range of colors and in wax-, water-, and air-soluble formulas. If you wish to remove any visible lines, be sure to use a nonwax formula.

USING A TRACING WHEEL AND TRANSFER POWDER

Pricking a paper template with a pattern tracing wheel along the design line followed by the application of transfer powder, or pounce, is a time-honored method of transferring designs (called the prick-and-pounce method). It remains an excellent method for transferring to any fabric stretched on a frame, as well as to thick, highly textured, or napped fabrics—such as velvet.

Dip a pounce pad—also referred to as a pattern pounce—into the loose powder and rub it gently over the surface of the pricked design. The powder sifts through the holes in the paper, leaving pinpoint markings on the cloth below, which indicate the lines of the design. Pouncing is followed up with painting or drawing in solid lines.

On small or relatively simple designs, an alternative to using the pattern tracing wheel is to create the holes by running the paper design through an unthreaded sewing machine.

Appendix B

Transferring Designs to a Stabilizer

Design transfer with stabilizers differs from transferring to fabric in that the surface of the fabric is not marked with lines for the design. Instead, you trace the design to a lightweight paper or water-soluble stabilizer. Then you iron or baste the stabilizer to the right side of the garment and keep it in place until the embellishment is complete. Upon completion, remove the stabilizer.

Less versatile than marking directly to the fabric, this method is useful when marking directly is difficult or undesirable and for various applications such as sewing on braid. It can also be used when extra stability is required and for napped or pile fabrics. One advantage of this method is that it takes less time than transferring to fabric, since the design needs to copied but once. Another is that the markings disappear with the template, which is removed when the design is complete.

Stabilizers best suited to this method include Solvy, which comes in clear plastic sheets, Stitch-N-Ditch paper stabilizer, and Totally Stable, which is ironed to the surface of the fabric and will keep the fabric beneath from shifting as the embellishment takes place. The larger the area to be embellished, the more critical this point will be.

MAIL-ORDER SOURCES

BEADS AND FINDINGS

Baker Bay Bead Co.
35633 Shoreview Dr.
Dorena, OR 97434
(541) 942-3941

Beadazzled
1522 Connecticut Ave. N.W.
Washington, D.C. 20036

Fire Mountain Gems
28195 Redwood Hwy.
Cave Junction, OR 97523-9304
(800) 423-2319

Garden of Beadin'
PO Box 1535
Redway, CA 95542
(707) 923-9120

General Bead
1010 Broadway
San Diego, CA 92101

Magnums
PO Box 362
Blackfoot, ID 83221

Ornamental Resources
1427 Miner St.
Idaho Springs, CO 80452

Shipwreck Beads
5021 Mud Bay Rd.
Olympia, WA 98502
(360) 754-2323

Universal Synergetics
16510 S.W. Edminston Rd.
Wilsonville, OR 97070-9514

TRIMS

Button Emporium
914 S.W. 11th
Portland, OR 97205
(503) 228-6372
www.buttonemporium.com

Classic Trims
1925 63rd St. East
Inver Grove Heights, MN 55077
(612) 552-9637

Exim Trims
13595 N.W. Overton
Portland, OR 97229
(503) 641-3431
(800) 291-3946

Ginsco Trims
242 W. 38th St.
New York, NY 10018
(212) 719-4871
(800) 929-2529
e-mail: mr.braid@worldnet.att.net
www.ginstrim.com

SPECIALTY THREADS

Hedgehog Handworks
PO Box 45384
Westchester, CA 90045
(310) 670-6040

Sew Art International
PO Box 1244
Bountiful, UT 84011
(800) 231-2787

Shay Pendray's Needle Arts, Inc.
2211 Monroe
Dearborn, MI 48124
(800) 813-3103

Speedstitch
3113 Broadpoint Dr.
Harbor Heights, FL 33983
(941) 629-3199
(800) 874-4115

Things Japanese
9805 N.E. 116th St.
Suite 7160
Kirkland, WA 98034
(206) 821-2287

Treadle Art
25834 Narbonne Ave.
Lomita, CA 90717
(310) 534-5122
e-mail: treadleart@aol.com

MISCELLANEOUS

Empyrean Beads
7129 34th Ave. S.W.
Seattle, WA 98126
(206) 937-4146
*Antique and unusual beads, electroplated char-
lottes, Japanese delicas and
cut beads, steel cut hematite beads*

Gripit Plus
125 50th St. N.W.
Albuquerque, NM 87105
(800) 347-5748
www.gripitplus.com
Scroll frames and frame holders

Lacis
3163 Adeline St.
Berkeley, CA 94703
(510) 843-7178
*Specialty needlework and beading supplies, as
well as trims, silk thread, tambour sewing supplies, and books*

Paris Southern Lights, Inc.
PO Box 374
Paris, Ont., Canada N3L 3T5
(800) 561-9731 (call for name of near-
est dealer)
*Maker and distributor of Eucalan No-Rinse
Woolwash*

Whole Customer's Catalogue
1998, 14th edition, Karen Dick
CBTB Press
PO Box 207
2860 Main St.
Beallsville, PA 15313-0207
*A compendium of mail-order sources and stores
that have costuming supplies, including
millinery, beading, fabric sources, and trims*

INDEX

Note: Page references in italic indicate a photo or illustration.